The Spiritual Gyre

Recurring Phases of Western History

Richard Sellin

Lost Coast Press

Fort Bragg California

For information, phone (707) 964-9520. For bookseller and library discounts or VISA and MasterCard orders, please call 800-883-7782. Or write to:

Lost Coast Press
155 Cypress Street
Fort Bragg CA 95437

Publishers Cataloging-in-Publication Data
(Provided by Quality Books, Inc.)

Sellin, Richard
The spiritual gyre : recurring phases of Western history / Richard Sellin. — 1st ed.
p. cm.
Includes bibliographical references.
Preassigned LCCN: 96-17397
ISBN: 1-8828971-9-6

1. Cycles—History—Philosophy. 2. Civilization—Forecasting. 3. Civilization—History—Philosophy. I. Title.

D16.9.S44 1997 116.0112
QBI97-40933

Cover design by Bill Sellin

Printed in Canada

First Edition

2 4 6 8 9 7 5 3 1

DEDICATION

To my wife Dianne
for her patience, faith and love

ACKNOWLEDGMENT

The author thanks those who contributed their time, views and interest in the creation of this book. Tim Cleary, Edwin Fisher, Jim Pyle, Paul Rinne, Dr. Tanis Thorne and Tom Wolfe read early drafts and offered their constructive criticism. Denise Martin, Joyce Polansky and Willow Sellin provided source materials and insight. Persia Wooley provided added insight into the publishing world. Dianne Sellin, a consummate speller and proofreader, provided the encouragement and spiritual support to see this project to its end. The editing and publishing work of John Fremont and Cynthia Frank of Lost Coast Press is also greatly appreciated.

CONTENTS

Turning and turning in the widening gyre
The falcon cannot hear the falconer;
Things fall apart; the centre cannot hold;
Mere anarchy is loosed upon the world . . .

from "The Second Coming,"
by W.B. Yeats, 1920

THE SPIRITUAL GYRE

Zeitgeist (n. German): The spirit of the time; the intellectual and moral tendencies that characterize any age or epoch (< G < zeit, *time* + geist, *spirit*)

Funk & Wagnalls, vol. II

INTRODUCTION

During our everyday journey in the pursuit of happiness and survival, we often forget that others have traveled and will travel our road. Whether driving a chariot or a Mercedes, we still need to stop, refuel and relieve our bladders. But these are only material concerns. The road includes hardship and happiness, love and hate that are as constant as rain and sunshine. These emotions recur in past, present and future. However, when in the midst of crisis or euphoria, it is of little concern to many that someone else has shared or will share our feelings. Technology clouds our perspective further by presenting new inventions and tools that change the material world. Many assume that the past, with its obsolete technology, translates into irrelevant ideas, philosophies, religions and feelings. But technology does little to alter questions dealing with emotions, feelings and spirituality as ancient as the first humans. French Jesuit paleontologist and philosopher, Pierre Teilhard de Chardin, stated in his 1955 book, *The Phenomenon of Man*, that a "thinking man" can not accept that there is nothing new under the sun. Chardin felt modern angst is based on recently expanded horizons brought to light through science and technology. He used this as evidence that thought or the "neosphere" was evolving toward a higher plane. When he stated, "...O man of the twentieth century, how does it happen that you are waking up to horizons and are susceptible to fears that your forefathers never knew?" (p. 228), he confused technology's expansion of horizons with human spiritual or emotional expansion. Whether forefathers and foremothers feared the Divine and the Hun, or currently people focus fears on space and chemical terrorism, the thoughts and emotions labeled fear and angst are timeless and ever present. When we do allow reflection, we are interested in understanding the past and applying it to the future. This is an aspect of humanity's survival mechanism and search for well being. In this capacity, society finds a purpose for historian and soothsayer. Historians, philosophers, sociologists and journalists create new labels for recycled feelings and ideas of the past.

Labels are useful for purposes of discussion and study. Labels are used in this book. Yet what many of us miss (including many historians), is that though the labels have changed, the emotional and spiritual game remains the same. This may give us the misleading impression that our feelings and spirituality of today are somehow unique in time. But New Agers have always existed to address realities beyond the conventional or traditional mythology, whether they were followers of Moses in the Exodus, Christians of the first two centuries or UFO observers today. Adam and Eve, before the Fall, were the original environmentalists. Scientists, agnostics and "free thinkers," often labeled secular humanists today, have always existed, inventing and expanding technology. They have imagined and delivered constitutions, democracies, republics and dictatorships in the Greek Golden Age, the Hellenistic Era, the Renaissance, and the Age of Reason.

The term "*Zeitgeist*" (spirit of the times) was introduced by philosophers and historians in an attempt to label what is difficult to describe or quantify for historians compared to documentation of dates, battles, or advances in technology. Feelings, emotions and spirituality, like air, are invisible yet do exist and must be acknowledged. Even the most rational person can be caught up in the emotionalism of the *Zeitgeist*.

Today there are anti-abortionists who also advocate capital punishment and state sponsored human sacrifice and murder by authoritarian or military means. Reason dictates that population control should be state sanctioned like war or the death penalty and seen as a necessary evil benefiting society as a whole. Who shall live and who shall die is an emotional issue in any society. The ancient German tribes dealt with overpopulation by requiring groups to leave the Fatherland and pillage and displace some other tribe or die trying. Who should be exiled was a decision often left to emotional whim. What is emotionally positive in a past age may be demonized in the next age. Evil is a subjective label. Evil spelled in reverse reveals the word live. Eighteenth century Romantics defined evil as separation from self, fellow humans, Nature, or the Divine.

A label is often employed to provide a rationale for the irrational. Anyone who works for, is contracted by, or is subsidized by the state is by definition a socialist. Thus the US trucking industry is by definition socialized. The costly right lane roadbeds are overbuilt to handle the weight of trucks and trailers on the federally funded, interstate freeway system. These asphalt and concrete ribbons are policed and maintained by government employees. The trucks are fueled by undertaxed diesel. The fuel tax provides only a third of the revenues needed for road construction and repair. The non-truck-driving taxpayer foots the rest of the bill. Yet few interstate truck drivers in the US would label themselves as anything but rugged individualists. Logic dictates that moving freight over land, long haul, would be less costly to society if the state subsidized maintenance of US railroad tracks and train depots. But shouts from anti-socialists extolling private enterprise will not allow this either. Those shouts are not based on logic or definition of terms, but the emotionalism and hypocrisy contained in the *Zeitgeist* of twentieth century USA.

Yet recurring changes in the *Zeitgeist* appear every 2000 years. This cyclical dynamic in Western Civilization is the focus of this book. There are three phases that Western Civilization's *Zeitgeist* has experienced. The West will again experience them. I have labeled them the "Theocratic Phase," which precedes our current "Secular Phase" and the fast approaching "Spiritual Phase." This work shall dispel any illusion that an "end time" will arrive in this or even the next generation. There will be no singular cataclysmic event or drama as predicted by fundamentalist Christians, millennialists, shamans or doomsayers. Yet profound spiritual change is beginning. The coming self-actualized spirituality existed 2000 years ago, but is mostly forgotten today.

Few in the West even recall life under a theocratic system anymore. In the US, the notions of past kings and priests controlling society are consigned to nursery rhyme, Disneyland's Sleeping Beauty's Castle, television or docudramas on England's royal family and Princess Di. For Europeans there are authentic palaces, castles and cathedrals which provide physical reminders of the Theocratic Phase. Yet in either geography, there are very few alive today who hold more than childhood memories of life under a czar or sultan. A personal history or memory leaves with the death of each individual, ultimately diminishing one phase of society's *Zeitgeist* until it is gone from society altogether and replaced by another phase.

Personal memory is best expressed as oral history. More is related than time or events of one's past existence. Personal memory involves oral expression, voice tone and body language that express genuine nuance, accent, emotion and spirit. I recall watching M.T.V. in the '80s at my grandmother's home when Paul McCartney's song, *Pipes of Peace*, came on. I called her in to view the music video. The message of the video was brotherly love, exemplified by an actual event when a Christmas truce was called during World War I. German and British troops crawled out of their trenches to exchange cigarettes, chocolates and play a little soccer. Just seeing the uniforms caused my 90 year old Oma (a German colloquialism for grandmother) to burst into tears saying, "So many good men died." I felt bad for bringing grief to her from something I thought uplifting and anti-war. I also felt her emotion which I could barely comprehend intellectually, though I was only two generations removed.

What emotions does a twenty five year old feel today concerning World War One, The Great World Depression, Pearl Harbor or Viet Nam? No one living today knows the experience of massive war on the soil of the continental USA. Such memory died with the last veteran of the Civil War or Indian Wars. The impact of war carried out on territories of the US is still felt by Americans via the surprise attack on Pearl Harbor. But this is very different from Europeans whose last experience of war in the home land was World War II or presently the Balkans. As a result, the approach to nationalism, sovereignty, war and militarism is different in the two societies due to living memory. Memory can be rekindled by reading history or viewing photos, but deep emotion comes from experiencing the unedited fear of invasion by a foreign enemy or from the euphoria of victory.

If the threat of invasion is lifted altogether, a myth of society's invincibility develops. A very long time with the myth of invincibility is the essence of the Spiritual Phase of the *Zeitgeist.* Allowed to continue for centuries, the myth of invincibility allows time for society to speculate beyond physical security and the *Zeitgeist* evolves in response to an attempt to actuate metaphysical ideals. After generations, the loss of personal memories of either the Secular Phase or the preceding Theocratic Phase is not available to serve as a guide for the future. Such a lengthy myth of invincibility was only last seen in Western Civilization during the Roman Empire and possibly two millennia before that. Today, fundamentalists, environmentalists and New Agers see a future end time in their metaphysical speculations. The demise of the secular, human centered, scientific system of present society is detailed in this work along with predictions of a future alternative system for society.

When looking at dates and events along with Western Civilization's *Zeitgeist*, its three phases exist within a 2000 year time frame. I arrived at this conclusion in 1970 when I created a time line which spanned 2000 years. On one side of the line I placed significant events starting with the time of Christ and Caesar Augustus and ending with the then recent landing of a human on the Moon. In choosing what was significant, I kept in mind events that academia has also acknowledged as turning points in history or human thought and mentality. A major foreign invasion creating a cultural shift, rise of a new theology, ideas represented by the life of a person and use of a political model were included. Then I placed on the other side of the same line events which occurred 2000 years before each event already listed. This double time line is illustrated in Part III of Chapter One. If these parallel time lines seem incomplete, it is because they are. I could have included Aristotle who died 374 years before the Christian Era and Age of Pisces and Francis Bacon who died 323 before the beginning of the Age of Aquarius. These great thinkers were separated by 2051 years. I invite the reader to make more comparisons. What I found was enough to confirm my hunch.

Within 50 years, plus or minus, I found any event before the Christian or Common Era (B.C.E.) had a counterpart 2000 years later in our present era (A.D.). For example, I saw that in the centers of trade and wealth, the Renaissance in fact did occur within the accepted dates of A.D. 1300-1600 and established itself as a major trend from 1450 to 1550. An identical Zeitgeist labeled today as the Golden Age of Greece (600 B.C.E. to 500 B.C.E.) occurred 2000 years earlier. I saw that though technology had developed and the geography of the areas affected by Western Civilization had increased in size over two millennia, the human cause and effect of events, ideas and trends of thoughts were remarkably parallel. It became apparent that all the trends and eras of the past fell within the three phases, the labels of which define a mega shift in the *Zeitgeist* and that they repeat themselves. Western Civilization's *Zeitgeist* is again beginning to establish a new cosmology, spiritual reality and "world order" to accommodate technologic changes and transcend past centuries of theocracy and secular humanism. This is the impetus for a Spiritual Phase which becomes the *Zeitgeist* of Western Civilization every two thousand years. I concluded that even though the coming Spiritual Phase was only just beginning, the weight of the past's revolving phases would carry us into a predictable future. The Spiritual Phase, in time, will be followed by yet another Theocratic Phase, leading to yet another Secular Phase, in a never ending cycle. This cyclical pattern seemed obvious and consistent with the operation of any other aspect of the cosmos and Nature.

I set my time line aside while I pursued the immediate demands of family support and career. Yet over the next 20 years I continued to be drawn back to my parallel time lines. I eventually developed a circular diagram which presented a better expression of the cyclical dynamic. I saw that while human technology did advance in a linear trajectory, the human *Zeitgeist* took a return journey. I remained disillusioned by the narrow way history was often approached. Most academic histories documented technology and artifacts which is only a study of modified matter. For documentation of human thought and emotion, selectively picked quotes used by historians validated history on a scientific model. I saw this did not make the story any less subjective (and thus scientific) than a preacher picking quotes from the Bible to support an interpretation. In the Secular Phase the art of history had been reduced to a science in order to be taken seriously by Western society's secular academia. And yet I found society as a whole had crossed certain mental and spiritual thresholds that even scientific historians had to recognize and had labeled (such as the Dark Ages or the Age of Reason).

I found a few twentieth century historians who accepted cyclical patterns. The German historian, Oswald Spengler, inspired me because he was brave enough to apply a human's life cycle to the universal operation of history and a Culture's cycle resulting in no lasting advance. He did not see the immortal soul or reincarnation as part of that life cycle, as I do. But he saw, as I do, the limits of ordering history in a systematic linear system. He was not duped, like the Romantics, into assuming humans would ever achieve perfection or idealized heaven on earth. Spengler looked at world history which today would be better labeled Western History, and noted that historians had systematically broken it into three major categories labeled Classical [B.C.E.], Medieval and Modern [A.D.]. Spengler felt that modern history had run its course and humanity was about to enter a new category which he left to a future historian to label. I believe that now, 75 years later, the new history has begun. There is no longer any separation between Western and global (world) history, as the Spiritual Phase descends upon us.

The British historian, Arnold Toynbee, believed in predictable patterns and general repetition of history. The American historians, Ariel and Will Durant, certainly felt lessons of the past had relevance for study of the contemporary and future activities of society. The limits of a scientific, secular age block a complete historical knowledge which should include emotions along with statistics. Art and imagination are primary in any society because they inspire new technology as well as provide a response to it. As difficult as it is to quantify fantasy and ideas, fantasy remains the source of invention, new tools and human adaptability. Fantasy must be accepted as part of any true story, including history.

Rather than sterile statistics, emotions expressed by the ancient bard transported the listeners' spirits back in time. The human voice and body retained something of personal memory, even if the original storyteller spoke generations earlier. It is not the documentation of a sixth century standard of living, but the interpersonal relations and spiritual questions which bring relevance, truth and reality to the legend of King Arthur and the Knights of the Round Table. When historians left the oral tradition to reach a wider audience through the written word, much of the emotional and spiritual voice of history disappeared.

I am living in these last days of the Secular Phase and my personal memory not only reflects who I am but influences this book. Like my grandmother, I am a product of environment and the *Zeitgeist.* In 1970, many of my peers were returning to a neo-fundamentalist Christianity. I recall an old US Coast Guard station overlooking the Pacific Ocean, at Table Bluff near the south end of Humboldt Bay, California. It was isolated on the bluff by fifty foot cliffs down to the beach and rolling pasture land. The only human neighbors were living at an Indian rancheria a mile inland and hidden from view. The property had been bought up from the government and the buildings were rented out. The facility was home to a commune of young "Freaks" (the most common self descriptive label used at that time for what the mass media labeled Hippies) trying to make a living by creating furniture out of redwood stumps that had washed up on the beach. Their utopia was subverted and then taken over by "Jesus Freaks" who had enough of LSD and revamped Romanticism. They had returned to "Old-Time religion" that was a scion of the Secular Phase mixed with uneducated notions of early Christianity which existed in the last Spiritual Phase. The Jesus Freaks subjected the original residents to proselytizing and constant badgering, forcing them to either join the Jesus Freak's brand of Christianity or leave.

The last hold out was a family living in a fine old structure that had been officers quarters. They were the most invested in getting the commune's furniture business going. With young children, they were less able to just pack up and leave. They placed a life sized picture of a Roman soldier on their front door. One day the father found a dead snake run over on the road. The father hung the carcass on the front gate. Seeing this, the Jesus Freaks began to kneel and pray, afraid to pass through the gate! In the end the Jesus Freaks did prevail and the old Coast Guard base lost its name as the Crazy Quilt Ranch to be renamed the Light House Ranch. It was eventually purchased by the Christians.

This became the Light House Ranch Christian group which later became a driving force in the born-again Christian movement that included Jerry Falwell and President Jimmy Carter. The same group became very active in missionary work in Guatemala. They supported the born-again Christian dictator, Rios Montt, who came to power in Guatemala in the 1980s. At present, the location on Table Bluff continues as a Christian training center.

My other peers looked to less traditional paths than fundamentalist Christianity for spiritual answers and effective change. College of the Redwoods in Eureka, California, which I was attending then, was presented the Peace Award in 1970 by then California governor Ronald Reagan. There was only one other community college that had seen no student disruptions in the California college system that year. Reagan may have assumed he would be speaking to a friendly or at least apathetic student body. What he didn't realize was that we were exiles from the violence going on elsewhere at that time. I had left the turmoil and student strikes at Los Angeles City College. Though peaceful, we were not apathetic. Reagan was apparently not conscious that he was basically laughed off the stage, assuming the jeers were cheers. After a lame joke about his days washing dishes in the girl's dormitory during his college days, he commented on how beautiful and unpolluted the Eureka area was. He apparently knew nothing of the foul smelling smoke which blew from the pulp mill or its waste which fouled the ocean. The nuclear power plant built on wetlands over a major fault was just being looked at. Reagan was from a past smokestack secular world and hopelessly out of touch with the spiritual realms we students were experimenting with at the time. He probably had no idea of why ours was a peaceful campus or what our reality and visions of the future might be.

Current events and technology were carrying society along rapidly in the late 1960s and early '70s. The anxiety as to the future sent many people into a desperate search for some definitive direction leading to a new reality beyond violence, secularism and science. Compassion for all living things and a search for quality of life over a life of material accumulation as a priority, became important. Ecology was a new term. Students devoured novels like Herman Hesse's *Steppenwolf* or *Siddhartha.* Romantic appeals to a seemingly simpler past abounded. Fantasy was embraced to be as valid as objectivity. J. R. Tolkien's books were popular. Thomas Berger's novel, *Little Big Man,* and the movie made from it, as well as Carlos Castenada's tales of a desert Indian shaman tapped interest in aboriginal peoples and shamanism. Study and practice of Eastern religions grew beyond the Beatles.

The words on this page fall short of the emotions behind them. If I spoke the words to my daughters, they would sense the depth of what I feel just as I sensed my grandmother's emotion when she told me her story. If my daughters related my story to my grandchildren, they might also transmit something of my emotion and the *Zeitgeist* of my times. Even if my oral accounts were videotaped for posterity, the complete truth would not come through because though I would be speaking from another time, I would be unable to elaborate, answer questions, touch or make eye contact.

To understand the past and future, one must balance rational research of quantifiable facts with personal experience of the qualitative practices, art and spiritual literature that are part of the global *Zeitgeist.* This book is an attempt to maintain that balance while explaining the road into the future. There are approaches to history other than the narrow systematic form of secular academia.

In Oswald Spengler's book, *Decline of the West,* he admitted he was a creature of his turn-of-the-twentieth-century time. Spengler dared to approach history in an organic "physiognomic" rather than usual systematic (scientific) way. He felt force of will found in primitive Culture dies once the Culture achieves civilization. He recognized the circular pattern provided by the romantic movement. But he did not see the closing of the circle as an advancement. I found this more pessimistic view refreshing though difficult for my Western ego to admit. Spengler wrote before the advent of Fascism or modern democratic socialism. He saw democracy exploited as an agent of the wealthy, which I can agree with. But he placed socialism above the influence of money and only concerned with power, which I don't agree with. Spengler saw ancient Greeks as being "ahistoric" while mentioning Herodotus or Thucydides as incapable of historical perspective. He did not see that these authors, who wrote about their current events or recent past, were reporters. The term "history" in Greek translates to "investigation". Spengler, like many historians, saw the Greeks as a fully evolved urban civilization. This view leads to comparison with ancient Persians or Egyptians.

It is more accurate to compare Greece with a tribal society whose past is recognized but not pinned down on a calendar. Such a society orally expresses mythology rather than written facts and dates. But the story is also digested as a current event with lessons for the future. This is actually an example of the "symbolism of history" that Spengler was attempting to explain. I do not agree with all his other assumptions, including his stereotype of women. I do not share his pessimism. But I also do not share optimism in the advance of human emotions or spirituality.

To describe what is not rational in rational terms is the folly of the West. Western science in the past has placed the source of emotion in the heart, liver and now the neuropeptides of the brain, still in the vain pursuit of discovering the source of love by rational means. Yet the West has in the past also fallen prey to the temptation of looking at reality in strictly metaphysical terms. This has created mythology, religion, theocracy and tyranny. Western feminism, missionary zeal, a systematic approach to problems, the low frustration level or impatience when Western systems don't work in non-Western societies, insensitivity and rudeness are the result of the logic, spirituality and *Zeitgeist* of the West investigated in this book.

As a native Californian of European immigrant parents, I am addressing this book from my Western perspective to the global community whose history I may not share completely but whose future we all share. It is my hope that non-Western readers of emerging nations will consume this work. They already experience the fads, technology and politics of the West. For many non-Westerners, there is personal memory of past rule of their lands by the West. I wish to help explain what must often seem irrational, even irreverent behavior not only of Western tourists, but government, industry and religion.

It is common in Western historical writing to capitalize Christianity but not Paganism. Since both are proper nouns for a belief system, I believe this represents prejudice. The original Latin definition of pagan translated to villager has passed long ago. Therefore Pagan is capitalized in this work. Nature will also be capitalized when used as a proper noun and as a spiritual place. In Western literature God is also capitalized as differentiated from gods. This presumes that God, whose name is Yahweh, Brahmin, Great Spirit, Allfather or Jehovah, is somehow more credible than the gods and goddesses, who also have names. I have used the word Divine capitalized or deity in place of God, gods or goddesses. I also found written history to be gender prejudiced. In this work the Divine is never written as "his" or "her" Divine unless quoting directly from another author. Likewise the terms "mankind" or "his" will not be found in this book. Instead the terms "humankind," "people" or "person" are used. Rather than using the titles "Third" or "Fourth Wave" or "Information Age" to describe the present technological epoch, I use the term "Silicone Age." This is consistent with the mineral analogy used in the labels "Stone Age, Bronze Age and Iron Age." It is time for story telling to become more sensitive. I am also directing this book toward jaded millennialists or utopians who have dropped out of the ranks of the fundamentalist Christians, New Age and environmental movement. This is a generalist, holistic, physiomatic work. This book is not for religious dogmatics, academic elitists or worshipers of science and technology, unless they can get beyond their paradigms.

We in the West are again seeing a time where the threat of foreign invasion is diminished. This feeling or *Zeitgeist* of invincibility usually lasts only 100 years or so, but can last for a period of 300 years. Such a 300 year time span has not been achieved by any empire since Rome, 2000 years ago. Such a prolonged period of physical security provides society time to collectively enter spiritual investigation that is the genesis of new religion. Today we in the West have the luxury of peace and liberty for speculation. Twenty years of hindsight and study have confirmed my assumptions and led me to agree with Christian fundamentalists, New Agers, the environmentalists and futurists who see Western Civilization coming to its end under Pax Americana. But while some see end time occurring in the present or next generation, I place a 200 to 300 year time frame for the time required to end the world as we know it. Yet I see no self-actualized improvement in human nature or Divine intervention. There is only the eternally recycling phases of the *Zeitgeist* adapting to advancing technology. This represents the mid path reality between pessimism and optimism and religion and science. Society's hybridization and rebirth of spirituality and creation of a new religion followed by a theocracy, will occur as Western Civilization is incorporated into World Civilization. Time is at hand.

> *"Study does not have to be scientific in order to be illuminating"*
>
> Arnold J. Toynbee,
> *Change and Habit, The Challenge of Our Time,* p. 8

CHAPTER ONE

THE PREMISE

1: THE CYCLICAL APPROACH TO HISTORY

Cycles are basic to the operation of Nature. Humans have studied this operation through the arts and sciences since the beginning of time. In the past, following the seasonal cycles of weather was a religious act. Today such observation is called the physical science of meteorology. The Greek word physis means Nature and is the root of the term physics. Each branch of science — physical, life and social — contain areas of specialization. Social sciences include cultural anthropology, political science, sociology and history. In the guise of science, history left the realms of art and oral tradition. It also lost its connection with cyclical, natural operation. As the Secular Phase of the West's *Zeitgeist* evolved, a linear, systematic historical approach was deemed more factual, objective and scientific.

In her classic work *The Greek Way*, originally published in 1930, Edith Hamilton writes about her contemporary twentieth century historian's approach in contrast to previous Western historians. She felt historians of her day "*generally rejected*" the idea that history repeats. She states:

> *The modern scientific historian looks at his subject very much as a geologist does. History is a chronicle of fact considered for itself alone. There is no pattern in the web unrolled from the loom of time and no profit in studying it except to gain information.*

> *That was not the point of view of the Greek historian... He* [Thucydides] *reasoned that since the nature of the human mind does not change any more than the nature of the human body, circumstances swayed by nature are bound to repeat themselves, and in the same situation men are bound to act in the same way.* (P. 184)

Perhaps the Greeks were on to something. They required more than facts to develop a clear picture. Karen Armstrong speaks of the ancient Greek approach to history in her book, *History of God*, when she states, "*Like the gods, reason is not denied but transcended*" (p. 31). She goes on to state that Greeks of Plato's day and later saw that, *"The most perfect motion, therefore, was the circle because it was perpetually turning and returning to its original point; the circling celestial spheres imitate the divine world as best they can"* (p. 35).

The cyclical approach to history is not unique to Western Civilization. Hindu history is expressed in cyclical terms. The ancient Mayan calendar allowed for 52 year cycles of history with the beginning and ending of time recurring every 20 million years. Hopi Indian mythology places the present in a "Fourth World" soon to be destroyed like the three previous "Worlds" that originated with the first humans. Greed, materialism and attacks on Nature are the reasons for the ending of each "World" (age), in a never ending cycle. The surviving humans of Hopi end time are to create the beginning of a "Fifth World." In *The Voice of the Great Spirit: Prophecies of the Hopi Indians*, the German scholar, Rudolf Kaiser states the Hopi approach:

> *They* [Hopi world ages] *form the basic mythological pattern of a cycle rather than a linear process, a cycle of humankind's ever-present experience of emergence, destruction and rebirth—as reflected in the rhythm of day and night, the seasons of the year, and human life as such—elevated to the dimension of world ages....* (Pp. 63-64)

Whether one accepts cycles as an artistic metaphor or scientific axiom, they are the fundamental mode of operation in both physical and spiritual realms. In any cycle, there is no beginning or end. Rain falls, warm air vaporizes the fallen water and the rising vapor condenses upon contact with cooling air. Clouds form and once again rain falls. In the arena of life science, biological study shows us that all life forms are born, mature, age and die. This seems to be a lineal progression to a dead end. But a complete observation shows that apart from transferring genes and genetic memory if sexual reproduction has occurred, the life form breaks apart on a molecular level into the earth or atmosphere upon death. The scattered atoms are absorbed by other life forms and live on within the new host. So the material life cycle continues beyond death.

A part of the life cycle that physical or life sciences cannot measure and thus do not address, is the continuation of the soul or spirit. Excluding physics, parapsychology or ethnobiology, scientific investigation only follows what is physically observable. This is unfortunate because this trend has led to the notion in the Secular Phase of the *Zeitgeist* that if soul or spirit can't be measured or observed, it therefore doesn't exist or is not worth study. During the Theocratic Phase, suppression of scientific inquiry was supported by spiritually based dogma. The Secular Phase slid away from the Theocratic Phase in the eighteenth century and Age of Reason. The Age of Reason's romanticism developed in an attempt to reconcile declining credibility of religion and ascending support of science.

The romantic philosophers and artists employed the circular model. They attempted to use secular terms and logic to explain the human thought process and consequential actions of society. The German playwright and historian, Johann von Schiller (1759-1805), felt the original fall from innocence, represented biblically by Adam's taste of the fruit from the tree of knowledge, was human separation from Nature. Thus set apart from other living forms, humans question the present, study the past and speculate on the future. Humans cannot go back to naive unity with Nature. Reasoning caused the division. Division equaled biblical evil. But Schiller optimistically felt that by using the necessary evil of reason, humanity would find its way back to a fully comprehended natural state. His contemporary, Immanuel Kant (1724-1804), attempted to reconcile science and religion. He felt pure religion which human reason had destroyed, would eventually return through continued use of human reason.

Kant's student, the nineteenth century German philosopher, George Wilhelm Friedrich Hegel (1770-1831), came up with a systematic historical pattern for human thought and actions involving the conflict between subject and object. His model operated as a turning circle, always returning to its original position, but advancing human understanding at the same time. He felt a return to the original position created the starting point for another, higher circle. This process continued, creating ever widening circles until three large circles, containing all the smaller ones, comprised complete knowledge. At this point, humans would return to the natural state of their origin and become one with divine reasoning — the biblical heaven on earth. He saw the beginning of each circle as an original idea, inspiration or state of being, which he called thesis. The thesis, inspected by reason, created an anti-thesis. When the process resolved itself in a complete understanding of the thesis and anti-thesis, an absolute idea — or synthesis — was achieved. The circle is closed, knowledge is increased and the individual and all humanity progresses. The digested synthesis becomes the thesis of yet another circle. Circles created by this process educate and advance human understanding in ever widening circles leading to an ultimate circle. Hegel termed "Absolute Spirit" as the ultimate human destiny yet to be attained by this dialectic process. The process included not only the opposition of subject and object, but also opposition between intelligence and Nature, conscious and unconscious, freedom and dependency and consolidation and dispersion.

Hegel's synthesis was the essence of the golden mean of the Greeks or Buddha's middle path. The Chinese Taoist's circle divided evenly by white and black, symbolizes the Yin (thesis) and Yang (anti-thesis), which together comprises the Tao (synthesis) and conforms to Hegel's wheel. Hegel and fellow romantics saw a parallel with the biblical alpha and omega. *"I am the Alpha and Omega, the beginning and the ending, saith the Lord, which is, and which was, and which is to come, the Almighty" (Revelation* 1:8). They applied secular terms to the human fall from grace, trials of redemption and return to grace. The romantics held that the return to the Divine or Nature would not be a naive primitivism originally given to humans. Instead, a recognition and full understanding of Nature was to be earned by human effort and education. The 19th century transcendentalists also recognized the dialectic paradigm. They advocated art and inspiration rather than science and facts as the means to resolve the dialectic opposites and develop a complete truth.

Many economists, social scientists, philosophers and historians have since supported the Hegelian dialectic. When applied to history, the circle starts with those in society who support the status quo (thesis). Reason pushes society toward a new system (anti-thesis). A clash of interests occurs, ending in some sort of compromise (synthesis). This synthesis becomes a new thesis when it is challenged by a new anti-thesis which arrives with the coming of the next social change.

Western thinkers applied Hegel's dialectic to humanity's recent historical behavior and current events. In eighteenth and nineteenth century Europe, the rising middle class, allied to the working class, was struggling against the aristocracy and church for political power in government and economics. The aristocracy naturally wished to maintain its position (thesis). Challenging the thesis was the anti-thesis represented by the middle class and workers who saw their nations financed by their enterprise, labor and taxes. They could not find champions among the aristocracy, so they called for secular, parliamentary government. They wanted the right to vote for representatives who would serve their interests. The American Revolution provided a model.

The events of the first half of the nineteenth century played out according to Hegel's model. Napoleon (anti-thesis) swept away aristocracy (thesis) except in Great Britain and Russia. The result was a new order (synthesis). Government was more responsive to middle class and workers. But the new order did not really achieve all their goals. They had to choose representatives from a politically correct group dictated by Napoleon. Napoleon had to continue fighting in an attempt to hold together this synthesis of conflicting interests. Finally, he crowned himself Emperor, thus reinstituting an aristocratic thesis. The new order thus became the new status quo (thesis) which was in turn challenged by the original aristocracy now allied with foreign nationalists, many of whom were middle class (new anti-thesis). After Waterloo, the new order (synthesis turned thesis) was replaced by a conservative, reactionary aristocratic establishment across Europe. The resulting synthesis became the next new thesis. It was again resisted by the middle class and workers, along with liberal aristocrats. These groups' new anti-thesis favored England's parliamentary monarchy or constitutional republicanism.

Nationalist republican independence movements liberated Greece and most of Latin America with the tacit support of England. Finally, in 1848 (the year Marx wrote his *Communist Manifesto*), middle class and worker revolts erupted all through Europe except in republican England and autocratic Russia. The resultant synthesis became a new thesis whereby the middle class got republican government with an aristocratic executive. The working class received little because the right to vote was based on wealth, property and gender. The wishes and rights of the workers (the next anti-thesis), would not be addressed until the turn of the twentieth century through the women's rights and labor movements and socialist revolutions. The nineteenth century events seemed to confirm Hegel's dialectic.

Karl Marx (1818-1883) used Hegel's terms but altered the evolutionary process to a revolutionary crossover to divine reason. He agreed with the apocalyptic change called for in the Bible, *"And behold, I come quickly; and my reward is with me, to give every man according as his work shall be" (Revelation* 22:12). He saw human attempts to achieve divine reason as a conflict between a minority's control of material resources (capital and technology) against the mass of humanity, separated from the end result of their labors and their reshaping of Nature.

This sets Marx apart from earlier romantics because they felt the highest expression of human progress was defined by the fine arts. Marx believed creation of any tool or object was a human reordering of Nature. He felt that once the workers who produce goods control that production as well, a utopian synthesis-thesis would result. Nature would be humanized and humans would also be naturalized (one with Nature).

In this romantic utopia, humans would return to a self-actualized communalism arriving full circle from the primitive communism they started with eons ago. Technology would thus be in harmony with Nature and humans. Anarchy would coexist with volunteer social order. Marx reflected the social Darwinism of his day by presuming existing aboriginal communist groups were not self-actualized. He idealized a state where all people would belong to one static class in a communist system. Either Marx was too urban to observe Nature's cyclical operation or ignorant of the scientific reality that nothing is truly static. Marx did not allow that within any class, greed and competition clash with compassion and cooperation often without reason. No amount of education will do more than recognize or label these conflicting emotions.

These natural, emotional traits were considered by another German, Friedrich Nietsche (1844-1900). He returned to the notion of the fine arts as the ultimate human expression. But he replaced Christian and romantic Divine-human unity with human "will to power" as the cause and effect and ultimate human goal. Nietsche's dialectic involved a battle between male and female aspects. Belief in the Divine was only a rationale disguising human will. Meanwhile, romanticism's optimistic dream of a new age was turned to pessimism with the failure of the French Revolution and revolts of 1848. Except for Marxists, literal political change was no longer a realistic expectation for human salvation. Personal change of consciousness became the romantic goal. Nietsche called for complete human responsibility in any social change unaided by a cosmic system. In step with the increasing scientific mode and systematic approach, twentieth century scholarship dropped the physiomatic, organic role of Nature or the Divine from social study. Though Marx had recognized the effects of technology, he did not move beyond it and the material plane as a reason for conflicts in the emotional realm. Because Hegel said humans end up at a more evolved self-actualized state at the close of a cycle, humans progress in time. But progress implies a lineal movement. Hegel's dialectic movement came to be likened to the mechanics of Newtonian clock pendulums, marking society's linear progress. Romanticism became as passé as Christianity. Cyclical history fell out of fashion or became irrelevant. Looking at the big picture was less important. Historians became specialists in their narrow areas of research. This was in keeping with the increase of new sciences and categorizing fragmented information to be tested by the scientific method.

Though Hegel's circle became a pendulum, the organic view was not completely extinguished. The English philosopher and sociologist, Herbert Spencer (1820-1903), saw society as an organism possessing organs such as those involved in nutrition, circulation or reproduction like any individual human. He felt that as society develops and becomes more complex, the separate parts increase in codependence as with organs in the complex biology of an individual human.

In the Secular Phase of the nineteenth century, science was employed as a rationale for conquest and imperialism no less than religion was used in the Theocratic Phase. During the Theocratic Phase, the notion had long been espoused by aristocracy that high and low birth determined divine favor and who should govern. This was used as a rationale for maintaining control of the masses. The governed masses traditionally believed, or at least accepted this theory or myth as fact. With Darwin's theory of evolution, social scientists applied the evolution of higher intelligence within the human species. Social Darwinism provided "scientific proof" for the idea that the white race was superior to other races. Evidence was provided by nineteenth century social scientists using the chosen facts of their day. White nations ruled all the black, brown and yellow peoples of the earth at that time. This was a central fact used in support of the Social Darwinists' theory. Thus the superiority concept was transferred to the Secular Phase in search of the Absolute Idea. Not until the twentieth century and the disaster of Adolph Hitler's adoption of Social Darwinism was that science discredited. Yet racists today still subscribe to the theory of Social Darwinism. Because an idea is no longer viewed as scientific, does not mean that belief in the idea is gone. Ethnocentric beliefs exemplify rationale passed off as truth, based on the *Zeitgeist* of the day.

Long before Darwin, without any scientific proof, the Cheyenne Indians saw themselves as human and other tribes as something other. Chinese believed China to be the center of the universe. Jews believed themselves to be chosen by Jehovah above all other people. To all these societies, such theory or myth was or is reality, with or without scientific support. The "scientific historian" is a legacy of the West's last and presently ending Secular Phase of the *Zeitgeist.* Romantics were too close to the fading Theocratic Phase. They were caught up in the Christian and/or French Revolution's optimism about a coming ideal millennium. Using Christian, Pagan and self-created terms, romantics served as a bridge into the Secular Phase where only material evidence was considered valid.

Currently, the shortcomings and validities of both Secular and Theocratic Phases can be reviewed in the perspective of time. If life cycles exist with individuals, then why not a society made from these individuals? If an individual's spirit lives on to reincarnate another day, and Spencer's view of organic society operating as an individual is applied, it follows that an entire civilization's *Zeitgeist* may also recycle.

In this arena, the arts become relevant to an accurate picture. Science explains the world through physical science, life science or social science. Art informs people through visual arts, performing arts or liberal arts and religion. Beliefs in artistic ideas and realities are based on subjective intuition and inspiration rather than on the objective physical world. Because history is often presented from a scientific, systematic standpoint, it takes artists like James Michener, Leo Tolstoy or Robert Graves to breathe life into history. Novelists use poetic license to bring a more relevant thus interesting, truthful and realistic vision of the past. Due to the scientific vogue, the art of storytelling has been split over time and institutionalized. In the form of a historical novel, storytelling lies within the field of the humanities, a sub caste of the arts. History as an academic subject is often part of the social sciences. As the West moves out of the Secular Phase and into a Spiritual Phase, change in perspective is affecting academia. At present history is increasingly placed within the humanities rather than the social sciences at Western colleges. But the Western approach to observation and theory continues to use the systematic linear model. Specialization prevails over an interdisciplinary approach to complete understanding.

Geology is a physical science specializing in the study of rocks. Orthopedics is a life science devoted to the study of bones. Orthopedists and geologists tell us that bones and rocks both regenerate, rebuild, decay. A complete observation shows that rocks experience life cycles and are *not* inanimate. The time rocks take to do this is so great that they may appear "dead." But with what is known today concerning volcanism and plate tectonics, we see rocks as alive as any bones. Rocks make up the skeleton of the planet as bones do for a biologic organism. Only ancient or primitive religion and poetic license allow the view of living rocks as a reality. But if we approach the study of our planet as though it were a living organism, we see it as a living being or Gaia. This is, in fact, a full circle return to the physiomatic, holistic approach of ancient and present animist religion that Christian theocracy or science has disregarded in the Theocratic and Secular Phases. Because scientists cannot quantitatively measure all aspects of Nature, does not eliminate a reality.

Any investigation within social studies must be factual and critical, but also open to all perspectives. History and sociology are not just a linear chain of events. The turn of the century German philosopher, Oswald Spengler, took the linear, systematic historical approach to task in 1922, stating in the introduction to his book *The Decline of the West:*

> *These Cultures, sublimated life-essences, grow with the same superb aimlessness as the flower of the field. They belong, like the plants and the animals, to the living Nature of Goethe, and not to the dead Nature of Newton. I see world-history as a picture of endless formations and transformations, of marvelous waxing and waning of organic forms.* (P. 18)

Spengler went on to state that the *"professional historian,"* wrongly views history as a *"sort of tape worm,"* adding one epoch after another without conclusion. Spengler felt the *"series of 'ancient-medieval-modern history'"* (p. 18), had run its course and was no longer needed.

Reality and truth must be based on scientific fact coupled with artistic imagination. The combining of art and science in all fields as well as History is not a new phenomena, and it should be a required approach for serious holistic study of any topic. British historian, Arnold Toynbee stated in his book *Change and Habit*:

> *It may be agreed that there cannot be a science of human affairs.... But to abandon the study of history on this account would be to pay excessive deference to scientific skepticism. Study does not have to be scientific to be illuminating.* (P. 8)

Past assumptions accepted by society because they were totally scientific (Secular Phase) or purely inspired revelation (Theocratic Phase) only presented half a picture in each case. Keeping this in mind, one must take a well informed leap of faith when applying natural cyclical operation to the study of history. When observing societies of Western Civilization's past empires, each follows a definite historical pattern and/or life cycle. But these are only part of the greater Western *Zeitgeist*'s 2000 year cycle. Through historical investigation, we see that with the guidance of able leaders organizing existing human and natural resources, a society develops an efficient system that allows enough prosperity and security to motivate maintaining and promoting that system for that society. This first generation of society builders is aggressive and will pursue its interests at the expense of older, existing neighboring societies. A process of conquest over other societies begins bringing increased material wealth to the nation builders and motivation for more conquest. The next generation continues imperial acquisition, but without the first generation's personal memories and emotions of harder times or the same appreciation and value given to material wealth. This second generation also begins the incorporation of ideas and values of those who were previously conquered. Leaving societal childhood, the third generation takes empire, wealth that it brings and the military might required to maintain protection as a given. They come to believe their nation is invincible. The society is deluded into believing that their empire and adolescence will continue.

Following adolescence come adulthood, old age and death. As generations continue, even the competing empires and foreign societies come to believe the myth of invincibility. But challenges to this primacy continue internally and externally. National defense and law and order are needed to maintain the status quo. The society's revenues are absorbed by the costs of the military, law enforcement, domestic subsidies and government bureaucracy.

Used to a high standard of living, the society purchases luxury and necessity items abroad at lower prices. An unfavorable trade balance develops. The fourth or fifth generation has tradition and prestige, but must struggle to keep an aging empire and high standard of living. These generations become entangled in tradition as there is no longer any societal, personal memory of any other type of existence. Their colonies become economic liabilities rather than assets. Finally the last tired generations, aware of the folly of maintaining the status quo, become apathetic or rebel. This may take the course of civil war or revolution. The empire is then ripe for the taking by yet another foreign society in its infancy or adolescence. We can apply this rise and fall life cycle to any empire of the past.

Spain's King Ferdinand and Queen Isabella led the final push of their generation to rid the Iberian Peninsula of the Muslims and then on to American conquests. Two generations later Spain ruled a global empire. They had outpaced older Muslim and Italian rivals but were being challenged by other groups such as the Portuguese. By 1588, Spain's myth of invincibility was in place. But it was short-lived. One hundred years (or three generations) after Columbus, successful independence movements against Spain raged in Holland and Portugal. Northern provinces were attacked and taken by France. As wealth left the nation through military spending and an unfavorable trade balance, Spain's empire was picked away at for another 200 years. In the early 1700s, France's royal family, the Bourbons, ruled Spain. England took Gibraltar. In 1808, Napoleon's troops finally conquered Iberia. Spain's myth of invincibility, that may have still existed in the minds of some, was extinguished.

In *The Decline of the West*, Spengler wrote that once a culture has reached its peak of civilization it automatically becomes static and is already in decline. Yet it continues under the illusion that it is still developing and virile. Spengler stated:

> *The dwindling powers rise to one more, half-successful, effort of creation, and produce the Classicism that is common to all dying*

> *Cultures. The soul thinks, and in Romanticism looks back piteously to its childhood....* (P. 75)

Spengler likened a culture's fall to a sort of mid-life crisis. After a brief rebound, the culture, like a person, succumbs to aging, death and disappearance of the soul. But is the fall the end? Does the soul die? Even if overrun by a foreign society, the old empire may accept new ideas introduced by the invaders and incorporate with the conquerors or even experience a revival with an evolved society. The Byzantine Empire's rise out of the previous Roman Empire serves as an example. In the sweltering humidity of a Turkish bath in Istanbul, one senses the ghosts of ancient Romans.

Spengler used the term "wave-cycles" to describe the washing away of one culture by another. He writes:

> *...the great Cultures accomplish their majestic wave-cycles. They appear suddenly, swell in splendid lines, flatten again and vanish, and the face of the waters is once more a sleeping waste.* (P. 73)

Apparently, Spengler was not a surfer. Had he studied hydrodynamics he would have known that waves do not disappear but reform. Calm water is not a static "sleeping waste." There is always some movement. But Spengler's analogy is still valid in that cultures or societies do build and flatten cyclically. Spengler was caught in the linear, systematic approach of his times that he criticized. He used the same stream of water containing the wave-cycles to symbolize past and future. He felt history, like the stream, comes out of a dark unseen source into the light of the present then flows on to disappear in the equally dark future downstream. Here Spengler was again not observing Nature completely. The source of any stream is ultimately rain from condensed evaporation which is the stream's ultimate end/beginning. The stream is only one component of a great cycle. Its past and future can be seen if the cycle is understood.

Spain revived after Napoleon, but never attained its former glory. Yet Spanish society still lives and exists today, incorporated as it is in the European Economic Community. The Spanish no longer hold the belief that they will never be invaded. But Spain's myth of invincibility lasted a century (A.D. 1500-1600). The length of time that a society can hang onto to the myth of invincibility is critical and significant. We shall see that a myth of invincibility usually lasts less than 150 years. Only one society within Western Civilization holds the myth of invincibility longer than three hundred years, in each 2000 year cycle. Such events may be documented in the linear perspective. But personal memory, emotions, ideas and values are difficult to measure scientifically. Study of the arts coupled with a cyclical historical approach can yield a valid description of the status of the empire's *Zeitgeist.*

A myth of invincibility held by one empire beyond 300 years, brings profound change in the *Zeitgeist* of the entire civilization. All friends or foes who come in contact with such an empire are affected. As a part of Nature, human individuals and, by extension, their societies and civilizations are subject to the laws of Nature. This is consistent with natural operation. History is a human creation subject to human subjective mentality and prevailing *Zeitgeist.* The prime law of Nature is that it, and all it contains, operates in cycles. Thus an historical cycle is no different from any other natural organic system. Arnold Toynbee stated at age 81 in his book published in 1971, *Surviving the Future:*

> *...human affairs now follow natural laws, like those that govern non-human affairs. And natural law means regularity, recurrence, and repetition. I think that, even when human control over human affairs is lost, the future does not become predictable, but some guesses about the future then do become more probable than others in the light of the patterns that are discernible in the course of past events.* (P. 74)

It is possible to document events and follow the West's *Zeitgeist* cycle into the future. Spengler's cultural decline and death or Hegel's Absolute Idea are not the future. Instead, each individual's, generation's or civilization's education simply recycles. There is no regress or progress of the eternal *Zeitgeist,* only new technology that humans create and then adapt to by applying the three succeeding phases. Each time the phase is applied, society comes to falsely believe it is on to a novel, new approach.

II: The Thesis

The West's empires rise and fall, technology advances linearly while Western Civilization's *Zeitgeist* spiral completes one revolution every

2000 years. At different points within the 2000 year time span, the spiraling *Zeitgeist's* cycle passes through three separate phases. These are the Theocratic Phase, Secular Phase and Spiritual Phase. These three phases represent not only major changes in how Western civilization's culture and society is organized and governed. The Phases also delineate fundamental, general change in the belief system and *Zeitgeist* by which individuals and societies see themselves and others, place value, hopes, fears and create governments. Technology's effect on the imagination and material world affects the *Zeitgeist* and visa versa. The events occurring during one phase lead toward the next in the continuously repeating three part cycle.

The Theocratic Phase is relatively long-lived, spanning 1400 years. Society embraces the belief that doctrines or dogma define truth, explain the Divine and in turn are divinely directed and ordained. This phase gives way to a reactive (anti-thesis) Secular Phase, lasting a mere 250 years during which religion is discredited and science replaces the Divine as the repository of truth. But society eventually loses faith in both theocracy and secularism in favor of the 350 year Spiritual Phase. It is during the Spiritual Phase that the myth of invincibility lasts long enough to bury personal memory of past events, defeats or victories. Personal memory is also lost concerning every day life and thought from the Secular and Theocratic Phases. This actuates a shift in the *Zeitgeist* which questions the authority of both science and religion. In the resulting Spiritual Phase, scientific and inspirational thought synthesize in the attempt to transcend both previous phases. But a new theology and eventually a theocracy evolve. This returns Western civilization full circle to a new Theocratic Phase in 2000 years.

Technology's history, in contrast with the *Zeitgeist's* history, develops in a straight line. Observers of technology's pattern have often wrongly assumed that all history develops the same way. But technology is only the material offspring of civilization's orbiting *Zeitgeist*. Because technology moves ahead into the objective future, the *Zeitgeist* spirals in tandem with the linear trajectory of technology. Technology is pulled by or pushed by or pulls or pushes the relentless, subjective, emotional, recurring and spiraling *Zeitgeist*. Technology's only effect on the *Zeitgeist* is a slight stretching or compressing of the spiral. The repeating *Zeitgeist* is thus bound with advancing technology into the future (see fig. 6 page 34).

III: The Diagrams

These six diagrams give a graphic understanding of the operations already introduced.

Figures 1 and 2 deal with Hegel's dialectic. Figure 1 shows the dialectic as modified through the Secular Phase to accommodate a linear approach to human history. In figure 2, the pendulum's motion, swinging from thesis to anti-thesis and back to synthesis has been returned to the circular model.

HEGEL'S DIALECTIC

(Swinging Pendulum Model)

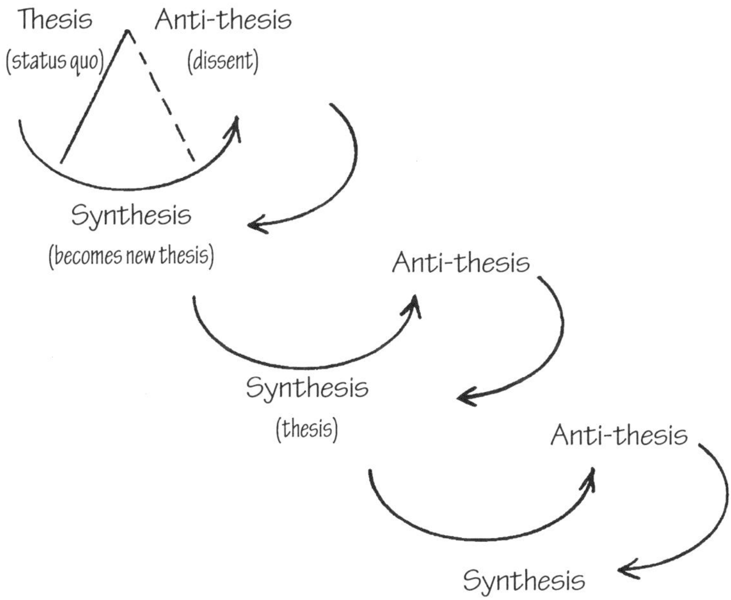

Figure 1

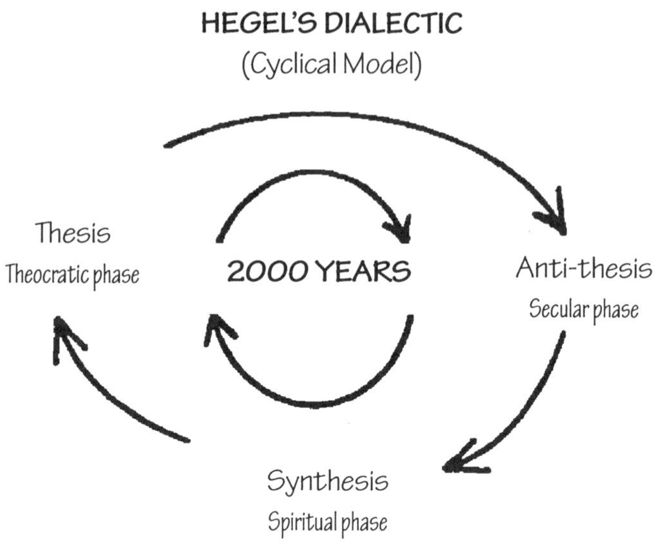

Figure 2

Western society cycles around every 2000 years within the three phases of the *Zeitgeist.* Each phase has been assigned to thesis, anti-thesis, synthesis. This represents another way to adapt Hegel's model. Nature operates in cycles. A child is dependent on parents (thesis), rebels against parents in the teen years (anti-thesis) then combines new ideas with those of the parent (synthesis) as the child reaches adulthood. The child in turn produces children, creating a new thesis status. Figure 2 applies this model to the dynamics of an entire civilization's society spanning 2000 years, including the string of separate empires that rise to administer the civilization.

The *Zeitgeist's* Theocratic Phase theocracy (thesis), whose right to rule is based on tradition and religion, is challenged by right to rule based on reason and science (anti-thesis) of the Secular Phase. The synthesis of the Theocratic and Secular Phases is the Spiritual Phase.

Figure 3 draws upon the 12 signs of the zodiac as handed down from ancient Persia (before 2000 B.C.E.) through Western myth and religion.

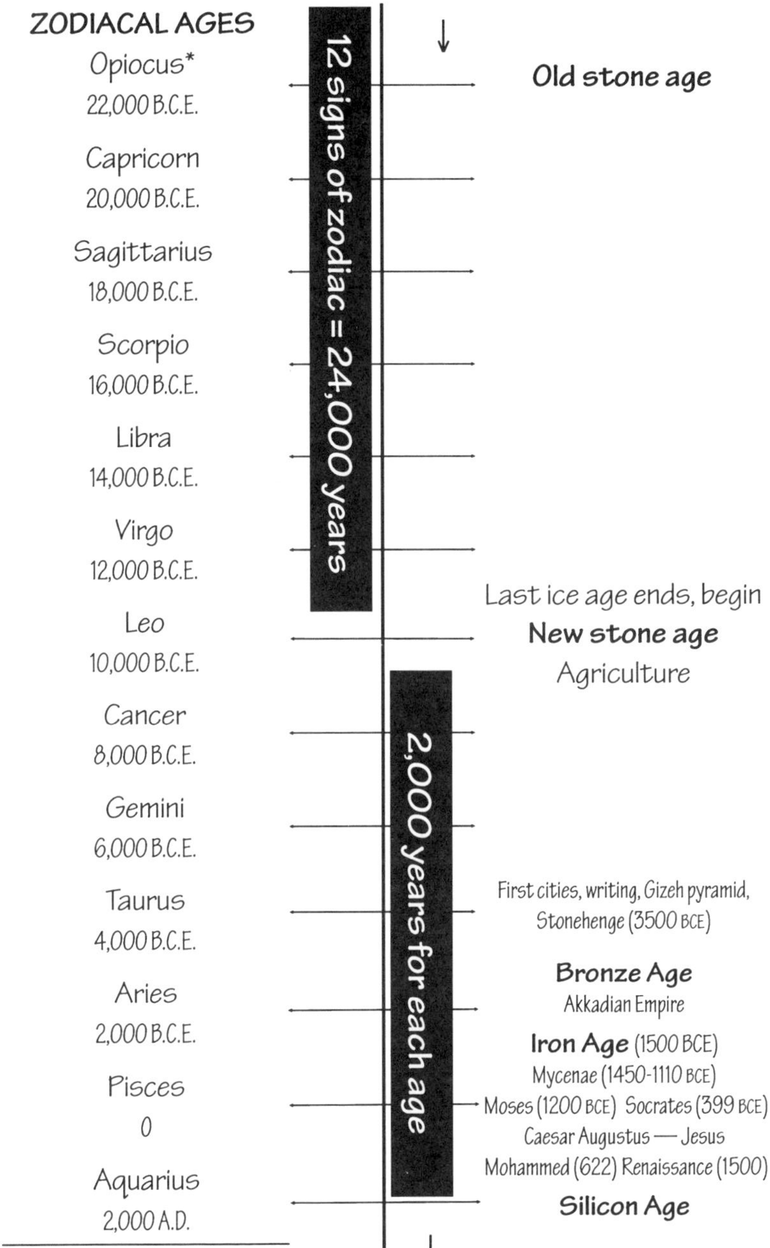

* *Opiocus is recognized by some astrologers as the 13th sign.*

Figure 3

The signs are used by modern astrologers and astronomers. Astronomers place the position of constellations in the night sky according to the time of year, using the 12 zodiac labels. Astrologers use them to predict the future. The number 12 holds an historical and mystical position in Western counting. Twelve inches to a foot, developed in ancient Egypt, remains the standard measurement in the US. Juries in the US court system number 12. Witch covens call for 12 members with a leader being the 13th. King Arthur had 12 knights of the Round Table. Jesus had 12 disciples. In groups of 12, Irish monks Christianized Pagan tribes in Medieval Europe. The Jews formed the 12 Tribes of Israel. Western Civilization has come to categorize its general history in 2000 year segments. Each 2000 year "age" is labeled by one of the twelve zodiacal signs. Breaking time into ages helps historians, paleontologists and geologists. It is a quick chronological reference when dealing with large time spans. As one goes back in time, the zodiacal titles follow each other in the same order as when going through the twelve months of a year. However, the direction is retrograde. Instead of Aries leading to Taurus and Taurus preceding Gemini, Taurus follows Gemini and Aries follows Taurus. Thus, the Age of Pisces precedes the Age of Aquarius.

Today, Before Christ (B.C.) or Before Christian Era and Before Common Era (B.C.E.) or Before Present Era (B.P.E.) are used with little religious connotation. The Piscean sign of the fish fit well with the church sponsored medieval historians. The Christian mission of saving souls was like catching fish in a net. No claim is made here to promote the zodiac's astrological, religious or astronomical significance. Yet the time before Jesus *is* labeled by historians as the Arian Age, and the 2000 years since has been the Age of Pisces.

The historical notations refer to technological progress and a few personalities are mentioned to give some chronological perspective. If 2000 years are multiplied by 12, the total is 24,000 years. At present, modern humans (Cro-Magnon) are believed to go back 40,000 years. We know little of what happened in human history even 4000 years ago. Presently some astrologers propose a thirteenth sign called Opiocus, which is also shown on the time line. Three human generations or the life span of any one human may exist in a 77 year period. If we allow this period to span the beginning and end of each age, a transition from the passing age to the dawn of a new age can be briefly held in personal memory. Thus feelings not just dry facts are carried into the next age. Only personal mem-

← 2000 YEARS DIFFERENTIAL →

	B.C.E.	A.D.	
Arian Age begins Akkadian-Babylon myth of invincibility Crete-Mycenae spiritual synthesis Greco-Pagan theocracy established — centered at Athens	2,000	0	**Piscean Age begins** Greco-Roman myth of invincibility Asian-European spiritual synthesis Roman-Christian theocracy centered at Rome and Constantinople
	1600	400	
	Theocratic Phase		
Dark Age Dorian invasions (Moses c. 1350) Greco-Dorian mix religion	1400-1200	700-800	**Dark Age** Arab & Norse invasions (Mohammed c. 650) Christian-Pagan mix religion
Greek culture replaces Mycenaen culture Athens rise — trade	900	1100	European culture replaces Roman culture Crusades begin — trade
Money replaces barter	700	1300	Money replaces barter
Golden Age Athenian, Roman republics Greek colonialism Defeat of Persia	600-400	1400-1600	**Renaissance** Venetian, Florentine, Swiss republics/European colonialism
Peloponnesian war ends Athenian revolution Conquest of Persia and Egypt	405	1650	Conquest of America 30 Yrs War ends English civil war, Virginia legislature Conquest of America, India, E. Asia
Hellenistic Age Divine right monarchy replaces theocracy (Alexander the Great c. 350) Ideal of one world Greek est. as international language	300	1700	**Age of Reason** Divine right monarchy replaces theocracy (Louis XIV c. 1650) ideal of one-world kingdom French est. as int'l language
	Secular Phase		
Divine right challenged by Roman republican law 2nd Punic war	225-200	1775-1800	Divine right monarchy challenged by US constitution-Napoleonic code Westward expansion
Science replaces religion Italo-Alpine, Gaul, Mediterranean & Aegean all under Roman military	100	1900	Science replaces religion N. America, Pacific and Caribbean, W. Europe, Japan, under US military
Pax Romana Disillusion with science, expo. and investigation of alternative beliefs Roman rise to single superpower Myth of invincibility begins	50	1950	**American Era** Disillusion with science, exposure & investigation of alternative beliefs US rise to single superpower Myth of invincibility begins
Piscean Age begins	0	2000	**Aquarian Age begins**
	Spiritual Phase		

Figure 4

ory can pass on the *Zeitgeist* of a past age. In time, a *Zeitgeist* carried by personal memory is extinguished as people die with their stories. Without personal memory, only written accounts and second hand feelings remain to draw on. History turns a page to a new age in the emotional and spiritual realm.

Recurring events come to pass generally every 2000 years. In some cases, a variable exists from one generation (30 years) to the greatest anomaly of 128 years. It was 2128 years after Rome became a republic (509 B.C.E.) that the republican House of Burgesses came to be in Virginia, USA (A.D. 1619). Examples of republican government did come about in Europe (Venice, Florence and Switzerland) within the 2000 year plus or minus a generation time frame. Other parallels are merely curious. Columbus sailed to America 2001 years after 509 B.C.E.

Figure 4 is a double time line representing the Arian Age next to the Age of Pisces shown in figure 3.

Along with naming ages, historians have placed labels on certain general trends, movements or periods such as The Golden Age, Pax Romana, Renaissance or Industrial Revolution. These have been assigned general dates affecting various geographies unevenly. The focus here is not to see, for example, how much and when the Lapps of Finland were affected by the Renaissance. This obscures the forest for the trees. What is important is that in the centers of trade and wealth, the Renaissance did occur within the generally accepted dates of A.D. 1300-1600 and established itself as the major general trend from A.D. 1400-1600. Within the time span variable of a generation or two, the Renaissance had been pre-played 2000 years before in the Golden Age of Greece 600 B.C.E. to 400 B.C.E. The use of money replaced barter in 700 B.C.E. and again, 2000 years later, in A.D. 1300. Some parallels listed may seem less apparent but will be clarified in following chapters.

Note should be made of the commonly accepted titles of trends, eras or ages listed which group the dated events. B.C.E., the Dark Ages lead to the Greek Golden Age, leading to the Hellenistic Age and then to Pax Romana. With the same sequence, time spans, and across the 2000 year leap, we find ourselves in A.D. with the Dark Ages leading to the Renaissance and then to the Age of Reason and on to the present American Era. The entire 2000 year period is bound by three groupings in parallel location on both the B.C.E. line and A.D. line. Labels given to these groupings are the Theocratic Phase the Secular Phase and the Spiritual Phase.

Figures 5 and 6 take the labels of trends, eras or ages as well as the three phases from the parallel time line (Fig. 4) and places them in a cyclical pattern. The flow and the recurring parallels are obvious.

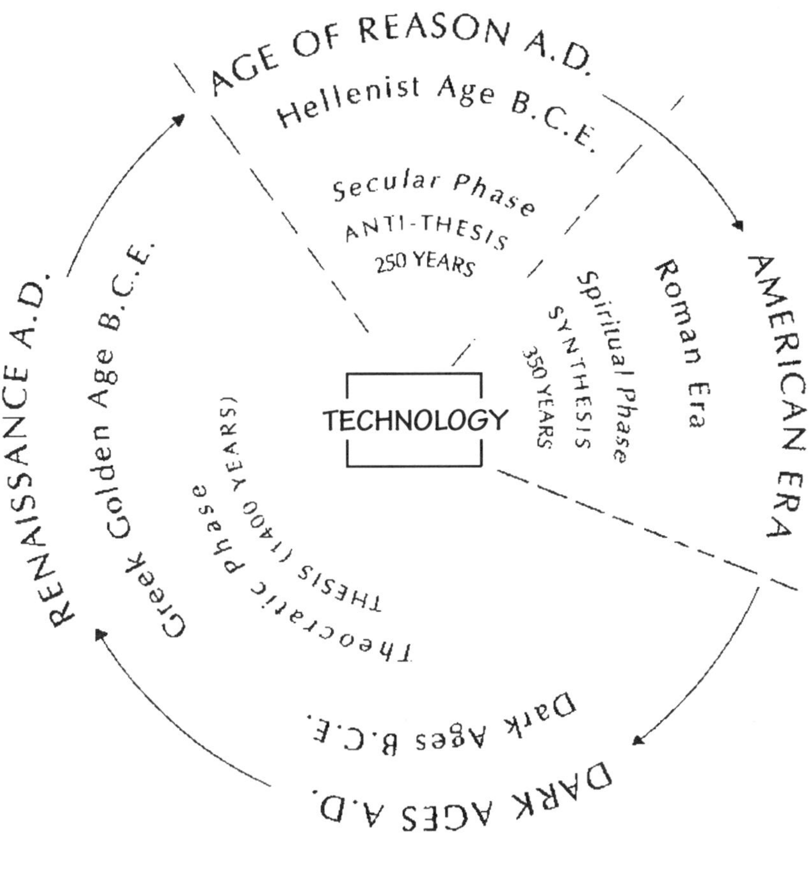

Figure 5

It should be noted that figure 5's view is an end view. The rectangle in the center is a cross section of the line of technology that is shown in a side view expressed in figure 6.

In figure 6, one phase follows the other. But the process repeats. The ellipse (or circle) is stretched like the coils of a spring. Following the coil, the Zeitgeist's movement passes through the phases then starts over again on the next coil. This symbolizes the separation in time of the returning pattern. The A.D. coil is currently ending the Piscean Age.

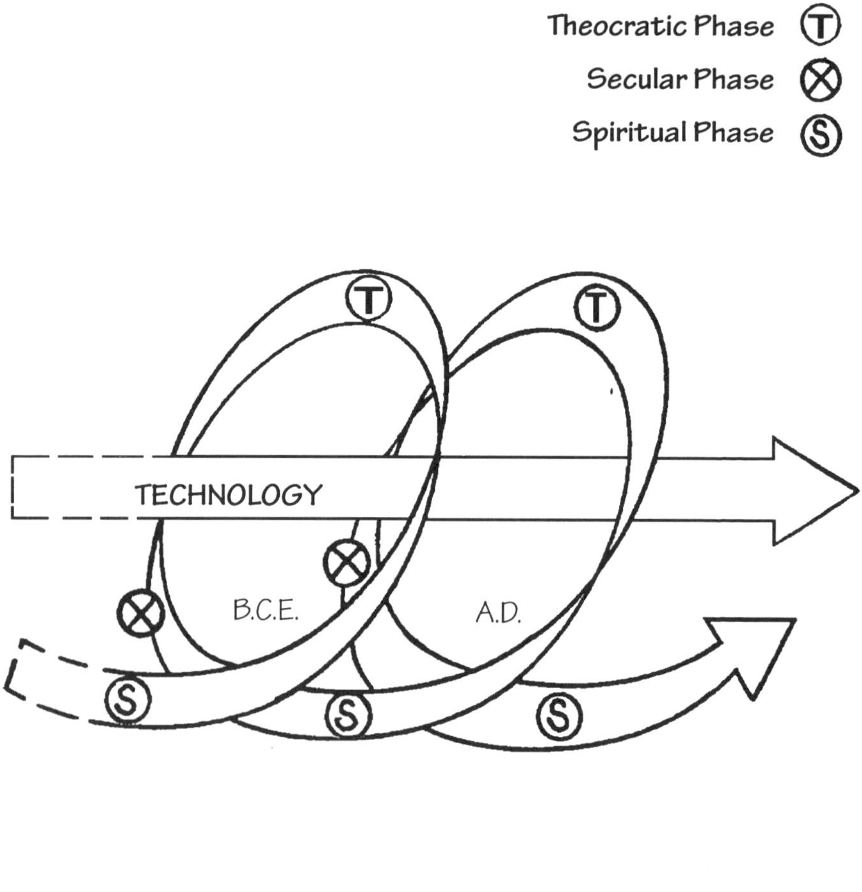

Figure 6

The next coil will be the coming Aquarian Age. But there is no progress in emotional understanding as Hegel and the romantics presumed. There is only the passing of one and the beginning of the next of the three phases of the eternal *Zeitgeist.* The *Zeitgeist* only appears to advance because it is adjusting to, or employing the prevailing technology.

Through the center of the diagram's coil, technology travels on a linear track into the future. Technological progress in human history has continually evolved while human thought and *Zeitgeist* has orbited around it. The pull or push of technology is constant. Sometimes fantastical visions like Buck Roger's space walks in the 1930s or Jules Verne's submarine in his nineteenth century novel, *Twenty Thousand Leagues Under the Sea,* pull technology until such flights of fancy become reality. Galileo's telescope and Copernicus's speculation that the Earth orbits the sun pushed Western society's *Zeitgeist* to accept scientific reality. Technology is either pulled or pushed by the coiling, orbiting *Zeitgeist;* it affects the politics of humans as they discover, create or use technology in its lineal race toward destiny. But the *Zeitgeist* keeps recycling, unchanged.

> *The thing that hath been, it is that which shall be;*
> *and that which is done is that which shall be done:*
> *and there is nothing new under the sun.*
>
> *Ecclesiastes 1:9*

CHAPTER TWO

TECHNOLOGY & GEOGRAPHY

1: TOOLS ON THE LANDSCAPE

Technology advances linearly while humans are left to deal with the spiritual changes it causes. The internal combustion engine answered society's dream of release from the less efficient horse. Geography became less of an obstacle; the Sunday driver was born. But the dream became a nightmare of wasted resources, pollution and traffic gridlock. In reaction, dreams of clean burning fuels and efficient, clean alternative transport push technology to further evolve.

Technology and geography affect human developments in both the material and spiritual realms. Conversely, materialism and spirituality affect the development and use of technology and geography. Diagrams 5 and 6 graphically show this process. This axiom is central to the study of the Theocratic, Secular and Spiritual Phases. In Western Civilization we term technological movement toward the future "progress." It has passed from Old to New Stone Age, to Bronze Age, to Iron Age, to the present Silicone Age. In the present, the technologies of these periods overlay and intermingle. Though no longer in the Stone Age, we still use stone (i.e., diamonds, silicone) in industry. Today's Stone Age slash and burn farmer of the tropics would probably not refuse a steel machete or a transistor radio. The urban, Silicone Age computer operator would probably not turn down a week of minimalist existence on an uncrowded tropical beach. Are people happier spiritually in a slash and burn society where perhaps minimum work hours are required to procure necessities? Or does spiritual well being come easier in an urban society where 40 hours or more of work a week is needed? Geographic location or level of technology does not dictate level of happiness or state of the *Zeitgeist.* Rather, the *Zeitgeist* determines geographic location and development of technology required to deal with geography and Nature.

In the midst of the Secular Phase, reasons for shifts in the *Zeitgeist* were pursued. It seemed logical to nineteenth century social scientists and philosophers, including Karl Marx, to surmise that class conflict and economics dictated behavior. Marx assumed that by eliminating private property, humans would act rationally and no longer have a need to be greedy. With greed eliminated, everyone would be self-actualized and happy. But the causes for emotions such as greed and happiness can't be reduced to logic. Consistent with the scientific, systematic approach of the Secular Phase, Marx dealt only with quantifiable realities. He disregarded the qualitative other than including with the fine arts all material created by human hands. Psychology might have helped Marx but it was then a new and untested science. By the end of the nineteenth century there was great working class solidarity throughout industrialized Europe and North America. This was logical and consistent with Marx's vision. Yet in 1914, workers went off to kill each other for "God and country." This nationalism was promoted by the aristocracy, industrialists and militarists who benefited from war at the expense of the workers. The most noble, self-actualized parent may produce the most base child.

In secular terms, the Crusades appear to be a series of imperialistic wars. They were motivated by the wish to secure a hold on lucrative trade routes and new territory for the Western European merchant class and aristocracy. There was little accommodation for or even slaughter of non-European Christians. Yet the Crusaders were exposed to Islam and the Mid East culture which presented advanced technology to the Europeans. Superior Damascus steel weapons and light cavalry halted European militarism. Advanced husbandry created Arabian horses that could handle the daily temperature extremes of the desert and required less water than European steeds. From the Arabs came the compass along with many other tools and sciences including algebra and the use of zero. The compass allowed accurate sailing at night and on cloudy days, doubling the amount of sea trade Europe could carry on. This in turn helped raise

Europe's standard of living and enhanced communication of ideas. The arrival of silk and fine chinaware, the technology of which was a mystery, created new desire, envy and wealth. Appeals to the senses and to envy are qualitative contributions to the *Zeitgeist.* New dyes produced a plethora of colorful alternatives to previously drab European textile shades. Cinnamon, cloves, nutmeg, mace, cardamom and other new spices shocked the sense of taste. Pepper became a new preservative of meat competing with smoke or salt. The new technologies forced the West to adapt sensually and emotionally.

So economics, technology and the control of geography were not the only reasons for the Crusades. Interest in the new ideas coming from the more urban, Muslim eastern Mediterranean also motivated spiritual shifts of the *Zeitgeist.* At the time of the Crusades, a rational approach to the Divine and study of classic Greek philosophy and science were tolerated by the Muslims. The Roman Catholic Church of that time reacted negatively to the Muslim acceptance of logic within its theology. The French King sided with the Roman Church and the abbot, Bernard of Burgundy. Bernard stated that love and reason were incompatible. It was threatening to Bernard and much of Western society, locked in the Theocratic Phase to see that atonement could be rationally explained and was not a mystery. Bernard's views had little to do with secular class conflict or economics and more to do with emotional theology, society's *Zeitgeist* and a search for doctrinal truth behind divine acts and purposes. He felt Christian faith would be destroyed if people believed they could understand or come to the Divine through their own reasoning.

The Muslim *Zeitgeist* of free thinking was nonetheless accepted by some in Europe. The philosopher Peter Abelard of Paris (A.D. 1079-1142) stated that Christ's crucifixion awakened compassion in humans and in so doing, humans (not the Divinity) created the Christ, a savior. Bernard, supported by the church and state, denounced Abelard. The universities, run by the church, followed Bernard's lead. The Muslim approach to understanding the Divine or rapture was deemed heresy. Bernard also advocated the Second Crusade in order to search for the Holy Grail!

Bernard's attitude was consistent with the Theocratic Phase which prevailed in Western society at that time. There were true believers and idealists in the Crusades who did not fight for riches or class status. They were motivated by the ideals dictated by Roman Christendom with little interest in new technology. Yet Muslim advances in science, navigation, math and medicine continued to intrigue some Europeans. This anticipated the Secular Phase's scientific and secular *Zeitgeist* by 500 years. Westerners like Abelard were intrigued by exotic knowledge. Dante's *Divine Comedy* may have been inspired by Mohammed's assent to heaven, described in the Koran. New ideas such as a rational approach to the Divine, whether reacted against or incorporated by European society, did affect Western Civilization's *Zeitgeist.*

Technology's use and Western society's *Zeitgeist* are played out on a given geography. Once the Secular Phase became established, the shift from having peasants and slaves to nineteenth century wage slaves and share croppers had more to do with the use of steam technology in factories, on iron rail and at sea, than it did with class conflict or spirituality. England's experience is one example.

England applied steam technology before other nations. Low cost of production and high profits resulted directly from steam powered textile mills. Steam ships and rail- roads provided lower transport costs fueled by England's plentiful coal and iron reserves. A strong currency resulted. This allowed net importation of cheaper grain. By 1850, England's people consumed more grain than they produced, but they didn't suffer the shortages and famine experienced by Ireland or Scotland. There was no longer need for wheat farmers. So land owning aristocrats drove yeomen farmers and peasants off their land, replacing them with a few shepherds raising sheep. This was legalized by the English Enclosure Acts. Grain was replaced by wool as England's bounty from the land. The farmers adapted by going to cities as wage slaves in industry, coal mines or the military. Some went to Australia and America. Thus England assumed an urban secularized *Zeitgeist*, ending serfdom for economic rather than ethical reasons.

In America, New York bankers and Yankee manufacturers saw little value in America's southern style feudalism. Farm commodities were delivered inexpensively by rail or steam boat. Cheap immigrant labor working land stolen from the Indians, supplied food and a market for manufactured goods. Acquisition of laborers with no housing, clothing or food costs borne by the employer was the profitable alternative to responsibilities and liabilities under the slavery system. This urban-industrial view was ultimately expressed by Lincoln's Emancipation Proclamation. Yet through all this technological rationale and materialist cause and effect, there were great emotional and spiritual acts of excessive brutality, martyrdom, heroism, unselfishness and greed as the agrarian *Zeitgeist* of the US was challenged and society adapted to industrialization.

Western Civilization's aristocrats, previously obliged to protect and care for peasants and slaves, expelled them from the land in the Industrial Revolution. Moralists who had preached against slavery for millennia, finally saw their dream come true. The urbanizing Western society saw captains of industry and bankers gain wealth and power by human effort rather than through divine help or birth right. The *Zeitgeist* of the West pushed technology which encouraged urbanization. Urbanization in turn pushed the *Zeitgeist* from belief in the Theocratic Phase's divine intervention to Secular Phase human empowerment.

While technology progresses, humans are born, mature, age and die. Individuals and society are born again from the genetic and cultural remains. Today's technology provides birth control and longevity, but the birth-death cycle continues. The changing phases of the *Zeitgeist* return while society is adapting or not adapting to the contemporary technology. (see fig. 5&6) Every 2000 years, technology expands human mastery over Nature and dependence on urbanization to where the resources required to maintain technology dwindle as does the human spirit that supports it. In the Spiritual Phase, humans come to feel technology controls their life rather than the other way around. The separation from Nature becomes acute.

A study of the past's urban geography and *Zeitgeist* that the Mediterranean World experienced B.C.E. compares with the urban geography and *Zeitgeist* of Western society A.D. Though technology has advanced and caused the world's geography to shrink in terms of travel time, a parallel spiritual experience recurs. Whether personal memory, emotions and ideas travel on Roman roads and galley boats or internet computer links and jets, the *Zeitgeist's* spiraling cycle continues to orbit technology's lineal advances.

Physical geography changes due to natural and/or human action. Like technology, geography also affects the *Zeitgeist*. Due to altitude, latitude, prevailing winds, availability of water, soil and other natural and human resources, a society living in a given area adapts and develops accordingly. Humans apply technology to reshape geography. In his exhaustive 12 volume work, *A Study of History*, historian Arnold Toynbee postulated his challenge to the natural environment thesis. He stated that civilization will not advance where the natural environment is so harsh that it overwhelms any human effort to adapt, or so pleasant that little effort is necessary to provide comfort and needs. Thus people in rain forests, tropical islands or temperate climates receive abundant food, shelter and clothing from fishing, hunting and gathering with relatively little effort or challenge. Such a society needs no technology to irrigate, store food or build cities. The human population does not outgrow the natural resources because disease, periodic famine or war keep population in check. Likewise, where a harsh environment provides little for even a small population, basic survival takes so much time that there is little time to contemplate or harness resources to develop technology. Thus we see the nomads of the desert (Bedouins) or the ice (Eskimos) wandering at a subsistence level. Toynbee felt a proper balance must exist between the challenges placed by the natural environment and technology for urban development to take place.

In the midst of a harsh environment, a natural resource like the abundant water of the Nile River provided an incentive to challenge the desert environment that would spawn the Egyptian civilization. Had the banks of the Nile been lined with rain forests, as is the case along the Amazon or Congo rivers, the population would not have been challenged enough to feel it worthwhile to build a civilization. Toynbee's idea still holds true today.

The rich alluvial soil of Southern California's coastal plain is trapped between snowcapped mountains and the Pacific Ocean. This provides the site of the Los Angeles Basin. It was initially identified by Spanish explorers as the Land of Smokes. Already smoke from the camp fires of the large native population was noticeable. Like today's LA smog, it was trapped over the flat land by westerly ocean breezes pushing against a mountain wall rising on the eastern edge of the plain. The native population was large but relatively peaceful. There were many rivers and springs and a mild climate. The plentiful oak trees provided an edible acorn staple. Game and fish were abundant. Life was fairly utopian in Stone Age terms. There was no need to develop a civilization or conquer a neighbor. In time population might have increased which would warrant changes. But the utopia was eliminated by the Spanish, who brought European civilization and technology.

Irrigation, the plow and the wheel, among other technologies, developed the basin into a prosperous farming and ranching area. Eighteenth century Spain, however, was not yet at a technological level required to create a large urban area and artificial seaport in a remote location. The agrarian population has grown to be the urban society it is today, because the technology was available to meet the natural challenge of insufficient water. In the twentieth century, electricity, internal combustion engines, dynamite, high dams, and steel all combined to deliver required water from eastern and northern California as well as the Colorado River.

Two millennia earlier, Roman urban centers also met natural challenges with technology. Concrete was first developed by the Romans in the second century A.D. The Romans built with the latest technology of that day and provided for urban society's efforts to adapt to the geography and environment. The aqueducts and roads they built are no match for today's California aqueducts or freeways but their technology impressed the world in their day as much as modern technology does today. Society in LA today enjoys a lifestyle with a high standard of living and leisure time. So did ancient Pompeii 2000 years ago. They share coastal climates with the specter of earthquakes and volcanoes (Vesuvius, in the case of Pompeii) as reminders of human subservience to Nature. But in the pursuit of material gain, neither gave sufficient consideration to Nature's power. The top priority in Pompeii, LA or any city is the activity of human relationships. This urban *Zeitgeist* is different from the agrarian top priority of human relationship with Nature. Today, Pompeii is buried under volcanic ash while the LA basin experiences devastating earthquakes, fires and floods. Technology apart, the lack of concern for Nature as part of the urban *Zeitgeist* was the same in the two periods separated by two millennia, different geographies and 6000 miles.

The creation and spread of an urban civilization are only limited by the technology of the day to serve the human population and deal with the environment. Modern technology has shrunk the world. When an ancient Roman referred to the world, it was the Mediterranean region and areas that bordered it. When a modern American refers to the world it is the planet Earth. The time it took to get a product from Athens to Rome in 100 B.C.E. was the same as getting a product from London to New York in A.D. 1900. A message by a fast riding messenger or carrier pigeon in B.C.E. wouldn't match the speed of electricity that telegraph or modern satellite communications travel today.

Human contact during commerce does not confine itself only to buying and selling. Trading of goods to satisfy material needs has always been accompanied by the spread of new ideas. Helped by technology, this process has kept pace with Earth's geometrically expanding population and distances between separate geographies under human control. Over the past two millennia, the speed and volume of trade and communication has accelerated. But has human mentality toward the material world changed? Today's geographic stage is larger, and the actors have different names. There are new tools. But the *Zeitgeist*'s phases remain the same, disguised by the technology which prevails at the moment.

II: The American Anomaly

Expanded geography does not change the *Zeitgeist* in terms of social, emotional or spiritual relationships. Dominant empires, however large or small, still affect society. Crossing the larger geographic stage of today takes no more time than crossing the smaller ancient one. The nation states of Europe today thus compare with the city states of ancient Greece. The continental nation state of the US is like the nation state of ancient Rome.

Both the US and ancient Rome were separated by water from their cultural source. Immigrants from the East (Greece B.C.E. and Europe A.D.) mingled with the native population's culture. From these similar beginnings both republics came to rule the urban Western world. Both developed a singular city that became the epitome of urbanity in their time. The metropolis of Rome and its port city Ostia was the financial and political center of the world B.C.E., only differing in size and technology from the New York City-Washington, D.C. megalopolis of 2000 years later. Cases can be made for any number of geographic comparisons. The Adriatic Sea and eastern Mediterranean Sea were for ancient Greece and Rome a watery barrier just as the Atlantic Ocean or Caribbean Sea are between modern Europe and America. The vastness of the ancient Atlantic or Indian Oceans were like today's Pacific for the societies clustered along the maritime shores.

Comparisons of modern England with ancient Athens or modern Spain with ancient Phoenicia or modern Prussia with ancient Sparta can be made. Iberian Spain and Portugal competed with France, England and later Holland to establish colonies overseas. Ancient Phoenicia and the Greek city states competed two millennia before. The spirit of adventure to gain personal wealth, a new life, spread old and new political and cultural values and religion — all these things were in the minds and hearts of ancient Greek colonists as well as those going to America 2000 years later.

Roger Williams, founder of Providence, Rhode Island, in 1636, exemplifies the *Zeitgeist* of his times in New England, America. Williams took a 65 day ship passage from England to find there a Calvinist theocracy. He felt it was as tyrannical as any theocracy. William's personal religion had gone from Anglican to Baptist to Seeker (a seventeenth century sect devoted to defining the truth). Yet he was not banished from Massachusetts Colony for his religious, anti-theocratic beliefs. He was ostracized because his personal relations with Native American Indians led him to call for Indian land rights. His call for freedom of religion and separation of church and state was an outgrowth of his political belief that protection of the dignity of *all* individuals and democracy should guide a limited, secular government. Rhode Island provided the first American model for the US in its creation of a sovereign, secular state a century later.

The idea of representative government was delayed from taking hold in colonial America. Yet it was being practiced in European cities and among American Indians. The Iroquois League set up a republican confederacy in 1570. This was 2079 years after the Latin Tribes did the same in Italy. Eventually the English-American colonies did start on the republican road with the establishment of a Virginia legislature in 1619. This was 2128 years after Rome's removal of their Etruscan king in 509 B.C.E. This delay resulted in a 128 year time span anomaly which added to the 2000 year span between recurring events and *Zeitgeist* phases. Usually a 30 to 50 year, plus or minus, variable exists. Technology had not yet compensated for the Atlantic Ocean's geographic obstacle. Before nineteenth century steam technology, the travel time between America and Europe was vast. This isolated and slowed news of current events and the exchange of ideas crossing the Atlantic.

In terms of contemporary geographic understanding, Italy was a known location to the Greeks of 509 B.C.E. This compares with accounts of Atlantis, voyages by Norse explorers, Irish monks and French fishermen which kept America more of a myth in the minds of Europeans before Columbus. Ancient Italy was part of the known world of the Greeks while America was a New World for modern Europeans. Such a profound concept takes time to digest into the *Zeitgeist.* But subsequent Renaissance technology, such as the printing press and inexpensive paper, sped communication. Mass written communication was a technological response to the pull of the emerging Secular Phase of the *Zeitgeist.*

The printed communication in colonial America compensated for isolation from Europe. The inevitable return of the Secular Phase came to pass under its own historical momentum. It arrived regardless of the delay caused by an unprecedented geographic barrier or limits of technology. The Zeitgeist pushed the advance of steam driven transport. Relative to the *Zeitgeist's* cyclical pattern, the concept that humans could run their own affairs without divine guidance spread in America and Europe. The self reliance required on the frontier and emerging urban centers contributed to the secular spirit in both Rome and America. For 13 of England's American colonies, this resulted in the removal of their king in 1776 and the creation of the United States of America.

The USA and ancient Roman republics both went on to establish their empires. Rome subdued barbarians, took barbarian lands and established a definable border. Rome continued to have problems with barbarians crossing the border. The US conquered the Native Americans and Mexico. In both cases, protection of settlers, national security and spread of Western Civilization provided the rationale for the blatant conquest of adjoining land and peoples. Both empires practiced genocide, at times, to achieve their goals. Technological "progress" was employed with the rationalized emotionalism of Roman Law, B.C.E. or American Manifest Destiny, A.D.

Technology has made Western Civilization's conquest of the entire planet Earth possible in a physical, geographic sense. The Euro-US society has also spread its *Zeitgeist* over the globe. Two thousand years before, the same *Zeitgeist* spread through the ancient Greco-Roman "West" over Central and West Europe, North Africa and Southwest Asia. In both A.D. and B.C.E., the known world presented ideas concerning human relations, spirituality and values which clashed and/or were incorporated with the West. The age old quest for defining spiritual and technological relationships with Nature and humans continues in its cyclical fashion.

(see fig. 6) In sequence, the three phases of the Western *Zeitgeist* follow each other through the 2000 year spiral.

> *Since we have admitted no substantial change in man's nature during historic times, all technological advances will have to be written off as merely new means of achieving old ends.*
>
> Will and Ariel Durant, *Lessons in History*, p. 95

chapter three

THE THEOCRATIC PHASE

1: Theocracy Defined

A society is theocratic if directed, adjudicated and legislated by persons acting as deities or the Divine, or as representatives of deities or the Divine. Whether self-appointed or chosen by another person or persons, the ruling authority comes from the Divine. This definition applies to the words theocracy or theocratic as used in this book. For a discussion of a Theocratic Phase, some documentation of its history and concurrent events are illustrative.

There is little data to clearly chart the *Zeitgeist's* 2000 year cycle prior to the ancient Minoans (Cretans) c. 2000 B.C.E. All that is left to us are artifacts showing us the level of technology, metallurgy, sources of trade items and level of personal wealth. There are stone works which date to 3000 B.C.E. contemporary with Egyptian pyramids and Stonehenge in England. From Asian cuneiform writing of the Tigris and Euphrates and African hieroglyphics from the Nile, we know that by 2000 B.C.E., these lands were ruled by priest kings or a priest class. The Akkadian Empire (see fig. 4) conquered and united all the cities of the Eastern Mediterranean and Tigris and Euphrates Rivers including Babylon (where the Tigris and Euphrates narrow their distance from each other). Akkadian Babylon was the Rome of 2000 B.C.E. Like Rome and the USA, Akkad was a society on the edge of the frontier that came to control the known civilized world. In terms of that superpower's influence in that time and location, little is really known today other than what the archeologists and the Bible tell us existed. Europe was certainly in communication with the lands of the Fertile Crescent (Nile, Tigris and Euphrates). Europe's geography contains the southern most Greek island of Crete in the Eastern Mediterranean.

Archeologists believe Crete of 2000 B.C.E. (see fig. 4), was ruled by a matriarchal Minoan society. Murals on the walls of the Minoan palace in Knossos, Crete, show porpoise in the sea interacting with humans and topless female acrobats gaming with bulls. The Bronze Age Minoans gained livelihood as farmers, fishers and merchants. Being able sailors, they established trade posts and colonies throughout the Mediterranean. Many exiles from the Akkadian conquests may have found their way to the safety of Crete. The Minoans had a complex written language with symbols representing syllables. Their math included the decimal system. A strong merchant class, wealth and international exposure to many ideas may well have led to a Secular Phase on Crete. This would have led to an extended period of peace and a Spiritual Phase, which ended during the natural disasters at Minoa's zenith of power.

On the Island of Crete, evidence suggests that the civilization declined following a catastrophic volcanic explosion. In 1450 B.C.E. the volcanic explosion of the nearby island of Thera was followed by a series of earthquakes. Volcanic ash and possible tidal waves devastated Crete's agricultural base and trade economy. Fifty years after the natural disaster, Mycenaeans arrived from the Greek mainland. They invaded and took over what was left of the Minoan empire. Human sacrifice came into practice as Minoan society desperately turned for help from the Divine. Using imported practices such as human and animal sacrifice may have helped its priest class institute methods of control. One hundred and fifty years later (1150 B.C.E.), the Mycenae empire also fell to foreign invasion. By 1000 B.C.E., Crete had become a myth. Crete's end might be shrouded in the story of Atlantis sinking beneath the waves. During the Minoan-Mycenaen decline, a Theocratic Phase developed, including religious dogma. Homer's stories provided the grist for the liturgy. But exact religious ritual eludes us.

Bulls played a large part in what has been determined as the Minoan religion of Crete. Minoan religion with a bull as a central figure is appropriate as the Cretan civilization originated in the Age of Taurus (see fig. 3). The origins of reverence for the cow is ancient indeed. The two previous ages had evolved an exalted place for "Holy Cows" alongside "Mother Nature" in the human spiritual psyche. Domesticated cattle supplied meat and pulled the plow (new technology 6000 B.C.E.). The ethnobotanist, Terrence McKenna, has postulated in his book, *Food of the Gods*, that cows gained an important position in human cosmology in pre-agricultural pastoral times. Before 10,000 B.C.E., McKenna sees small groups foraging and ingesting the psychedelic mushrooms found only in the cow dung. This, he feels, spawned much in human development including language and religion. By the time of Crete, opium and ergot (a fungus on grain that causes psychedelic reaction) as well as mead and beer were known and may have performed a function within Cretan religion.

Drugs may not have played as important a role as McKenna suggests. But Homer's description of opium eaters is probably based on more than fantasy. Homer's Iliad and Odyssey stories came out of Mycenaen-Minoan/Cretan oral history. For later Greeks, Homer's stories served as a sort of Greco-Roman Bible.

As for physical remnants of religion from before 2000 B.C.E., there are cave paintings and female forms represented in statuary. There are the mysterious standing stones used by the Canaanites in Moses' time, destroyed in Arabia by seventh century Muslims or found today from Tara, Ireland, to Toraja in Sulawesi, Indonesia. They were revered by the ancients in the West as they are today by Hindus in Bali and India. For Hindus, these "lingums" are stone phallic symbols tied in with the mystery and recognition of fertility and the male.

Today the sacred pools, arcades and general layout of Hindu temples are very similar to the ancient temples of the Mid-East and Greece uncovered by excavation. Though Brahmin of the Hindus and Kronos of the ancient Greeks have different names, they both occupy the position as a single Divinity from which all the incarnations, deities and creation originate. Hinduism, as practiced today, may be our last link to religion of the Age of Taurus (see fig. 3). Lingums, pyramids and Stonehenge may be religious artifacts of a Theocratic Phase and a preceding Spiritual Phase. The science involved in their construction may indicate a scientific, Secular Phase. Perhaps the constructions were used to satisfy the needs of all three phases as the *Zeitgeist* revolved. After the Taurusian Age, the following Arian Age produced the monotheism introduced briefly in

Egypt and then by the Jews of Moses. This monotheism existed in the Mid-East during the Arian Age but only spread over Western Civilization in the current Piscean Age. Monotheism was an alternative view of the Divine. It emphasized Kronos (Yahweh) and reduced the incarnations to the status of angels rather than deities. But Jewish monotheism was nonetheless employed as a rationale for a theocracy in keeping with a Theocratic Phase.

In the Arian Age, a priest class and theocracy operated in Greece as well as throughout the eastern Mediterranean by 1600 B.C.E. Natural disasters and foreign invasion had dissipated what was left of Mycenae-Minoan civilization's power. However many Minoan-Mycenaen cities (such as Mycenae or Troy) survived into the Arian Age. Their beliefs continued and mingled with the beliefs of invading waves of rural Dorian (Celtic) society (see fig. 4).

The story of Western theocracy two thousand years later (c. A.D. 400), compares. The priest class assumed control of a descending Roman Empire in the face of invasion from a rural Germanic society. In both cases, (Dorian invasions of Greece 1400-1300 B.C.E., and Arab and Germanic invasions of Rome A.D. 600-700), technological progress slowed, trade ebbed and literacy dropped. Money ceased to be used as trade and barter took over the economy. The Theocratic Phase was institutionalized. Assimilation between rural conquerors and the conquered urbanites took place. Modern Europe's Dark Ages (A.D. 600), and the Dorian Invasions or Greek Dark Age, (1400 B.C.E.), are the titles given to these general trends and events, 2000 years distant from each other (see fig. 4). The conquered Greek city states of B.C.E. as well as those cities that were bypassed by the invading Dorians all eventually shared their languages, ideas and religions during this time. Similarly, two thousand years later, Western and Eastern Roman cities assimilated with the Arab tribes invading from the south and Germanic tribes who invaded from the north.

In the respective Dark Ages, myths, values, priests and families were shared by both conqueror and conquered. These were also persecuted, co-opted, blended and destroyed until a new mythology synthesized in both A.D. and B.C.E. Theocracy prevailed because government, run by illiterate warlords, was consecrated by a priest class. The literate and organized priest class was the last vestige of a past world government and tradition. Theocracy was forced on, or accepted by, society as a function of the Divine. Divine law-giving was sanctified and advised in the Arian

Age by sibyl or druid and two millennia later in the Piscean Age, by bishop or Pope. In both periods, there were only one or maybe two generations who felt safe within a short myth of invincibility during the Theocratic Phase. Western society, struggling for physical survival, had relatively little time to allow contemplation of divergent or alternative spiritual matters. Efficient protection was top priority. The issue of whether a divine rationale for a system of government was valid or not became secondary.

II: Greek Theocracy

The ancient Greeks are recognized for their humanist attitude advocating direct, skeptical observation of Nature and democracies. A form of rationalism rose in Greece that may appear secular. But this was only the Arian Age seed of a truly Secular Phase yet to come. Athens's first attempts at secularism in its Golden Age (c. 500 B.C.E.) must not be confused with an end to the Theocratic Phase. Individuals were postulating ideas that would only later be applied to the Hellenism of the approaching Secular Phase. Two millennia later the Renaissance (c. A.D. 1500) played the same role, pointing the way to the Age of Reason of the Secular Phase in the Piscean Age (see fig. 4). Modern historians in the West have also wrongly assumed Greek secular humanism to be unique. Edith Hamilton states in her work, *The Greek Way: "In that black and fierce world a little centre of white-hot spiritual energy was at work. A new civilization had arisen in Athens, unlike all that had gone before"* (p. 16). But this view is ethnocentric. Like many Secular Phase historians, Hamilton was locked into her specialty. The Minoans may very well have had a humanist Secular Phase before 2000 B.C.E.

Athens's Golden Age was not unique in its own time period either. Buddha also had ideas similar to Athenian belief that human will and labor toward the good could bring a human close to the Divine. Lao Tsu placed emphasis on natural environment and its relation to humans just as ancient Athenians and the animist societies existing then and today. Buddha in India and Lao Tsu in China were members of societies contemporaneous with Golden Age Greece. Historians have labeled this period containing Lao Tsu, Buddha, Zoroaster of Persia and Socrates of Greece, as the "Axial Age" (c. 500 B.C.E.). Greece did not exist in a vacuum.

Cities in Persia or Egypt, at this time, already had a millennium old, established and unbroken urban theocracy. The Persian king was seen as a direct representative of the Divine. The Pharaoh was considered a deity. Greek society had only vague memory of a long gone Minoan urban society whose last remnant was the city of Mycenae. They had lost personal memory. Following the Greek Dark Ages and the fall of Mycenae (1400-1200 B.C.E.), urbanism was relatively limited in Greece. The free individualistic spirit found in the tribe and village was still alive.

Democracy is found in any tribal society where leaders are elected. In a tribal society, shaman, story teller, artist or musician are equals and often the same person. Specialization of labor is minimal. Pursuit of divine reality and truth is an individual quest. These tribal traditions were still evident in the classical Greeks 500 B.C.E. It was this tribal spirit of freedom and the sibyl's blessings which fortified the Greeks in their victory over the Persians (see fig. 4) at the Battle of Marathon in 490 B.C.E. It was also a European tribal spirit and Christian religion that inspired Europeans in their victory over the Turks at Vienna, 2039 years later (A.D. 1529). Had the Persians won the Battle of Marathon and the Persian Wars, Greek cities would have become western outposts of established Persian urbanity, including Persian style theocracy. Had Vienna fallen to the Turks two millennia later, much of Western Europe would have followed. Muslim theocracy would have administered Central Europe.

The Roman, Greek, Phoenician, Persian, Canaanite and Egyptian deities, along with tribal deities including Yahweh of the Jews, were all known and recognized by one another (c. 800 B.C.E.). By 500 B.C.E. the Greeks were skeptical of the magic found in barbarian religions. This makes Golden Age Greeks seem analytical or less superstitious. It may appear that Greeks broke from dogma or other institutional trappings of theocracy and embraced free thought. Athens seems to have had a generally speculative society championing individual liberty. But the appearance is superficial. Greek beliefs were not considered fantasy by Greek society. Homer chronicled the acts and magic powers of deities we call mythology today but considered divine in Greece of 500 B.C.E.

The stories of Homer were read more in the context of a holy book or Greek Bible, displaying Greek values and morals worthy of study. The use of dates by early Greeks was not important. This is also consistent with traditional, cyclical, tribal history which is used for study of the past, for the future and any current event. A present account of cyclical, tribal history is provided by Kaiser. In his book, *The Voice of the Spirit: Prophesies of the Hopi Indians,* he states:

> *And for the Hopi all this is related to the unfolding of "seeds" that have been part of cosmic motion since the beginning of time. In this sense, mythical past and future are one, and prophecy actually becomes a myth for the future.* (P. 64)

Deities from Greek religion were utilized in Greek plays. Today we see or read those Greek plays and view the deities as mythological. The plays are a vehicle to gain insight into human nature and relationships with the Divine. It is tempting to assume that all Greeks interpreted the plays in this secular way. Some Greeks no doubt did. But the general society probably took the characters and stories literally. This is similar to audiences today watching an open air production of a Ramayana drama played out in Bali or on TV in Hindu India. In Hindu village society, artists, actors and musicians hold as high a station in society as priests. The theater is a religious as well as an entertaining experience. In ancient Athens, theater shared this form of preaching and religious control of society. Greek ethics and morality were espoused in the context of the religion of the time. Greek humanism was not secular humanism.

Free from Persian or Egyptian control, the Greeks crawled out of their Dark Ages to develop urbanism and spirituality on their own. They gradually left their rural lifestyle while retaining dim memories through oral tradition of urbane Mycenaean past. This is similar to how the legend of King Arthur reflected dim memory of a post Roman past for modern England. Greece had historians before Herodotus, "the Father of History," but we would label them story tellers today. Herodotus is important because he attempted to be as clear, systematic and factual in his writing as possible. Herodotus dealt more with current events or very recent history. Because of this, in the twentieth century A.D., Spengler determined that the Greeks were "ahistorical." But Spengler missed the connection that the Greeks had with tribal society in regard to the art and purpose of history. Herodotus tried to break the holistic connection discounting tribalistic myth and magic. As a result of his limited scientific approach, he could not find credible earlier historical accounts filled with mythology. In time, other Greek histories were discounted or lost, except for Homer's.

A city was also seen as an aspect of the Divine. The Greeks demanded sacrifice for the defense of their cities no less than their urban neighboring empires. Expulsion from the city was a sentence worse than death. Arian Age city folk felt their town had a divine connection. Every city had a protecting deity. Today many cities in the West have a patron saint serving the same purpose. The ancient protectors included Jehovah for Jerusalem, Athena for Athens and Sparta or Diana for Ephesus. Unlike most Greek cities, freedom of speech and thought was central to Athenian urban development. For this reason, historians have seen Athens as above theocratic dogma. Edith Hamilton wrote romantically about the Greeks, without recognition of tribal mentality or Buddha:

> *They would have no man to dictate to them and being free from masters they used their freedom to think. For the first time in the world the mind was free, free as it hardly is today. Both the state and religion left the Athenian free to think as he pleased.* (P. 42)

Initially free speech provided some equity in government. Euripides could speak against slavery. Aristophanes wrote an anti-war play at the height of Athens's life and death struggles with Sparta. But these free thinkers were elite members of a mostly illiterate society. Athens did exist in a theocratic world and its theocracy did have limits. Socrates took freedom of speech to that limit. He was condemned to death for introducing a new concept of the Divine and corrupting Athens's youth. Those corrupted youth were not the rabble of society, but the children of the wealthy and powerful merchants and aristocrats, supported by the institution of slavery, who could afford to pay for an education. Though literate, even the wealthiest woman was not allowed citizenship.

Athens was not the only city in Greece. As in the Venetian Republic or Florence of Europe, 2000 years later (see fig. 4), scientific inquiry and the seeds of the Secular Phase were evident. But other Greek cities held fast to old tradition and theocracy. The poet aristocrat Pindar of ancient Thebes placed no merit in democracy. The narrow, singular martial mind of Sparta was perhaps socialist, but the state had definite Divine authority and religious guidance.

Democracy of the male elite did not serve Athens well in war, where emergencies of defense do not benefit from the luxury of public debate. Ancient Athens is called a democracy because all male citizens were allowed a political voice and vote like Switzerland or Iceland today. But in reality, Athens was a limited republic whose representatives did not include non-citizens, slaves or women. What is called Greek humanism today, was for the most part confined to Athens.

Though early humanism could be found in any merchant controlled free state city in sixteenth century Europe, the Pope, or at least the Christian mythology, was recognized if not fully accepted by most of society. The Christian mythology was taken symbolically or literally depending on the person interpreting it. The common folk went to worship dutifully at church. The schools were sponsored and controlled by the church. Aristocracy and priests sat in judgment, ruling society and representing the Divine. Art retained religious themes. Even the irreverent work of Hieronymus Bosch was filled with religious symbolism.

It is romantic to assume that the general population of Athenian Golden Age society, much less all of Greece, held the lofty views of Plato. This would be like assuming Renaissance European society saw the world the same as their genius contemporaries, Galileo or DaVinci. Statues of deities looked down upon the students and Socrates in the gymnasium. Apollo, the deity for poetry, music and art held a high station with Athenians and was worshipped at Delphi. Upon the temple was inscribed "Nothing in Excess." This tenet, expressed in Buddhist wisdom as "following the middle path," is an example of Greek attitude and dogma. The Eleusinian mysteries was an institution with all the appearance of religion. We know little about it because members were sworn to secrecy. We do know one tenet was that the soul is immortal. Alexander the Great was a convert of the Eleusinian mysteries, and the cult existed well into the Roman period. The Greek priest class probably had more in common with Europe's shamanistic Druids than the Mid-East's oriental priests. Evidence suggests Pythagoras was at least influenced by Druid philosophy. The study of Nature was not secular initially. Toynbee aptly stated in his book *Surviving the Future*: *"For instance, early Greek science is really mythology translated into terms of physical and psychic forces, and it is easy to translate those forces back into gods and goddesses"* (p. 45). Some Greeks may have questioned the priest class and religion, but society was still regulated and governed by divine sanction and was therefore a theocracy. This clearly places Greece's Golden Age within the Theocratic Phase of the *Zeitgeist*.

Greek theocracy spent funds and labor on houses of worship as well.

Hamilton compared the placement of Greek temples to a European Gothic cathedral that *"stands low down in the midst of a huddle of little houses...where it is marked by its incongruity with its surroundings"* (p. 304). She continued, "*But to the Greek architect the setting of his temple was all-important. He planned it, seeing it in clear outline against sea or sky, determining its size by its situation on plain hilltop or the wide plateau of an acropolis"* (p. 304).

Hamilton is trapped in her twentieth century view. She continues to presume the uniqueness of the Greeks. Not only does this statement counter Hamilton's earlier view that Greeks were not held by priestly dictums, but it ignores what stood on the actual site of the cathedral she condemns. The cathedrals, including Notre Dame and St. Paul's were built on the sites of earlier Pagan temples. When those original Pagan temples were built there were no cities. A rural, tribal society had placed them with as much care for Nature as the Greeks. Later a city and urban society grew up at the holy spot and constructed the cathedral monstrosity with typical urban disregard for place and Nature.

Using Hamilton's comparison in contemporary terms would be to place, for example, the steel and glass skyscraper church called the Crystal Cathedral of Southern California on the acropolis in today's metropolitan Athens. Many would see this as an abomination. There is little regard for the Indians who once foraged, or the citrus rancher who farmed where the Crystal Cathedral stands today. Gothic cathedrals no doubt appeared sacrilegious to devout Pagans in the Middle Ages. Greek architectural geometry and proportion drew from equations found in Nature. Still cognizant of Nature's place in their rural past, the Greeks built the temples with Nature in mind. But we must not romanticize the Greek connection with Nature either. The stone columns were a replacement for wood that no longer existed. The urban Greeks depleted available natural resources, including their forests.

The urban centers of wealth and power rose from the ashes of the Greek Dark Age past. There was a need for governmental organization due to the rise of agriculture, commerce and cities protecting stored commodities. A common idea of the Divine provided a common interest, which bound government and the governed. The governments were ordained and guided by the Divine expressed as deities by the priests and aristocratic families. This is a definition of theocracy. Athens became a principal location of wealth, culture and of priestly administration by

900 B.C.E. as were the cities of Rome and Constantinople two thousand years later in A.D. 1100. Greek wars against Persia (B.C.E.) and the Crusades against Arabs and Pagan European tribes (A.D.) were sanctified by the priest class in both times, two millennia distant. Expanded trade was the economic result of these wars. Money came back into use by 700 B.C.E. and again in A.D. 1300, two thousand years later (see fig. 4). With money and commerce followed both the Golden Age of Greece, (600-500 B.C.E.) and the Renaissance (A.D. 1400-1500).

Socrates and DaVinci were participants in parallel eras, two millennia distant. Much of the Renaissance learning and investigation was based on what little remained from before the Dark Ages. The ancient Greek city states pushed back the Persians in Anatolia. The Arabs were pushed out of Iberia (Spain and Portugal). Greek colonies were established throughout the Black Sea and Mediterranean as were modern European colonies throughout the Atlantic, Pacific and Indian Oceans. The Black Sea B.C.E. became as the Indian Ocean A.D., bringing trade from the East. The ancient Greeks competed commercially with Phoenicians. Modern Europeans competed with Arabs. After two thousand years, only technology had advanced. City states gave way to nation states as a political unit reflecting an expanded geography. But Western Civilization was replaying its *Zeitgeist.* With greater physical security and material wealth, leisure time became available for contemplation. In both A.D. and B.C.E., people other than the narrow elite of aristocrat and priest would find time to think and question. The idea that others than the divinely chosen could share in government and its regulation of wealth and power became a realistic alternative. But this secular notion took time to spread. Meanwhile society continued in its Theocratic Phase.

III: The Decline of Theocracy

Theocracy was the status quo (thesis), during both the Renaissance and Greek Golden Age. But the beginnings of the coming Secular Phase (anti-thesis) of the *Zeitgeist* emerged in a few locations. Athenian democracy and elected Spartan dictators ruled in those cities. Across the sea, Romans got rid of their king and set up a republic (509 B.C.E.). Rome's rival in North Africa, Carthage, had a Punic republic. Two thousand years later, Switzerland broke from Austria to form a confederated democracy (c. A.D. 1300) and Venice had a less democratic republic run by nobles and the merchant class. The creation of merchant controlled republics also developed in other North Italian cities like Florence or Genoa. Merchant-republic cities, such as Hamburg or Bremen in the Baltic region of North Europe, confederated into the Hanseatic Free States.

In England, the move toward representative government had been in the making since the Magna Carta of A.D. 1216. At that point English nobles were able to put limits on the monarchy's power. Republicanism finally took hold in Holland and England's American colony, Virginia (c. 1600s). Virginia's republic began with the establishment of the House of Burgesses (A.D. 1619) while Rome's republican birth date was 509 B.C.E. The unique geographic and technological differences caused the time anomaly of 78 years beyond the allowable 50 year maximum (128 years total) added to the 2000 year period. This anomaly was covered in the last chapter. The point of significance here is that Western examples of the governed electing their governors, creating laws and judging peers came into practice again after 2000 years. The *Zeitgeist* was again looking toward a Secular Phase.

The merchants and wealthy land owners who made up the ancient Roman senate and assemblies had no need for royalty to carry on business. Two millennia later, the members from the same class, who ran the Virginia House of Burgesses in America, felt the same. Across the Atlantic during the wars of the Reformation, the English monarchy was disposed of by a Parliamentary sponsored revolution. Parliamentary republican rule quickly turned into a theocratic dictatorship under the Puritan (Calvinist), Oliver Cromwell, in 1645. Virginia's republicans continued to run their colony while London's religious dictatorship was consumed in turmoil. When monarchy was restored in England, Virginia's government proclaimed loyalty to the returned monarchy. One of the biggest Virginia land owners, George Washington, led Virginian volunteers against the French in support of the English King during the French and Indian War (Seven Years War) in 1763.

But 130 years of American distance from the king in London had kept royal authority at a minimum. Decisions for the everyday needs of frontier America could not wait for the king's dictation through his appointees. American loyalty lasted only as long as its ruling members assumed new land west of the Appalachian Mountains could be taken from the Indians for development. When the king closed western lands to American colonists and protected the Indians for the lucrative fur trade, the Virginia House of Burgesses dropped any pretense of loyalty to the king. Virginia colony joined the US revolution against the king along with the twelve other colonies. Monarchy in non-Canadian, English America was ended. After two thousand years, Western society again had examples of secular republicanism showing an alternative to the institution of monarchy.

In the last days of the Theocratic Phase, monarchy's claim of divine sanction to rule was being challenged. But religion and the priest class still held authority in the Western *Zeitgeist.* The Divine was often called upon and religious leaders at times assumed prominence. The republics in ancient Greece and Rome and modern Europe and America, kept their limited republicanism alive through the religious wars that followed the Greek Golden Age and Europe's Renaissance two millennia later. Those religious struggles were the Peloponnesian Wars (ending 404 B.C.E.) and the Reformation (ending A.D. 1648).

Comparison of the Peloponnesian Wars with the Reformation's Thirty Years War is valid. Both conflagrations occurred after the foreign threat of invasion subsided (Persian or Macedonian B.C.E. and Arab, Viking or Turk A.D.). In both cases "civilized" Europeans set about fighting among themselves. New wealth from trade and foreign conquests had not been evenly distributed through society in the eyes of both the needy and the greedy. In both cases B.C.E. and A.D., theocracy lost credibility and declined as secularism ascended.

During the Peloponnesian Wars the ancient Greek city states and colonies battled over trade routes and resources. Though economics played its part, spiritual and religious emotions also ran high. Each city state had their Baal/Saturn, Athena, Mars, Diana or any number of incarnations of the Divine to aid them in their causes. The Athenian leader Alcibiades was banished by his own followers for allegedly destroying sacred images of Hermes. In this case religion took precedence over military success. Alcibiades was about to lead Athenians in a war against Greek colonies in Sicily. Later Pericles brought social, political and economic reform in Athens. But he also ordered the construction of the temple of Athena Nike and the Parthenon for religious reasons. Athenians sentenced Diagoras to death for his "godless" writings. Socrates may seem today to have been an icon of secularism. But even he stated he was an instrument of the Divine. Though wealth and energy spent in war led to Athens's political decline, it remained a cultural and religious center long after the Peloponnesian Wars. The last Pagan school in Athens was not closed until A.D. 529 by a Christian Roman Emperor (Justinian). Athens's long lived cultural-religious status parallels Rome's position two thousand years later. After the Thirty Years War, Rome lost economic and political clout, but the city retained its cultural-religious status.

The Reformation's Thirty Year War may be cast as a religious war. In England, Oliver Cromwell, like his Athenian predecessor Pericles, set out to reform society and purify traditional theocracy and religion. In England this resulted in the murder of Catholics and witches. However, there was an economic element in Cromwell's actions. Lands and wealth of the persecuted were confiscated by Cromwell and redistributed to fellow Calvinists. Calvinists (Huguenots in France or Puritans in England) subscribed to the ideas of John Calvin of France. One of Calvin's tenets contained a belief in the virtue of individual wealth. To be wealthy was a sign of the Divine's favor.

This Calvinist view relieved the expanding merchant class in Western Europe and America of any guilt previously laid upon them by the Roman Catholic Church. The Roman Catholic theocracy asked for tithes as a means to place excess wealth into its own institutional maintenance and cathedrals for the glory of the Divine. Calvinists denounced the accumulation of wealth and land held by the Roman Catholic Church. The biblical statement by Jesus in *Mark* that *"it is easier for a camel to go through the eye of a needle, than for a rich man to enter the kingdom of God"* (10:25) was not emphasized by Calvinists. The idea that wealth should be in the hands of individuals rather than the church was also a secular notion. But it was a restrained secular notion because Calvinists felt that wealthy individuals were divinely chosen. Cromwell's campaigns were only part of Europe's overall thirty year conflagration.

The Lutherans of Germany and Scandinavia also joined in. During the Thirty Years War, a Calvinist or Lutheran Protestant divinity aided the esprit de corps of the armies supporting European powers and their colonies at war against kingdoms supporting Roman Catholic divinity. European politics encouraged the struggle for souls by military means. But control of society, resources and trade was often the economic motivator of the rulers. By the end of the wars, religion took a second place after economics and rising nationalism. Eventually Catholic France joined Protestant Sweden against Catholic Austria and Rome for economic and political reasons. Across the Atlantic, the Americas received exiles of these European wars just as Italy had received Greek exiles from across the Adriatic during the Peloponnesian Wars, 2000 years before. Yet secular nationalism had not taken complete hold of society's *Zeitgeist.*

Though the Peloponnesian and Thirty Years Wars had economic causes with consequences in the material plane, the rationale that mustered the imagination of the general population and armies was spiritual. Since the wars were divinely authorized, the events lie within a Theocratic Phase of the *Zeitgeist.* In both cases (Greece B.C.E. and Europe A.D.), subduing, enslaving and converting groups occurred at home and abroad. Society's common people were initially willing to do this in the belief that they were being led by the Divine through their theocratic governments. By the time these religious trade wars ended (404 B.C.E. in Greece and A.D. 1648 in Europe), a new world order was developing. Western society's mentalities and *Zeitgeist* had made incremental shifts toward secularism. People were disgusted with the waste and bloodshed to support priests, aristocrats and wealthy merchants. The combatant populations saw that a hoped for new, utopian millennium had not arrived. The approach toward who and how the people should be governed was questioned. The world had not experienced an end time, but the Theocratic Phase was ending.

IV: Theocracy Challenged

How the Divine of A.D. or the deities of B.C.E. ruled the affairs of humans was challenged, synthesized and redefined in the Thirty Years and Peloponnesian Wars. The Greek Golden Age and the European Renaissance had unleashed new wealth and also a scientific approach to the study of Nature. The observable material world began to be systematically dissected. A secular, systematic method to promote and organize scientific terms and logic was heralded by Aristotle (384-322 B.C.E.). His works were compiled in an *Organon.* A similar approach was presented 2000 years later by Francis Bacon (A.D. 1561-1626) who published the *New Organon.* At the conclusion of the religious conflicts, there was no scientific proof that destruction of an enemy's city or its people killed the Divine's entity that the enemy believed in. Society needed another approach to divine interaction with human affairs. Two different kings, two millennia distant, rose to the occasion.

In ancient Greece, Alexander the Great arrived on the heels of the Peloponnesian Wars. In modern Europe, Louis the XIV reigned after the Thirty Years War (see fig. 4). Their rise to power differed. Led by Alexander's father, the Macedonians conquered and unified Greece. Alexander (356-323 B.C.E.) led the Greek conquest of the Mid-East. Under Louis, France did not conquer all of Europe and beyond. Louis (1638-1715) reigned from A.D. 1643-1715 (72 years). Alexander lived only 33 years. Louis died 2038 years after Alexander. Yet, the effect of both Alexander and Louis on the *Zeitgeist* of their times was significantly parallel.

Alexander sponsored secular advances in the sciences, but was revered postmortem as a deity. This Divine sanction provided a rationale for Greek theocratic rule, through Greek aristocracy. This system prevailed until ended by Roman conquests. Cleopatra Ptolemy of Egypt was the last Greek ruler to fall (30 B.C.E.). Two millennia later, Protestant kings and even the Catholic French monarchy no longer accepted the Roman Pope as a temporal ruler. But society came to accept Louis's idea that he, the "Sun King," along with other kings (and by lesser degree aristocrats), were chosen and directed by the Divine. This "Divine Right" system did not end until the American, French and Russian Revolutions. Rule over the common population by virtue of birth was maintained in both cases.

Both Alexander and Louis supported a theocratic political system based on a theocratic myth. Yet both accommodated the advance of rational investigation and knowledge in the physical and biological sciences. This ushered in the Hellenistic Age (c. 300 B.C.E.) and the "Enlightenment" and Age of Reason (c. A.D. 1700) two thousand years later. With Alexander the Great, Greek became the international language for trade, diplomacy, culture and science right into and in tandem with Latin of the following Roman Era. Under Louis XIV, the French language assumed the same role into the present American Era. Under Louis and Alexander, the ideal of one world united under one political-economic system was seriously entertained by the rulers, if not yet all of society. In each respective period "Things Greek" and "Things French" came to be placed on a cultural pedestal and incorporated within Western society's *Zeitgeist.*

The belief in Divine Right A.D. or human deities B.C.E. are represented today in England's monarchy and by the Dalai Lama. But in the West these vestiges of the Theocratic Phase no longer govern absolutely or at all. Many soldiers and church congregations sang the nineteenth century Protestant Christian hymn, "Onward Christian Soldier," all through the wars of the twentieth century. But after World War I, the national armies were being directed and governed by secular, democratic, republican, socialist, or fascist governments. Western society's twentieth century A.D. crusaders' idealism came filled with the secular belief that they were making the world safe for democracy or liberating the workers of the world. Patriotic nationalism for the people and senate of Rome was employed to secure a superior Roman state and the advance of Roman Law, B.C.E.

Alexander's human deification theocracy and Louis's Divine Right theocracy were the status quo (thesis) of the *Zeitgeist* at the end of the Theocratic Phase. Hellenism and the Roman Republic B.C.E. were agents of the Secular Phase (anti-thesis) which eventually washed away that Theocratic Phase. The Age of Reason, including American, French and Russian Revolutions contained by the Industrial Revolution, were the anti-thesis events A.D. which again returned the Secular Phase to the West's *Zeitgeist.*

> *The replacement of Christianity with secular institutions is the culminating and critical result of the Industrial Revolution. That states should attempt to dispense with theological supports is one of the many crucial experiments that bewilder our brains and unsettle our ways today. Laws which were once presented as the decrees of a God-given king are now frankly the confused commands of fallible men.*
>
> Ariel and Will Durant, *Lessons of History,* p. 48

Chapter Four

THE SECULAR PHASE

1: The Ascendance of the Secular Phase

The term "secular" as applied to the Secular Phase denotes adherence to a non-Divine based mythology by society. With this secularism (or humanism), morality of society is based on the present well-being of humankind in the material world rather than the spiritual world or hereafter. Government does not control a church, nor is it under the control of a church, but transcends the church. Government derives its authority from the consent and efforts of humans and not the Divine or humans representing the Divine. However, government control of, or influence from, religion does occur occasionally in the Secular Phase. This is because religion is a human invention, subject to secular exploitation. The Secular Phase is the anti-thesis to the thesis expressed by the Theocratic Phase (see figs. 1&2). When Western Civilization lost faith that the Divine could best govern the governed, faith was transferred to science and reason to answer sociopolitical and even spiritual questions.

Science is based on human investigation and observation of physical evidence and data found in Nature. From the gathered information, theories are created and applied to advance knowledge and develop systems and technology. A look at the thoughts of Marcus Tullius Cicero (106-43 B.C.E.) illustrates the shift from faith in the Divine to faith in observable Nature in his time. Cicero was a contemporary of Julius Caesar, writer, stoic, republican politician and part of the established ruling elite of republican Rome two millennia ago. In his letter, *On Old Age*, Cicero says, "*...I follow Nature, the best of guides, as I would a god, and am loyal to her commands.*" This exemplifies the lofty position the direct observation of science assumes in a Secular Phase. Deities may be disposed of altogether.

With such faith in science and reason, it was a short leap of logic for Western society to assume science could supply a rational and just form of government. Secularists of B.C.E. and A.D. felt rational mortals could run a government without divine help. Many felt scientific research had developed technology, which if continued, would solve any problems in the future. Science served the present. Many believed science provided theory rather than myth about the past and future. Secular humanism gave hope for the future as well as any traditional religion did. Secularists saw philosophy, agnosticism and atheism as replacements for religion and divine myth.

When investigating the Greco-Roman Secular Phase for comparison with the modern world, it should be noted that only about one percent of ancient literature B.C.E., including history, exists today. Pieces must be filled in and a more generalized approach must be taken due to lack of information. Modern history to eighteenth century A.D. provides more information to draw upon. This history is far enough distant in time to allow objectivity, hindsight and the establishment of general trends that all can agree on and label. Comparisons will be made in this chapter that involve the nineteenth and twentieth centuries A.D. This later period is near enough in time to involve personal memory and recent family history of the reader and author. Thus personal prejudices enter in. Even though there are more facts and material available, it is difficult to develop a clear picture of the recent past. More facts and resources challenge the determination of what is a real, inconsequential, trivial or passing historical trend. At the cost of being too general, the trees from the nineteenth and twentieth centuries' forest of historical facts must be winnowed while meager resources from the last two centuries B.C.E. are pulled together to facilitate comparisons 2000 years distant.

In the last two centuries A.D., new labels for groups or movements have appeared. Technocrats, who believe science and technology will solve all of Earth's problems; Humanists who believe science and human logic will explain mysteries and advance society; Romantics, who hearken to a past Golden Age when humans and Nature were one with the Divine and believe humanity will regain Eden through human effort; Communists, who feel the past, present and future can be determined scientifically in purely socioeconomic terms; Fascists, who favor secular authoritarian rule and individual subservience to the organic state and its union with big business; Fabians, who advocate a secular, democratic socialism.

Secular mythology also exists. The scientific method replaced the Ten Commandments in establishing and defining what is valid or correct. Divine miracles lost credibility in the Secular Phase because science and human thought seemingly created miracles. Though most of the miracles were on the material plane, there was strong faith that science could eventually explain every mystery in the universe. In the eighteenth and nineteenth centuries A.D., it was liberating to shed guilt or fear established by religion in one's childhood. Psychologists became the secular priest class and Jehovah became what Sigmund Freud called Id. Science became a new religion. It altered, blended and competed with existing religions. Today we have examples of this synthesis expressed in the names of new, Secular Phase religions such as Christian Science or Scientology.

In the nineteenth and twentieth centuries A.D. and the last two centuries B.C.E., the Divine became less and less relevant to the everyday operation of society. Not only was government secularized, but art, literature and education lost church sponsorship and control. Today we see artists financially supported by private patrons and government grants, not the church. In Europe, governments regulate church operated schools by contributing a large part of the cost of the school's operation. In the US, public funds are not used at all. But regulation comes in the form of state accreditation and tax-free status if the church school remains non profit.

Cicero is available within the tiny one percent of ancient literature left for us to read. But what was available to Cicero? We do know that 2000 years ago the Druids of Europe believed in reincarnation and immortality of the soul. Druids were described by the Greek writer Posidonous. But only secondhand references to his 52 books are left to us. Book 23, (c. 120 B.C.E.) described Celtic religion and Druid thought. Posidonous was writing well into the first century B.C.E. Like Cicero, Posidonous belonged to the Secular Phase of that time. Cicero alluded to those who disregarded his notion of the immortality of the soul. In his letter, *On Old Age*, he said:

> But if I am wrong in thinking the human soul immortal, I am glad to be wrong; nor will I allow the mistake which gives me so much pleasure.... But if when dead, as some insignificant philosophers think, I am without sensation, I am not afraid of dead philosophers deriding my errors.

Apparently the "insignificant philosophers" Cicero mentions were cynics that he decided not to name. Perhaps the Roman poet philosopher, Titus Carus Lucretius (c. 95-45 B.C.E.) was one. He was an atomist who championed the Epicurean view that the world operated without any Divine design or rule. He held no belief in reincarnation and attempted to dispel fear of the Divine and death. We have only his long poem, *On the Nature Of Things* , to ponder.

Atheists were unpopular in Roman society. Atheism, then as today, placed faith in secular humanism and science. Neither blame or merit can be ascribed to the Divine. This is a heavy responsibility for most humans. Cicero also touched on other human needs in the face of cynicism. Those human needs are solace and purpose. In Cicero's case, he preferred faith in theory or myth rather than the devastation of accepting that all human endeavor and learning ends with death. Reincarnation may have been a prevailing "scientific theory" in the Roman era no less than Social Darwinism was in the nineteenth century A.D. It may also have been a sort of Roman "New Age" idea indicating an approaching Spiritual Phase.

The genesis of today's Secular Phase came with the end of the most recent Theocratic Phase. Martin Luther, John Calvin, Oliver Cromwell and the Protestant Reformation (A.D. 1500s-1600s) challenged the status quo theocracy, but the protagonists were still fighting to maintain, alter or replace theocracy with another theocracy. The Secular Phase emerged from the trade wars of the first half of the 1700s. Here mainly British, French and Dutch nations preyed on the empires of Spain and Portugal. As Spain and Portugal declined in power, the French, English and Dutch fought each other, culminating in the first global war. This conflict is known as The Seven Years War or French and Indian War (A.D. 1763) in which England won North American and Indian colonies from the French. Shortly thereafter, England ended any military resistance to conquest in Scotland or major economic-military challenges from Holland. This was not unlike the process that Hellenized the civilized Western world 2000 years before, through the conquests of Alexander the Great. The Greek city-states, like eighteenth century European nation states, competed for economic gain with declining regard for sponsorship from the Divine.

The secularist American and French Revolutions followed the Seven Years War. More revolution to bring about constitutional rather than Divine Right governments continued in Europe and the Americas right through the nineteenth century and the Russian Revolution of 1917. Few supporting the American or French Revolution held any illusion that the then-recent Seven Years War was over which religion, king or nation the Divine favored. The French felt humiliated. The white Americans felt thwarted in their own expansionist designs west of the Appalachians. They also felt estranged from England. In terms of class conflict, both French and white American working class and middle class people were taxed to pay off debts incurred by the Seven Years War. Yet Divine Right kings, aristocracy and clerics were allowed to carry on their lifestyles with little economic sacrifice.

Anti-clericalism and freedom of religion were major tenets in both the American and French revolutions. Some in society thought they were going against divine will by going against the king (Theocratic Phase). But increasingly society had been attracted to the secular *Zeitgeist* (Secular Phase) and wanted a clear separation of church and state. In the revolutionary Paris of 1793, the atheistic worship of the Goddess of Reason was established by the government only to be soon replaced by a deist worship of Rousseau's Supreme Being. Unlike the US, France had no peace following their revolution. Napoleon's dictatorship provided a defense against invasion. For pragmatic reasons including organization needed for national security, Napoleon returned to theocracy by proclaiming himself emperor. In signing a concordat with Pope Pius VII (1801), he restored the Roman Catholic Church in France. France possessed a short lived myth of invincibility for only a decade under Napoleon. Meanwhile the young US entered into a second war with England (1812-1814). The American and French Revolutions supplied inspiration for, and examples of secularism's successes and failures. This encouraged and influenced later nineteenth century secular revolts against Divine Right monarchy in Europe and Latin America.

Latin American republican revolutions fell to Creole oligarchy in the 1820s. These revolutions against the Spanish monarchy and Roman Catholic theocracy were supported and exploited by the capitalistic interests of the U. S. and Britain. Through economic and military support of oligarchies, the US and England achieved economic control of Latin America. Still, Latin American nations did eliminate Divine Right rule and established separation of church and state. By less violent means, England became a constitutional monarchy by the mid-nineteenth century. Although British citizens today still refer to themselves as subjects of the monarch. In Russia the monarchy was violently eliminated in 1918. Religion was deemed the opiate of the people by an elite Marxist-Leninist secular dictatorship. The Holy Russian Empire became the Union of Soviet Socialist Republics. The Secular Phase of the *Zeitgeist* prevailed.

Western powers rose along with the nationalism of the expanding Secular Phase contained in Western society's *Zeitgeist.* After 1815, republican France, Holland, US, England and theocratic Russia took or gained control of the rest of the remaining non-Western world. This imperialism included the new worlds of America and Australia. Control through annexation, alliance, or economics of the "known world" by Western Civilization has occurred before. This was 2000 years ago, during the years B.C.E. and A.D. labeled the Roman Era.

When we go back 2000 years before the eighteenth and nineteenth centuries A.D., we find a different yet hauntingly similar world (see fig. 4). Rome concluded the three wars with Carthage by physically leveling the city (146 B.C.E.). Two thousand and eleven years after the demise of Carthage, during the war between the states in the US, General Sherman's March to the Sea destroyed Atlanta, Georgia. His troops then devastated a 60 mile wide path stretching from Atlanta to the Atlantic Ocean. The US would not again level an enemy city for another 75 years when Hiroshima, Japan, was destroyed during World War II (the British allies destroyed Dresden and Hamburg). After Carthage, Rome went on to fight and win wars against Celtic tribes in North Italy. Rome helped the Greek leagues in their successful wars against Macedonia and Syria. Two millennia later, the US took one third of Mexico's territory, conquered American Indians, conquered Spanish colonies and helped European nations in World War I, World War II, the cold war and recent Balkan wars of the 1990s. Comparing exact dates of individual events show some flip flop in corresponding parallel sequences. The wasting of Hiroshima and

Carthage were separated by 2086 years. But the other events correspond to the two thousand year cycle within the 30-50 year variable.

Rome's wars with Carthage over trade and territory (c. 265-146 B.C.E.) secured Sicily, Spain and western North Africa for Rome. The Anglo-American-US involvement with French and English trade wars and Latin American revolutions against modern Spain (c. A.D. 1735-1854) was experienced two millennia later. In Greece, the Aetolian League and the smaller Achaean League (290 B.C.E.-262 B.C.E.) united the Greek cities with secular rule by elected representatives and annual democratic assemblies of all free citizens. But these city states fell into rivalries and rule by oligarchy. Rome became involved in these inter-Greek wars. Finally Rome's senate or their Greek allies disbanded any remaining democracies or leagues in Greece. The Roman senate instituted rule by approved tyrants, chosen by local oligarchies in the conquered lands. Two thousand years later the United States and republican France and Britain were engaged in the same form of control as Rome in Greece by supporting puppet leaders or war lords in Europe, Asia, Africa and Latin America who were friendly to Western military and economic interests. By A.D. 1860, the US delineated its immediate imperial borders though Civil War. Forty more years of Indian wars lay ahead. Rome secured Gaul 2000 years earlier. Both nineteenth century US and Rome were engaged in gaining territory. Both ancient Rome and the USA were the juggernauts of secularism and realization of the Western *Zeitgeist's* Secular Phase.

Given the 128 year US-Rome anomaly (Chapter 2), general economic-political comparison can be made within the 30-50 year variable. In modern Europe various secular leagues or confederations had been formed. This was also the case in ancient Greece. In modern Europe, mutual commercial interests forged republican cities in north Italy. On the Baltic and North Sea coasts, republican cities formed the Hanseatic League. Whole cantons confederated into a democratic Switzerland. Others combined to become the nation state kingdoms of Spain, Portugal, France and England. The US had plenty of contemporary examples to compare secular republicanism against theocracy when creating a Constitution. In response to Napoleon and in reaction to secularism, European theocracies entered into a Holy Alliance (1815) after Napoleon's defeat. But this was only one of the many ongoing shifting alliances of European states determined by economic-political issues that were comparable to those of ancient Greece.

These issues were trade, territory, international prestige and loyalty to their homeland and society. The soldiers' allegiance to a king or religion was gradually replaced by nationalism. There were popular revolts against oligarchic-aristocracy as democratic-republicanism challenged monarchy. European wars culminated in World War I (A.D. 1914-1918), before the United States, (like Rome 2053 earlier), sailed an army across the sea and dictated a new order. Roman Law was placed on Greece. President Wilson's 14 Points and the League of Nations was the US solution for Europe. The US government policy held that reason and US democracy would save Europe. Rome felt rational Roman Law would save Greece B.C.E.

The actions of the Roman Senate destroyed democracy in Greece by instituting tyrannical rule in Greece. Ironically the inaction of the US Senate allowed tyranny in Europe by voting not to allow the US to join the League of Nations that President Wilson had initiated. Except for a brief incursion into the USSR, US troops were ordered home. The US followed a policy of isolation from political involvement in Europe. This permitted European political and economic chaos. The chaos increased due to the inaction of the remaining European republics. Law and order was established by Europe's ascending secular socialist or fascist dictatorships. Within 14 years after World War I, only Scandinavia, Switzerland, France, England, Ireland and Czechoslovakia remained republican.

The competition between the secular dictatorships of Germany, Poland and the USSR ignited World War II in Europe. Republican England and France chose to defend Poland by attacking only Germany, though the USSR had joined Germany in the conquest of Poland. France was quickly defeated. England asked for US political, economic and finally military involvement in Europe to defeat Germany and Italy and establish secular, representative governments in Europe. Even with a discrepancy of 50 years we come within a generation of parallel events, separated by 2000 years. The *Zeitgeist* of Western society had recycled. World War II also involved Asian colonies ruled by Western powers. Japan's conquest of these colonies, including the US owned Philippines, brought US intervention to the Australian and Asian continents. By whatever means, the USA had come to the same place in relation to Europe and the world as Rome had in relation to Greece and the known world 2000 years earlier.

There are similarities in the rise and fall of all great and powerful empires and their societies. Note should be taken that every Western empire (and republic) since Rome has likened itself to Rome. They all experienced the initial struggle against the natural environment, foreign enemies and finally the conquest of any competitors while increasing their wealth. The new wealth, power and subsequent myth of invincibility included strains that forced a civil war or substantial internal strife. Finally, colonial acquisitions were no longer economic assets due to the costs to maintain and police them. New independent foreign societies emerged to compete for their day in the sun. The myth of invincibility commonly faded in a century or two. Ultimately, the society of the now aging great power became a lesser player in some new empire's scheme or it was absorbed completely and lost sovereignty. This has been outlined earlier with the example of the Spanish Empire in Chapter One.

But Rome's myth of invincibility is unique because it lasted 300 years. This is longer than any empire has experienced since. Economically and technologically, the US has the resources to maintain a strong military and myth of invincibility for 300 years. Like Rome, the US uniquely rose without monarchy and divine authority. For both empires, power was based on wealth rather than birth. The implications of such an extended myth of invincibility shall be examined in Part Two of the next Chapter. Along with imperial acquisitions, other similarities between the US and Rome should first be examined.

II: Rome and the US

Rome, like the US, was isolated from its locus of Western Civilization, culture, and philosophy by a large body of water. The Aegean, Adriatic and Mediterranean Seas lay like natural moats between Italy and Greece. The Caribbean Sea and Atlantic and Pacific Oceans were America's barrier to Europe 2000 years later. Rome began with the Iron Age Etruscans and Latin tribes mixing with Greek colonists and traders in their midst. The US started with European traders and colonists in the midst of Stone Age Native American tribes. This comparison exposes differences in technological status (Iron Age vs. Stone Age). Yet commonality between the US and Rome is found in the mixing of the indigenous and colonial groups, in isolation, at the fringe of urban civilization. This created an environment that resulted in a hybrid frontier republic in both situations, A.D. and B.C.E. The Latin Tribes of Rome formed a union not unlike the Iroquois Indians of America. Greeks in ancient Italy, like modern Europeans in North America, brought advanced technology, science, culture, religion and philosophy. Rome came to be the first European nation state of monumental geographic size and duration compared to the tiny city states of Greece. Asian Persia or African Egypt and Carthage were not European. But within Western Civilization they played a role. In William McNeill's biography, *Arnold J. Toynbee: A Life*, he says Toynbee compared the cold war between Rome and Carthage to that of the US and USSR. A better comparison, conforming to the 2000 year cycle, is the cold war that existed between Persia and Rome. The US was also the West's first continental size nation next to the small kingdoms of Europe, other than mostly Asian and theocratic Russia or Ottoman Turkey.

There is also a parallel between the US and Rome expressed in their agricultural and economic interests. In ancient Rome, soil depletion eroded the small family farm's grain production. The small family farms were replaced by more profitable cattle ranches and vineyards. The estates were worked by slaves and owned by the wealthy (latifundias) of Italy. Rome turned to the recently conquered provinces of North Africa and Gaul for needed grain. Soil depletion in the US South caused cotton and tobacco farming to move westward in search of virgin soil. This movement eventually went as far as Texas, bringing slavery along with it. The large plantation system employed by Southerners expanded. The North's small family farm filled up the west that lay north of the Mason-Dixon line. US expansion into Mexico and Indian lands of the Mid-West, Great Plains and Rocky Mountains was the combined result.

The US Civil War ended the Southern plantation system. But it was replaced by the share cropper system. This form of feudalism gives a share of the farmer's crop to a large land owner in lieu of rent. In the North, the small farmer began to fall victim to wealthy absentee farmers administering from urban locations. Wealthy farmers held sufficient capital to afford expensive farm machines and technology. Slavery in the ancient world played the role of today's farm machinery. In A.D. and B.C.E., the large estates created more wealth for the wealthy who had capital to invest in slaves or machinery for agricultural enterprise. In Rome, crop rotation and increased use of slaves created revolutionary rates of production which impacted the ancient world. In the US, the McCormick Reaper, Ford tractor and genetics similarly affected our age.

Abundant food supply for the two empires was guaranteed. Initially the backbone of both the US and Roman republics were rural, free farmers supplying food and a citizen's army. This generated wealth and produced an ever-expanding trade across the seas and land. This expanded the entrepreneurial class and free enterprise capitalism. This capitalism initially had little government control or regulation.

In Rome's empire, the grain shipping cartels prospered. Wealth came to contractors building the ships and famous Roman roads that carried the trade. Continuing territorial expansion and protecting the trade and provinces necessitated a constant supply of arms and material. This created the money making enterprises of Rome's military industrial complex. The newly taken lands, like the American West two millennia later, provided land for settlement and a new start for the colonist/pioneer. Protecting trade, supporting settlers and establishing an empire provided the rationale for canal and railroad construction and the arms industry in the US.

By clearing the seas of pirates and competitors, Rome greatly increased trade and communication. The Roman roads and signal fires sped communication across the relatively smaller geography of the Roman Empire. The windjammers and later steamships did the same for the US. The first steam-powered Atlantic crossing was in 1819. The crossing was shortened from sixty-five to seven days. Steam-powered trains and riverboats also sped and increased the volume of trade. Newspapers and telegraph sped and spread information. Like the contractors building the ancient Roman roads, the great robber barons and corporations constructed the railroads (and later freeways) built in the US. In the US and Rome, big business, industry and agribusiness were subsidized by the state through land grants and contracts. Small farmers and small business lost their struggle against big business in Rome, as they are losing in the same struggle today.

In both Rome and the US, attempts were made to save the small farmer. The Homestead Act of 1862 in the US gave 660 acres of land taken from the Indians to anyone who would settle and farm the parcel. In Rome, 1995 years earlier (133 B.C.E.), land reform was legislated which blocked land trusts and limited to 600 acres the maximum parcel to be held by any one family. These acts helped small farmers, but they only slowed a trend. Ending US farm subsidy programs in 1996 meant farmers could no longer depend on bottom line prices for staple crops they produced. Under the subsidy system, the state had previously paid farmers for not producing, thus reducing supply and keeping prices up. This provided farmers with economic stability and a steady food supply for all of society. With the free market determining demand, only corporations with the latest information, technology, capital and volume of production are able to ride the economic swings of the world market.

Wealth generated by Roman or US agriculture and industry was the genesis of a secular aristocracy based on wealth, not blood line. Given a few more generations of inherited wealth, blood line or divine blessing would have become a rationale for aristocracy to assume a hereditary station in US society. The US Civil War destroyed landed aristocracy and established that only wealth, not birth, provided the rationale for the aristocratic class. This wealthy class continues to directly or indirectly make up the elected members of the US plutocracy today. A similar millionaire's secular plutocracy also ruled in Rome B.C.E. The wealthy class control of capital eventually ended the small family farm except in specialty crops. Small farmers could not compete with corporate capital resources. People in Rome and the US left the farm and crowded into the cities looking for jobs. This started an unemployment problem in the growing cities which changed the *Zeitgeist* of the respective empires. People were removed from a connection to land in exchange for the anonymity, sophistication, complexity and chaos of the city. The need for large families, or the family unit itself, diminished. Sanitation and water delivery systems were developed along with more taxes, regulations and building codes. Less personal liberty, more socialization, crime and law enforcement resulted.

The migration to urban centers has been going on since the first cities. But urbanization was accelerated in the Western world of the Roman Era and again 2000 years later in Western Europe and the US. The far flung cities of Rome and the US came under a central government and treasury. This was massive relative to single city states like Jericho and the ancient Greek cities or even the first cities that united along the Tigris and Euphrates in Asia, or the Nile River in Africa. Mining operations, soil depletion from intense agricultural activity and nearly complete deforestation of Mediterranean coastal lands were the prices paid B.C.E. by Rome's need to supply its war machine, industry and urban population.

Today the planet's urban population has grown from 20 percent of the total world population in A.D. 1925 to 45 percent today, taxing Earth's resources. The last remaining forests are under attack. Only three percent of Earth's surface is used for agriculture to feed the cities. A handful of nations have enough surplus food for export to the more than 200 nations importing food. World urbanization continues to increase. The use of Earth's resources by the US far exceeds its per capita ratio relative to the nearly six billion people who populate the planet. China's Cultural Revolution attempted to reverse urban capitalist influence. Muslim fundamentalism in Iran or Afghanistan have risen in reaction to Western influence. The Khmer Rouge attempted forceful de-urbanization of Cambodia. But these extreme examples are isolated and short lived. India's ban on Coca Cola was lifted in 1996. The US urban consumer market and the industries supplying and advertising it, have clout if not direct influence upon the entire globe. That influence affects decisions as to how the Earth's resources are exploited. Even with meager resources, people of the non-West aspire to the urban consumptive materialism and lifestyle of US society.

In Kenya, the author saw a fifteen year old lad walking along a crowded Nairobi street, wearing a tee-shirt adorned with the "Stars and Bars" across chest and back. He had no idea that American Blacks would never wear this one time flag for Southern rebellion and symbol of past slavery in the US. Perhaps he had seen a re-run TV show, "Dukes of Hazard," showing "good ol' boys" having fun racing a big car in the US South. The shirt came from donated clothes sent to Africa for American missionaries. For that boy it was an identification with America, mistaken as it was. In Bali, a young moped rider wore a helmet with "fuck you" written across its front. Perhaps some tourist gave him the phrase. But it was an English phrase denoting some sense of adolescent rebellion. This Balinese James Dean probably didn't know any other English words. Today the initials O.K. and the word "hello" are international. Fashion and things American have replaced things European; even in France. The known world also emulated things Roman, which replaced things Greek two millennia ago.

Within the ancient Roman world and the US sphere, a single language (Latin B.C.E. and English A.D.) prevailed, becoming the international language for trade and diplomacy. But language and fashion were not the only things emulated. Universal 'Roman Law' was a major contribution to the ancient world. Constitutional law is a model in the American Era. Though laws were not always carried out or may have been unjust at times, statutes were legislated by a representative body of mortals rather than monarch or priest class in Rome and the US. This rational, egalitarian approach is the child of a Secular Phase in which the laws were made by humans for humans and the world's nations at least display the charade of representative, secular government.

In both Rome and the US, the representative body was initially made up of only the male property owning class. Over time and through violent and peaceful protests change came which allowed the common citizen to participate in government. Rome's republican experiment ended before women could vote. The ancient world could find no technological replacement for a slave class. Slavery finally came to an end A.D. due to the advent of the steam engine. Steam and electrical technology created the factories utilizing the assembly line. Low skilled labor employed in these factories earned subsistence pay. They could not save money to build capital or find time to advance in training and education (12 hour work days, six days a week was common). Thus the wage slave class we have today was created. Yet Roman slaves and Western workers were not submissive.

In the twentieth century A.D., the working class responded through the secular labor movement and women's movement. Labor laws and higher wages elevated many of the working class in the US to a middle class standard of living. Today this situation is challenged in the face of inflation, robots and cheap overseas labor outside the immediate borders of the US. A minimum wage (six dollars per hour) provides less than $1,000.00 a month. This pays for rent, utilities, food, transportation and little else. Even with voting rights, citizen groups in Rome found it difficult to organize just as do groups in the US today.

Periodically, the poor unite to effect some socioeconomic reform. But the wealthy elite have resources in terms of capital, information, the mobility to relocate resources and operations. Information is needed to make informed decisions and actions. The vast majority of wealth, and thus information in the US is controlled by a small, influential minority. It was the same in Rome. Political views are only defined or validated through incorporation by two political parties. Occasionally a third party has risen without achieving victory. The platform or reforms offered by the third party are co-opted or ignored by the two main parties in search of popular votes. Reform is incremental. Very few in the US can expect to become representatives at state or federal levels unless they join the

Democratic or Republican parties. Women have achieved legal and educational status. Isolated examples of female wealth and power exist. But only five percent hold high corporate positions. Income and power still generally remain in male hands.

In Rome, the Senate's republican sentiment was still strong enough to reject Julius Caesar's bid for monarchy, 44 B.C.E. The fear of executive power in A.D. 1962 may have been behind the yet to be resolved J. F. Kennedy assassination, 2006 years after Caesar's death. A decade earlier, the US Congress and states amended the Constitution placing term limits on the presidency. Only one re-election for the Presidency was legislated in reaction to Franklin D. Roosevelt's three re-elections. Following the Vietnam War, the length of time a President could put the military in the field without Congressional approval was limited. President Nixon left office before impending impeachment by the Senate. However all these republican actions competed with society's need for increased domestic subsidy and security. President Jefferson's Louisiana Purchase without congressional approval, President Jackson's forced removal of the Cherokee Indians against Supreme Court judgment or President Theodore Roosevelt's establishment of game preserves and national parks counter to big business wishes are a few examples of arbitrary executive power.

Elected legislators often become dupes of special interests through the complexities and bribery found in a giant imperial government. Like the small farmer, the individual's social and economic power becomes subservient to big government and big business. In both Rome and the US, the legislative body appears as a forum for partisan politics and personal egos, rather than an agent serving the needs of society. The US big government, charged with preventing monopolies, and health, labor and environmental exploitation by business, is presently under attack. Consequently, government regulation on business has declined. Big business's power increases. Bank mergers centralize capital. Mass media networks and publications merge with big industry and compromise free press. The military-industrial complex persists even with the ending of the cold war. In 1995 Congress funded seven billion dollars more for the military than what the Pentagon asked for!

Big business and the media tolerate but also attempt to manipulate the secular, republican government. NBC network TV evening news *In Depth* segment reported on 11/8/95 that the 1992 presidential campaign cost the two candidates (Clinton and President Bush) $55,200,000.00 each. The average cost for campaigning for a House seat was $500,000.00 in the 1994 race. Special interest lobbies supplied 44 percent of these funds. The news commentator, Tom Brokaw, smugly noted that the last four Congresses attempted and failed to legislate against such monetary influence. He smiled as he stated that the present Congress would try again to change the rules of the Washington, D.C. game. Thus the wealthy elite maintain a plutocracy through the Congress and President. The 1996 presidential race cost the Republican and Democratic Parties nearly $600 million. The most expensive Senatorial race cost $20 million. The most expensive House race cost $7 million.

In January 1996, (after the term for statutes of limitations expired), investigations revealed that President Bush used illegal campaign funds in his 1988 election campaign. This caused no great furor even though the President's job is the enforcement of federal law. President Clinton, like Nixon, won re-election in spite of mounting investigations into criminal activity. Corruption is seen more as the status quo by a cynical population. Frustration with Congress grows as tax revenues continue to be funneled into "pork barrel" projects added to bills in order to buy support from individual legislators who vote the bill into law. There is popular appeal in hoping for a single elected leader who can cut through all the bureaucratic confusion and special interest influence. There is a desire within society to set the government on a path responsive to the vast majority of society that make up the middle, lower-middle and poor classes. In response to this dream, Congress gave the power of line item veto to the President in January 1997. The President could then pick and choose what parts of a tax spending bill are signed into law. This may eliminate pork barrel measures, but it will also diminish republican law making power. The power vacuum left by any reduction in big government will be filled by big business. The plutocracy continues.

Citizenship seems less of a political advantage when society recognizes the plutocracy as a pseudo republic. Only a third of the citizens actually participate in politics, whether de facto in the US or due to Rome's laws. The voter turnout for the 1992 US presidential election was only 36 percent. This indicates that 64 percent of the voting population was either apathetic or disaffected. The 1996 Republican and Democratic presidential conventions were media events providing free advertisement. Rather than arguing over the candidate and platform choices, the candidates and party platforms were established before the conventions began. TV viewership for these predetermined events were a relatively low 12 percent. For many, change through the ballot box is widely seen as futile except on the local level.

But citizenship does hold economic merit. Illegal and legal immigrants strive for jobs that citizenship permits. This has caused friction with those who are already citizens. In 1994, 59 percent of California's voters democratically passed Proposition 187 in an attempt to withhold publicly-funded educational and medical services from illegal immigrants. The 1996 Republican Presidential nominee candidate, Pat Buchanan endorsed Proposition 187 in his campaign. Restrictions on employers who hire illegal aliens was not addressed. Thus the plutocracy is aided by the middle and working class divisions over economics, xenophobia and racism. The working class is split and rendered less effective politically and economically. Big business continues exploiting the workers competing for jobs. Yet in both republics, A.D. and B.C.E., citizenship was valuable and sought after. Non-Romans and barbarians outside the empire who could obtain Roman citizenship, tried. This was not to gain the right to participate in politics, but to have a stake in the economic benefits presented by Roman industry and trade. The *Zeitgeists* in ancient Rome and the US are similar due to the economic opportunities and general high standard of living relative to other nations.

The higher standard of living allows time for recreation, mindless hedonism and entertainment for the masses. Though human sacrifice was banned in 97 B.C.E., Rome's population crowded into coliseums to witness mortal combat. In the US today, witch burning, dueling and boxing without gloves are no longer legal. But people see violence on the evening news reamplified again in violent dramas shown on the same TV or in a movie house. This incurs the same base, detached fascination with bloodletting that passes as entertainment. Sporting events today are a great pacifier of the masses to a per capita extent seen previously only in ancient Rome. Noam Chomsky addressed this in his book, *Manufacturing Consent.* Chomsky in a televised program (KQED, San Francisco, August 8, 1995), described sports as a training in irrational jingoism and a place to focus on for the 80 percent of the population who follow orders. He said, *"Mentality is the same since Genghis Khan, only the factors have changed."* One factor is technology. Like Roman chariots, race cars today put the spectator vicariously on the edge and exclaiming when an accident actually happens. Keeping the mass of society distracted by entertainment and sporting events is beneficial for a political-economic elite who wish to keep power.

The US and ancient Rome also share other sinister similarities in the republican nation building period. While possessing and extolling representative government at home, the US, like Rome, supported or installed tyrants, dictators, oligarchies or monarchies in any foreign land they allied to or annexed. The US laid waste to Dresden and Hiroshima during World War II as effectively as Rome's obliteration of Carthage at the end of the third Punic War. Neither republic advocated human sacrifice. But Rome sacrificed plenty to gladiator conflict for the public entertainment. The US replaced witch burning with lynching as politicians looked the other way. Genocide was inflicted on Native American tribes that resisted US conquest. Survivors were left with marginal land, alcohol or a job in a wild west show. The genocide, devastation and land grab carried out by Rome in the Mediterranean, Mid East and south of the Rhine and Danube Rivers, compares with the conquest of lands west of the Appalachians, Hawaii and north of the Rio Grand River including Alaska. Virtual control of resources and trade by the US in Latin America came under the guise of protection via the Monroe Doctrine (1830s). This doctrine prevented conquest of a Latin American nation by any European nation. But this military security was paid for with economic and military dependence on the US and Euro-US banks.

Freedom of religion was touted by both republics. Yet with Rome there was persecution of the Celtic Druid priests. Though allowed to practice in exchange for Druid recognition of Rome's conquest of Gaul in 18 B.C.E., Druids were denied Roman citizenship. Druidism was eventually outlawed in A.D. 54. As the tolerance in the republic and later empire dwindled, Jews and Christians were also persecuted. The US banned the Ghost Dance religion of the Native Americans, Hawaiian's Hula dance and polygamy among Mormons and Muslims. Whether these negative aspects to conquest and nation building are any better or worse than those of other empires is irrelevant. The US closely compares with Rome when considering a society extolling republicanism, equality and freedom of religion while subjugating other societies and its own people through a plutocracy's control or misinformation. Rome and the US are partners in hypocrisy.

Success is often *the* rationale for conquering other societies when building a nation. Empathy or compassion for foreign societies gives way to broad terms of "might makes right." Some rationalize imperialism as a positive way for the imperial power to bring the conquered society to higher, happier standards. The conqueror offers its idea of civilization, trade and industry to the conquered. Superiority is claimed by the imperialist as self evident. Historian H. Last is quoted in Stuart Piggott's book, *The Druids*, as follows: *"Romans counted the suppression of savagery as part of their service to mankind"* (p. 109). Conquering Romans felt favored by Jupiter, Saturn, Minerva and Mars. Jehovah and Jesus were given to the Manifest Destiny which led the US. That the citizenry followed any specific religion was irrelevant as long as it did not conflict with the secular government's view of humanitarian service. Thus, in the Secular Phase, spiritual expression is tolerated and often encouraged by the secular government.

The plutocracies tolerate spiritual pursuit as long as it pacifies and amuses the masses or the rich. In Rome's cities the old Celtic Nature-based religions were blended with Greek urban religion and pantheon of deities. The mother goddess incorporated by Rome assumed names like Aphrodite, Isis, Ishtar or Anat. The Sun became the focus of official religion just before Christianity did. In the US A.D., the already blended Celtic-Christian tradition celebrates holidays like Christmas, Easter, May Day, Halloween, Thanksgiving and Valentine's Day. These blend with the naturalism of the Native Americans and European Romantics. In the expanded scale of US geography, whole forests are set aside (Yosemite, Yellowstone, Grand Canyon) rather than a mere sacred grove or hilltop as was the case in ancient Rome. For those in the Roman world who only accepted a secular rationale and rejected theocracy or traditional spiritual expressions, there was philosophy. Urban Greece provided epicureanism, gnosticism or stoicism. Modern Europe's anti-clericalism, atheism, deism and agnosticism came to the US two millennia later. Astrology, occultism and hedonism also had a following in both times and places.

In a Secular Phase, Western society becomes cynical, disenfranchised and hedonistic spiritually though material blessings continue. Scientific, engineering and medical advances progress alongside. Oswald Spengler saw the secular parallels when he noted twentieth century disenchantment with nineteenth century secular urbanism. In his book, *Man and Technics; A Contribution to a Philosophy of Life*, he says, *"It is the spirit of Rome in the Age of Augustus. Out of satiety of life, men take refuge from civi-*

lization in the more primitive parts of the earth, in vagabondage, in suicide" (p. 97). The Secular Phase in Rome and the USA turned the *Zeitgeist* from optimism, based on human reason and faith in science, to cynicism directed toward the secular institutions of big business, big government and theocratic traditional religion.

III: RURAL TO URBAN

A shift from an agrarian nation to an urban one took place in both Rome and the US. The shift in perspective, religion and *Zeitgeist* from rural, nature based time and values to urban, human based time and values is an important aspect of the Secular Phase. It is more important for an urban dweller to get along with fellow humans in the city than deal with Nature's cycles and demands. Spengler observed in his 1931 publication, *Man and Technics*:

> *Even today the peasant is slow of speech as compared with the townsman — who is so accustomed to speaking that he cannot hold his tongue and must, from boredom, chatter and make conversation as soon as he has nothing else to do, whether he has anything really to say or not.* (P. 55)

The Christian church bell, Muslim call to prayer and, more recently, the clock dictate time for human activities more than the position of the sun, moon, stars and clouds. Anonymous strangers of the city present different realities than an extended family and long time neighbors in a rural village. The city person can exist under the illusion that humans are not affected by Nature other than by an occasional natural disaster or annoyance of too much rain or heat. Rural society is fully aware of human dependence on Nature for income and survival. As cities grow and multiply, the society divorces itself from Nature and Mother Earth.

We must not romanticize agrarian life either. Sustenance was earned at the cost of hard labor. Human sacrifice finds its origins in the belief system of an agricultural society where the example of taking life is required to continue life in an endless cycle. All ancient cities were created as a result of agricultural success or holding strategic locations that controlled the flow of commodities including food. Rome and the US both experienced a long period of super agricultural abundance. This surplus food was the paradoxical undoing of agrarianism.

In *Food of the Gods*, Terence McKenna addressed the changes in spiritual focus caused by quantity, procurement and types of food available. McKenna placed biblical Eden among the Stone Age pastoral hunter-gatherer societies. Such pre-urban groups cooperatively foraged. Human sacrifice was not be tolerated since each individual was an important gatherer or hunter for the survival of the whole. McKenna theorized that eating psychedelic mushrooms, which greatly aided these societies in the general human evolution of speech, self consciousness, visual arts and the ability to visualize past and future, gradually ceased with urbanization. McKenna provided evidence that honey was originally used by a rapidly expanding, sedentary population to preserve dwindling supplies of the mushrooms found in the now domesticated cow's dung. McKenna felt the psychedelic mushrooms were gradually replaced by alcohol created when the more plentiful honey fermented. In the village or urban setting, only a select group continued with psychedelics. McKenna believed the decline in availability and use of psychedelics slowed human evolution, encouraged the ego and began a trend toward male dominated societies.

With agriculture's arrival, over production of food created over production of people. This allowed the luxury of establishing classes within the society and a mythology calling for sacrifice of plant, animal or human (usually the first born in each case). Organization and routine was needed to get up with the sun and tend crops and livestock. Such regimentation of labor did not operate well in a society continually in a state of mushroom induced ecstasy; priest class excepted. Fermented honey, grain and fruit alcohol became a religious sacrament, replacing increasingly less plentiful psychedelics. Alcohol, monumental temples, theocracy and cities all came with agriculture. Urban regimentation of labor, dictated by the leadership, created division between humans and separation from Nature.

McKenna placed Crete, the last example in the West, as an agricultural society still holding onto the female values of the cooperative pastoralists and Eden lost. In *Food of the Gods,* McKenna stated:

> *Agriculture brings with it the potential for overproduction, which leads to excess wealth, hoarding, and trade. Trade leads to cities; cities isolate their inhabitants from the natural world. Paradoxically, more efficient utilization of plant resources through agriculture led to a breaking away from the symbiotic relationship that had bound human beings to nature. I do not*

> *mean this metaphorically. The ennui of modernity is the consequence of disrupted quasi-symbiotic relationship between ourselves and Gaian nature. Only a restoration of this relationship in some form is capable of carrying us into a full appreciation of our birthright and sense of ourselves as complete human beings.* (P. 56)

Restoration of positive human to human and human to Nature relationships is also a motivator of a Spiritual Phase. The genesis of a Spiritual Phase may be found through the investigation of a Secular Phase just as the origins of a Secular Phase are found contained in a Theocratic Phase.

Comparisons of the urbanizing Secular Phase in the Greco-Roman past and Euro-US continue. The A.D. 1860s correspond to the 140s B.C.E., separated by 2000 years in the cyclical model. The last 140 years of US history is held up to the mirror of the last 140 years of the ancient Roman Republic before Jesus and increasing urbanism and optimism turned to cynicism. In the Roman case, urbanity that provided material strength and the myth of invincibility paradoxically created cynicism which broke down the validity of the secular, systematic approach. This move out of the Secular Phase is the path for the US as well.

Change from ruralism to urbanity expressed itself spiritually, economically, and politically. The Roman Tiberius Gracchus was assassinated 1998 years before Abraham Lincoln by different technology. Both events were cheered or mourned by three factions which would continue to vie or ally in the political arena depending on where their interests lay. Politics after all is the art of getting along with fellow humans. Cities are the locus. The US two party political system monopoly, with occasional third party influence was outlined in Part II of this chapter. Rome had political factions also. These were: Populares, who favored reform in civil rights and welfare of the common people and the poor; Optimates, who being the old established wealthy families, wanted no reform — they tended to be ideologues hearkening to the virtues of old Rome developed during the agrarian empire building period; and Equites, who were mostly the new rich wanting more political clout equal to their economic status. The Equites wanted reform for the masses if it helped their own interests. Yet they often resisted change otherwise. The Equites strove for a broader more pragmatic plutocracy. This same three way split existed in the US. In 1912, this manifested into a three-way presidential race. The contender parties were the Democratic (Populares), Republican (Optimates), and Bull Moose (Equites) parties.

Abraham Lincoln was elected after a unique four party race (1860). Under President Lincoln's administration, centralized federal power and industry increased along with the emancipation of slaves. Social reform nearly died after Lincoln's assassination. In Rome 2000 years earlier, reform was put on hold after the Gracchus brothers (10 years after Tiberius, Gaius was assassinated). Yet, US and Roman society continued to demand change. In Rome relief came to the poor by sponsoring resettlement abroad in conquered lands. Grain subsidies were supplied for the urban poor. Rome's new wealthy class (Equites) got more political power in the provinces including the lucrative tax collection positions. In the US, citizenship was expanded for ex-slaves though wage slavery continued. More "free" land in the West was opened to the poor willing to risk the challenges of the environment, conflict with angry Native Americans and lawless Whites. The rich were allowed full laissez-faire capitalism. Only the Sherman Anti-Trust Act (1890) and Hepburn Act(1906) curbed monopolies and inflated railroad shipping costs exacted on farmers. Large national parks and game reserves were established to halt environmental destruction by industry. But the privately owned Federal Reserve Bank monopoly was established by an act of Congress (1913). By the turn of the respective centuries (100 B.C.E. and A.D. 1900), big business interests continued to hold a major influence in the respective governments. In Rome and the US, the poor could vote, but few had the leisure, connections or money to run for office themselves. Legislatures were urban rich-man clubs, making laws for rural and increasingly urban, secular society.

The Republic of Rome waged battles on the frontiers, quelled revolt in Greece and carried on a war with Persia up to 100 B.C.E. The US fought Indian wars and rebellion, Hispanic revolt in Texas, war with Spain and the Mexican Revolution (involving US troops) through A.D. 1900. Both Roman and US cities provided population and industry for well equipped, standing professional armies and navies. This ended the dependency on the citizen militia. The military-industrial complex became well entrenched. During the period between A.D. 1854-1917 and 146-88 B.C.E., two millennia apart, Rome and the US came into their own militarily and internationally.

Within respective 58 and 57 year periods, 2000 years distant (146-88

B.C.E. and A.D. 1860-1917), both Rome and the US had a civil war. They both conquered the lands across the sea (Europe and Greece) whose urban culture, religion and science they had originally aped. Rome was asked to aide in inter-Greek wars resulting in eventual Roman control of Greece at the beginning of this period (146 B.C.E.), corresponding to the two millennia period (A.D. 1854). The US would do the same by "liberating" Europe at the end of the period (A.D. 1917), corresponding to 83 B.C.E. In another chronological flip flop, the US would fight its War Between the States (A.D. 1860-1865) at the beginning of the half century period. Rome experienced its civil war, labeled the Social War (91-88 B.C.E.), at the end of the period. The demands for socioeconomic reform, shifts in populations from rural to urban and ascendancy to world leadership are strikingly the same! More importantly the *Zeitgeist* of Western urban society's place in the world order was set. For both the US and Rome, nationalism, hubris, sense of purpose and hope for the future was built, along with cities, by the two generations of that period (c. A.D. 1855-1900 and c. 145-100 B.C.E.). In that time the newly enfranchised members of society felt optimistic, confident that reason and human effort, with an obvious benign divine blessing, would carry on eternally into their secular futures. In the following century, a myth of invincibility was born on the heels of more conquests and urbanization. Cynicism and separation from Nature was the price paid.

IV: The Last Secular Century

During the respective last centuries of the two republics, events continued to coincide within a generation or less. World War I and II demonized the Germans, Japanese and later Russians and parallels Rome's war with and demonization of Persians, Germans and Gauls. The US and Rome's growing power of big business, central government and executive branch continued along with urbanization. In both cases the central government's executive power was tested but increased. There was pressure from society for a more assertive central government to address socioeconomic needs and organized crime. Within the respective time periods (c. 88-0 B.C.E. and c. A.D. 1917-2000), Rome had slave revolts, such as one led by Sparticus. There was rebellion in Spain and piracy on the high seas. The US experienced the labor movement, civil rights movement, Cuban revolt, various other independence movements and international or domestic terrorism. The US government responded with the "New Deal" and the FBI (Federal Bureau of Investigation). Laws were passed giving more civil rights in both Rome and the US. Protection of slaves through limits on slavery's worst abuses and citizenship to Gauls was carried out in Rome. The US came up with minimum-wage labor laws to protect workers. The right to vote and citizenship for women and Native Americans came to pass. In both cases the small farm continued to disappear, even as more material resources went to aid the poor and failing middle classes of the cities. The wealthy continued to increase and consolidate their wealth and influence. Public works continued and national pride increased. The Senates and assemblies of Rome and the US continued to be mostly peopled by the wealthy. Overseas dictatorships and domestic crime continued as capitalism became more regulated and socialist contracts were made.

Global involvement increased as US banks loaned funds to prop up European currencies and fought World War II in Europe and Asia. The US redressed the League of Nations' failure with the creation of the United Nations (UN), Marshal Plan, North Atlantic Treaty Organization (NATO) and South East Asian Treaty Organization (SEATO). To contain new threats from China and the Soviet Union, the US involved itself in the "cold war" featuring the Korean War, Cuban Missile Crisis and Vietnam War. For its part, Rome finally conquered the "demon" Gauls, pacified Asia (present day Turkey and Mid East) and unified with Egypt. This set the rough limits of Roman borders until its decline 300-400 years later. The Roman and US generations experiencing all these events and victories felt proud but guarded. Fear continued to strike Roman hearts at the mention of the Gauls, Persians or Germans. In the US 2000 years later, society was paranoid and sensitive to the Indians, Mexicans, Germans, Asian "Yellow Peril" and finally the Russian's "Evil Empire" before A.D. 1990. But, not sharing these living memories, the '90s generation has felt only the unabated myth of invincibility.

Once defeated, held in check, or pacified, the foreign demons disappeared. Viet Nam and China, who once stood up to the US militarily and politically, court US economic favor today. This phenomena is not unlike the way ancient Petra, in present day Jordan, was brought into the Roman fold. Petra's king willed his city to Rome upon his death. Knowing the naturally protected city could hold out militarily, he saw that they would be economically isolated from the Roman world if the city didn't join it. The lack of trade would be as fatal and destructive as any military invasion. The economic and political world order was set with military support.

The reality of one world order under one superpower has once again become part of the world's *Zeitgeist.* This mental and emotional consciousness has not been dreamed of by Western society since Alexander the Great and 2000 years later by Louis the XIV. The last actualization of a single superpower, unmatched militarily and economically for 300 years, was ancient Rome. The Roman world government ruled in the micro geography of the Mediterranean World. Two millennia later, the US is the acknowledged de-facto, undisputed, single, world superpower over the entire globe. The future will determine if the limits of US control have been reached. Time will tell if the US will continue as the only super power for the next 300-400 years, as was the case with Rome.

However, being the world's superpower does not equate to domestic tranquillity or spiritual peace. The general society in B.C.E. and A.D. came to distrust their secular government. Fear of foreign attack could be dispelled, but not meaningful political participation. This cynicism developed in Rome and recently in the US. Distrust was urban society's response to plutocracy's control of government and business. Hard won rights gained by the common person, were buried under large bureaucracy, corruption, taxes, influence of special interests and the general influence of wealth.

In Rome as today, society yearns for compassion and accommodation amid divergent material interests and societal problems. But what ancient Romans saw and contemporary US society sees, is mostly partisan politics and inaction by impersonal government or business. Turning to the Twelve Tablets in Rome or their counterpart, the US Constitution, keeps most disputes in the courts. But increasingly expensive, slow and frustrating legal battles continue to demoralize the population's sense of justice. Thus faith that humans can efficiently, honestly and fairly rule themselves declines.

Secularism fails when institutions of government and business, created and guided by people for people, can no longer guarantee hope for equity, reason or compassion in the future. After generations of a plutocratic-republican Secular Phase, society's combined personal memory of rule by monarchy or theocracy fades into history and myth. With the

Theocratic Phase in the mythic past and discontent with the present Secular Phase, society searches for a new way of ordering society.

The future US central government may continue to be run by a series of executives sharing power with a congress, or one long serving executive (as with Caesar Augustus) sharing power with a republican legislature. But Rome's story shows that the plutocracy continues. The governed eventually become cynical about receiving reform after agitation only to be subverted in the future by moneyed interests. This translates to a feeling of little personal power. Faith in logic, science and human ability subside. Reason is replaced by increased urban alienation of the individual within society. Transcending secularism and no longer having a personal memory of the negatives of the theocratic model, a partial or even complete divine guidance becomes idealized as an alternative. This presents the danger of demagoguery and a cult of personality. The end result is dictatorship. Society quickly forgets what it didn't want in the past. It takes for granted what it has. It demands of the future what it doesn't have. In this lies the seed of society's expectations for, and consequential disillusionment with, science and the Secular Phase. Today society's individuals continue to feel unrepresented, insecure and ultimately spiritually unsatisfied. The human ego demands human significance within a cosmology. This motivator is bound up in the general life force and will to live.

The recent Euro-US Secular Phase disillusionment with faith in pure science and humanism was initially expressed by eighteenth and nineteenth century romantics and through the creation of fundamentalist Christian churches. The Age of Reason's deism, acknowledged that the Divine exists and created matter or life, but the Divine was passive as to the creation's operation. Humans were left to develop by their own efforts. Pure science was atheistic or agnostic. Spiritually insecure with these cold notions, Romantics returned to the Theocratic Phase *Zeitgeist* in search of a lost naturalism and unity with the Divine through study of neo-Gothic Christianity or a revival of Greco-Roman mythology.

Unwilling to deny an active Jehovah, Christian fundamentalists nonetheless accepted the Secular Phase *Zeitgeist*'s rationalist need for data to substantiate proof. The Bible's literal interpretation served as an instruction manual proving Jehovah's existence rather than a metaphorical book of poems and moral lessons. This was blended with interpretations of visions, prophesy and acts such as speaking in tongues or laying on hands.

The literal interpretation of the Bible led to new churches such as the Seventh Day Adventists (1863), Jehovah's Witnesses (1884) or Pentecostal Church (1903). From the Methodist Church evolved the Church of the Nazarene (1908). Stressed by the liberalism of his Presbyterian congregation, an oil millionaire, Lyman Stewart, funded the publication of *The Fundamentals* in Los Angeles, California (1909). This voice in support of biblical literalism coined the current "fundamentalist" label.

Having won leisure time and the material world, the old religions of the agrarian period, pure reason, humanism or philosophy all fell short of providing spiritual peace for Western society. The need to have divinity enter politics more directly than simple religious tolerance was the result. In response to the spiritual vacuum, secular governments found it advantageous to invoke divine sponsorship as society became disillusioned with deism or the religion of science. It was never forgotten that the Twelve Tablets of Roman law were handed down by deities. Omens and the sibyl's divination became more important to decision making in the last days of the Roman Republic. In the 1950s "under God" was added to the pledge of allegiance to the national flag of the US.

Society's turn toward divine guidance sends people searching for alternatives beyond the context of the prevailing Secular Phase or long past Theocratic Phase *Zeitgeists*. The field is shared by science, established religion (polytheism with ancient Rome and Christian-Judaic monotheism with the US) and new ideas of divinity flowing into the empire along with trade. As the myth of invincibility continues, society feels secure enough to investigate and practice established foreign religious belief systems. The Greco-Romans gained interest in Persian Zoroastrianism and Mithraism, Egyptian, Indian, Jewish, Nordic and Celtic beliefs. The Euro-US alternatives to traditional Judeo-Christian religions include Islam, Baha'i, Taoism, Hinduism, Buddhism, Native American, African and European shamanism. There are also new ideas influencing the search for compassion and justice currently contained in the universalistic labels of "New Thought" or "New Age." For Rome, new ideas were held within what came to be called Mithraism, Manichaeanism or Christianity.

After two millennia, spiritual questions are again posed which Western Civilization has the peace, security and luxury of centuries to resolve. Past answers are no longer sufficient. If the US sponsored world peace begun in the 1990s (Pax Americana) can hold as long as Pax Romana (250-300 years), the expansion of multi-national trade will continue.

The resultant networking of groups that operate on and hold a one world view will increase. Based on the Roman example, the appeal of human cooperation and security will become greater. As the myth of invincibility endures, society's desire for physical risks, individual independence and nationalism shall diminish.

The drive for rationalism to provide equality and society's material well being led to secular experiments in government (democratic, republican-capitalist, fascist, democratic-socialist and communist). These fell short of society's emotional or spiritual needs. Society remains in a quandary. Today's questions are fundamental. Should Western governments be completely rational, influenced by science and humanism or guided divinely by an empowered state religion? And if society veers toward divine guidance, shall it be through traditional domestic religion, established foreign religion or a completely new religion? Can traditional religion and traditional science form a new synthesized belief system to serve the changing present and bring hope for society's future?

Presently societal spiritual happiness or utopia remains unrealized. The individual still seeks compassion, hope, some sense of divine mystery and spiritual and physical well being. The individual longs to belong to or synchronize with a societal *Zeitgeist.* The individual's soul longs to be one with the Divine. As the US leads the West out of the Secular Phase, the Spiritual Phase will fill the void in Western Civilization's *Zeitgeist.* In Rome 2000 years ago this shift was personified in Caesar Augustus (representing established religion), or his contemporary, Jesus Christ (representing new religion). Today Jesus represents established religion as Zeus or Jupiter did two thousand years ago. No single avatar of new religion or established religion has been credited by society or state sanction yet. Perhaps none shall. Instead we may see an institution or group of individuals playing the role of the new Augustus and Jesus.

> *Before us there stands a last spiritual crisis that will involve all Europe and America. What its course will be, Late Hellenism tells us. The tyranny of Reason - of which we are not conscious, for we are ourselves its apex - is in every Culture an epoch between man and old - man, and no more.*
>
> Oswald Spengler, *The Decline of the West,* p. 22

Chapter Five

THE SPIRITUAL PHASE

1: The Meaning of Spirit

The word "spirit" originates in the Greek word for breath. This is an appropriate expression for such an illusive yet real entity. The breath vibrating through vocal chords and channeled by tongue and mouth creates sounds and words. Breath is required for trumpets and flutes. We know breath exists and we can feel it against our skin. We can only trace it when its heat generated by our body strikes cooler air and condenses into a mist. Condensation in the manufacture of liquor brings forth alcoholic "spirits." We can blow smoke. According to *Funk & Wagnalls Dictionary*:

> Spirit (spir' it) *n.* 1. *The principle of life and energy in man and animals, at one time regarded as being composed of an especially refined substance, such as breath or warm air, separable from body, mysterious in nature and ascribable to a divine origin.*

The breath acts as an entity revealing only the manifestation of its existence. Breath provides us with life-giving oxygen on the inhale. We exhale poisonous carbon dioxide required by plants. Athletic training recognizes the importance of breath control to elevate mental focus and strength. Breath awareness and control is primary in Eastern religious meditation. Hindu-Buddhist religion presents "the Word" expressed as Om. This is very similar to Amen (with a soft A) used to end prayers in present day Christianity. The use of a hard A is unique to US fundamentalist Christianity. It is stated in the Bible that in the beginning there was the "Word." *John* 1:1. Words exist and can have power, yet like the spirit, we cannot touch them or hold them physically.

Though we can record spoken words, we cannot evoke the emotion behind them. We must often experience or feel a word in order to come to a full understanding of it. This comes into play when personal memory is verbalized. Words like love or hate may be defined but never truly understood until one experiences love or hate. In English translation, the *King James Bible* goes on to state, *"the Word was with God and the Word was God." (John 1:1.)*

In the Greek translation found in *The Kingdom Interlinear Translation of the Greek Scriptures,* John states, *"In beginning was the Word, and the Word was toward the God, and god was the Word."* Interpretations of the lower case "god" used in John's statement include; godlike, divine, of a divine kind or a god. Thus, to approach the Divine is to feel the Divine's breath. Words emote truth or reality as felt by the writer or speaker. Words expressed through poetry or music can evoke a spirit that carries metaphorical truth while at the same time they seem whimsical or fictional. The religions, philosophies and cults that have risen in the West were spawned from words elevated to the emotional level, often transcending reason. How a word is spoken is often more powerful than the word itself. The spoken word expresses human attempts to communicate emotions and divine communication through sounds, generated by the breath. This is biblically recognized in the Bible's book, *Joel, "And it shall come to pass afterward, that I will pour out my Spirit upon all flesh; and your sons and daughters shall prophesy, your old men shall dream, your young men shall see visions."* (2:28) Even secular, rational ideas like self government or no taxation without representation needed words such as "Life, Liberty and the Pursuit of Happiness" to provide the inspiration required to fight and die for them.

This spiritual truth contained in words may be in conjunction with, or transcend the secular systematic approach. The systematic, secular method employs only reason and science when investigating the truth. The spiritual or "physiognomic" (as Spengler labeled it) approach to history brings into question more than just how secular political systems and their rationale for existence match society's needs. The emotional, often irrational human nature is holistically considered. In the Spiritual Phase, ethics, morals and values can no longer be dictated. Each individual member of society is allowed to investigate their own spirit. Not just a few mystics, but society as a whole attempts to explore and experience what cannot be defined rationally. Society as a whole attempts to realize its full physical and emotional potential.

In this context the Spiritual Phase can be defined as a period when society feels safe enough to actively self-actualize a full experiential and intellectual understanding. An updated definition of the Divine is attempted. This secure speculative environment found in the Spiritual Phase of the *Zeitgeist* results from an extended myth of invincibility. The Theocratic and Secular Phases synthesize to become the Spiritual Phase (see figs. 2 and 5).

Earth's resources appeared inexhaustible or indefinitely renewable at the onset of the Secular Phase. Faith in miracles or divine will gave way to faith in science and technology. Passion for mystery and understanding the Divine's will was transferred to the belief that science holds the future direction for understanding all reality. Science offered a believable reality using theory based on observation. This caused past mythology to seem irrelevant. There was faith that science and human effort would answer *any* questions. But belief in science and the "progress" it created also turned into a myth or religion of its own. Humans have difficulty with having no belief system. As with any religion, science also developed dogma.

Secular Phase society has found solace in believing that the Big Bang created all matter in the universe. Secular faith dictates that humans arrived through the process of natural selection (Darwin). Scientific history or social science is nothing more than the interplay of social classes divided from each other and Nature by economics (Marx). The whole universe can be explained in terms of math and numbers (Newton). But such notions deal only with the material plane. Eventually society feels that the Divine is distant and apathetic to human emotional needs. This deism resulted from the demands of scientifically driven technological progress and definition of truth which lacks recognition of the human need for spiritual feeling. This lack of concern for emotion has taken its toll even on the material plane. The use of Nature's resources in Earth's finite environment for a geometrically expanding human population is now beyond reason. Without solutions that include major lifestyle changes, war and genocide, science today offers declining solace. Western society continues to be increasingly skeptical of both past myths and scientific statements of human purpose. In logical terms, the Earth continues with or without humankind. Cynics see humans as a spreading cancer killing the planet. As the Secular Phase plays out, individual effort seems meaningless. The Divine is increasingly seen as the transcending, impersonal mechanic of Nature.

But the human ego seems incapable of sustaining human insignificance for long. The Spiritual Phase evolves as an attempt to bring order to the mental chaos and spiritual anxiety of not knowing. Thus new myths and deities, with human characteristics, that guide or affect human behavior and destiny are conjured. But the deities of the new theology must also be credible to compliment or compete with contemporary science and Theocratic Phase mythology. Science and the Secular Phase hands society many formidable facts. Given time, speculation on those facts sends spiritual quests beyond science and religion. Emotions, like the breath of life, do not lend themselves to a systematic study. Terms such as love, compassion, passion, belonging, alienation, jealousy, revenge, selfishness, loneliness and hate express emotional realities that must be recognized when investigating from a spiritual perspective. A humanist education (including psychology) is the Secular Phase prescription for needed understanding of these emotional terms. But such a purely systematic stance is losing credibility. The Western World is once again in a position to actually attempt to pursue a contemporary spiritual reality through the investigation and re-defining of the Divine. Creation and sanction of new deities take a minimum of three centuries protected by a myth of invincibility.

In the Spiritual Phase, society searches for a balance between reason and emotion, transcending science and religion. This is what early Christians and their contemporary cults were attempting in the first three centuries A.D. There was no lack of detractors who held onto past Secular Phase views or traditional religion in those days either. Emperor Julian (A.D. 361-363) made the last official attempt to restore Paganism. But Emperor Theodosius (A.D. 379-395) finally made Christianity the state religion and persecuted Pagans. Persecution did not end Paganism but Christian dogma and theocracy was established. Paganism continued alongside Christianity after the myth of invincibility ended. Armstrong wrote about this in *A History of God*:

> *During the fourth and fifth century, 'heretics' such as Apollinarius, Nestorius and Eutyches asked very difficult questions. How had the divinity of Christ been able to cohere with his humanity? Surely Mary was not the mother of God but the mother of the man Jesus? How could God have been a helpless, puling baby? Was it not more accurate to say that he had dwelt with Christ in particular intimacy, as in a temple?... The remote God of the Greeks, characterized by the divine Apatheia, seemed an entirely different deity from the God who was supposed to have become incarnate in Jesus Christ. The orthodox felt that the 'heretics,' who found the idea of a suffering, helpless God deeply offensive, wanted to drain the divine of its mystery and wonder. The paradox of the Incarnation seemed an antidote to the Hellenic God who did nothing to shake our complacency and who was so entirely reasonable.* (P. 125)

Western Rome's end of the myth of invincibility came with the sack of Rome in A.D. 410. By the end of the fifth century and the fall of Western Rome (A.D. 476), balanced investigation had evaporated into new mythologies. A strengthening theocracy and dogma gradually eliminated spiritual speculation for political reasons. This ensured emotionalism's eventual demise of the Spiritual Phase synthesis or Secular Phase scientific rationalism.

II: A 300 YEAR MYTH OF INVINCIBILITY

Two ways that a society's religion or basic belief system can be replaced are by foreign conquest or through a long period of peace and security (300 year myth of invincibility). If conquered, adherence to the foreign invader's religion may result. This was the case with the Muslim Turkish conquest of Christian Constantinople (Istanbul). The Christian European conquest of Muslim Moorish Spain is another example. An alternate example lies with Rome whose military might remained long enough to establish a myth of invincibility among her enemies and Roman society alike. In their Spiritual Phase, society attempted to actualize a lasting shift in Western Civilization's *Zeitgeist* and belief system. This required a minimum 300 year period of peace and relative physical security. Such a period occurred as Rome evolved from a frontier republic to an imperium and finally a theocracy based on a new religion. Military action was still required by the Romans during their empire's life span. But during the myth of invincibility period, these engagements were felt as more of an acknowledgment of overwhelming strength than as a real challenge to national security. Friend, foe and the empire's society came to believe the empire was invincible. The defeat and slaughter of Roman legions at the hands of German tribes in the Teutoburg Forest, was a reversal that tested faith in the myth of invincibility. But few doubted that ultimately the empire would prevail and continue. A 300-year myth of invincibility and a Spiritual Phase occurred in tandem. During this period Rome was consolidating and maintaining its empire. Only old stories and history books provided any reality to the fear of foreign invasion. As personal memories of such a threat faded, invasion of the homeland by the enemy was not seriously entertained by 10 B.C.E. in Rome.

Two millennia later (A.D. 1990), fear of invasion by a foreign power left the consciousness or *Zeitgeist* of the under-30-year-old age group within Western society. At the close of the cold war, the Hollywood movie *Red Dawn* depicted a Russian invasion of the US, using Cuban allies. This seemed more fantastic than real to young movie-goers. Support for President Reagan's "Star Wars" defense technology declined precipitously. Speaking English and wearing the Western suit and tie have become the norm for carrying on the planet's government and business. American Indians wear cowboy hats today and eat deep fried white flour. This "Indian fry bread" is a vestige of reservation life and US government handouts. Two millennia ago in the Mediterranean world, Latin was spoken and the toga was worn. Pants were identified with barbarians. For ancient Rome, past foes eventually emulated Roman dress, literature, culture and religion after a few generations under Rome's world order. Roman citizenship was coveted. Rome was held by its enemies in irrational awe. Even long after the end of Rome's myth of invincibility, tribal chieftains who invaded Rome's empire continued to pattern their dress and titles on Roman models. In A.D. 452, Attila the Hun's army stood at the gates of Rome. Bishop Leo and the clergy went out to meet the enemy unarmed. Attila was so impressed by the Romans' aspect and words that he left Rome untouched.

During Rome's 300 year myth of invincibility, democracy in the Christian congregations disappeared along with personal memory of a more tolerant past. Literacy also declined in the empire. Theocracy was well established by time the barbarian chiefs took over and needed to administer their newly conquered parcels of the civilized world. All that remained of Roman Law and ethics was held by the few literate Christian bishops and clerics who still had some books. For practical bureaucratic reasons alone, the church theocracy was maintained by the warlords of the rural invaders and the invaded urban society alike. Three centuries of national security plus a century of theocracy had allowed time for a new system to become established without personal memory of any alternative way.

Empires before and after Rome attained peace and prosperity. But they were not able to hold the position for more than a century or two before a rival power would rise, compete and more often replace it. Even when the former power had a revival, it never quite matched the glory of its original nation builders. Any search by the empire's society for new spiritual guidelines fell short of the creation of a new religion. Peace and security ran out. Western society only altered or revived fervent dedication to the established, traditional church of the time. This happened when Rome was briefly challenged near the end of their 300 year myth of invincibility. After Goth raiders had sacked Athens (A.D. 267), then burned the temple of Diana at Ephesus (A.D. 269), Roman priests reverted to human sacrifice to appease and obtain protection from the Pagan deities. The raiders were defeated and Rome's myth of invincibility continued. If the Goths had shattered Rome's myth of invincibility, "old time (Pagan) religion" would have prevailed and Christianity would not have been allowed to develop. Instead, by A.D. 350, Rome created a new theocracy based on a new cosmology and mythology called the Roman Catholic Church today. It was this new theocracy that Rome fell back on when their myth of invincibility ended and the Dark Ages got under way. How this Roman experience replays in the future of the USA is yet to be seen.

In order to see where the future of the US may lead, a study of the effects of a long peace and unified world order in Western Civilization is essential. Akkad-Babylon, Greco-Rome and Euro-US realized the super power dream, each separated by intervals of two millennia. Rome is the most recent example. For comparison and perspective, a survey noting other empires' myths of invincibility before and since Rome's is worth documenting.

The Akkadians created the first multi-cultural, unified empire in the West that we know of (c. 2200 B.C.E.). In *Change and Habit*, Toynbee calls it the "*Sumero-Akkadian world-state*" (p. 67). It stretched over modern Persia and Iraq to the Eastern Mediterranean coast. Akkad had provided an example of world conquest and one world government 300 years before the rise of Babylon. In accordance with the 2000 year cycle, Greece did the same 300 years before Rome became the world's single super power. Two thousand years after Rome, Europe showed the US the same example. Akkad was absorbed into the rising power of Babylon much as Greece melted into Rome's empire and Europe is melting into the US world order. Akkadian Babylon felt secure enough to have experienced a minimum 300 year myth of invincibility by 1600 B.C.E. Reflecting the Spiritual Phase of the *Zeitgeist* of that time, the Babylonian king, Hamurabi (c. 1728-1686), presented a constitution (code). Hamurabi's Code, written in Akkadian, established law subject to written dictates rather than oral tradition, priestly dictate or royal whim. There were 300 different statutes and regulations ranging from secular concerns like debt and taxes to spiritual matters like witchcraft. The guiding Spiritual Phase ethic was protection of the weak from the strong. This is similar to the Christian ethic that gained popularity and state sanction 2000 years later in Rome. The reign of Hamurabi and Babylon's Golden Age was 1850-1650 B.C.E. This conforms with Rome's last two centuries of a myth of invincibility and Early Christian Era, 2000 years later (A.D. 150-350). Western Rome's fall to foreign invaders (A.D. 476) came 1991 years after Akkad-Babylon fell to the same fate (1513 B.C.E.).

Minoans on Europe's island of Crete enjoyed a 300 year myth of invincibility contemporaneously with Akkad-Babylon. Crete had been home to an advanced agricultural and merchant society since 3000 B.C.E. Protected from Akkad-Babylon by a watery barrier, Minoans developed freely in the eastern Mediterranean Sea. There was no warrior cult. Yet they were not culturally isolated. Exiles and trade connections from Akkadian-Babylon to the East and Egypt to the South, no doubt influenced the Minoan cosmology, religion and *Zeitgeist.* The political exiles and traders immigrating to Crete may have related their personal memory of invasions and conquest. This would have served to make Cretans aware, but not necessarily afraid, of danger across the sea's horizon. Crete could have easily experienced an urban Secular Phase in tandem with Babylon, preceding their Spiritual Phase. Cretans could have provided an example of enlightened government for Hamurabi. The Cretans (Minoans) developed a matriarchal theocracy by the end of their myth of invincibility. During Crete's end days, religion turned to human sacrifice. This may have been an imported idea resorted to as society came under stress from natural disaster (1450 B.C.E.), followed by Mycenaen invasions. Whatever secular or spiritual movements the Minoan economy of surplus agriculture and mercantilism had underwritten was synthesized and turned into a religion. This Minoan religion and theocracy was adopted by the conquering Mycenaeans of Greece's mainland to the north. The Mycenaen myth of invincibility only lasted 200 years (c. 1350-1150 B.C.E.) before they were in turn overrun by Dorian tribes. The Minoan religion endured as the Greek Dark Ages descended.

In Africa, Egypt's great pyramid building period of the Old Kingdom had ended by 2000 B.C.E. Though periods of peace and prosperity would follow 2000 B.C.E., none of the reformed empires to come out of Egypt would maintain a myth of invincibility for the minimum 300 years (as Babylon or Crete did). There was perhaps a 200 year period of hubris and feelings of invincibility felt by Egyptians from the reign of King Thutmose III (1490 B.C.E.-1436 B.C.E.) to King Akhenaton (1367 B.C.E.-1350 B.C.E.). This myth of invincibility period was sufficient to allow speculation among at least the elite. However spiritual upheaval occurred when Akhenaton tried to enforce upon Egyptian society his belief in monotheism. The critical third century of national security was not to be forthcoming. Egyptian society did not have the time to digest a concept like monotheism or establish a theocracy to enforce it. Monotheism in Egypt officially died with King Akhenaton.

A generation later, monotheists led by Moses left the empire as political intrigue and rebellion within the established theocracy broke Egypt into separate small states. In the face of uncertainty and their loss of the myth of invincibility, the Egyptian society fell back on traditional religion. The exiled monotheists eventually established a kingdom and theocracy (Israel), based on monotheism. Jewish monotheism was refined and retained as that nation's supporting traditional cosmology. But the Jewish monotheism had to wait to be incorporated into Western cosmology until Western civilization's next Spiritual Phase. A 100 year myth of invincibility came to the Jews under Kings David and Solomon (1020-933 B.C.E.). Eventually Israel was absorbed by a revived Babylon in 597 and 598 B.C.E.

Babylon's revival (626-539 B.C.E.) gave them only a 100 year myth of invincibility. In Egypt following Akhenaton, foreign invasions kept any myth of invincibility at bay. From 940 B.C.E. to 30 B.C.E., Egypt was conquered in turn by Libya, Sudan, Assyria, Persia, Greece and finally Rome. Except for Rome, these conquerors of Egypt never held the myth of invincibility longer than 200 years nor changed their basic pan-polytheistic cosmologies.

In Rome, revolution at home and disturbances on the frontier or in the colonies were usually dealt with militarily, insuring national security and order within the empire. As generations and centuries passed, society in the Roman world felt safe and then free enough to enter into spiritual contemplation without any guilt or fear of divine consequences. Society's personal memory of past invasions or their ancestor's material struggles disappeared. More of society than the wealthy elite were allowed the mental leisure to contemplate philosophy, religion, Nature, the Divine and science. In time, hedonist orgies, circuses and foreign military adventures did not even hold enough distraction or inspiration to counter society's dreams of a more spiritually satisfying world. The Pax Romana (27 B.C.E. to A.D. 180) provided 200 years of peace. This created a myth of invincibility and Spiritual Phase which carried on another century. Unlike Egypt, Rome maintained its domain a crucial 100 years after Pax Romana (total 300 years). By A.D. 280, 300 years of speculation and synthesis had brought Christianity to the point of official acceptance by Western society (Edict of Milan, A.D. 313). The 300 year old myth of invincibility died slowly over the next century. Rome's military leaders fought each other and Emperor Diocletian split the empire by dividing its administration (A.D. 286). Emperor Constantine followed by reuniting the empire, constructing Constantinople (A.D. 330) as a new capitol and legalizing Christianity. The empire was officially divided again in

A.D. 395. Yet through all this internal strife, foreign invasion was prevented until Rome was sacked by foreign invasion in A.D. 410.

After the Western Roman Empire's fall in A.D. 476, Rome along with its new state religion Christianity, continued into the European Dark Ages and concurrent Theocratic Phase. The Eastern Roman Empire (Byzantine Empire) continued to fight for survival. This empire was greatly reduced in geographic, military, and economic size. Latin language was replaced by Greek. However, Byzantium still held the military and commercial geography strategically centered at Constantinople. The Byzantines held on to Anatolia, Syria, Palestine and Egypt. But the myth of invincibility was gone. This new empire tried to collect and protect remnants from the old empire while foreign powers whittled away at it. The remnants included a Greek Orthodox theocracy. A good defense was made by the Byzantines for the next 300 years (A.D. 400-700) against first animist Huns, then Zoroastrian Persians, Muslim Arabs and Pagan Franks. The Byzantines lost Egypt and Syria to the Arabs. Byzantium did not possess an extended myth of invincibility. Their society was constantly concerned with physical survival against foreign invasion. Maintaining the existing Christian religion was synonymous with cultural survival and patriotism. Spiritual contemplation, investigation or changes were left to the priestly elite.

Meanwhile in Europe outside Byzantium, an initially Pagan Frankish Empire evolved in Western Europe from the conquering German tribes who had taken the Western Roman Empire. The Frankish warlords became a new aristocracy. The old state religion of Rome (Christianity) mingled with the Pagan faiths of the Franks to form a new hybrid theocracy and religion named the Roman Catholic Church. During the 150 years of the Frank's life span (A.D. 700-850), the Roman Catholic theocracy grew and separated from the Byzantine Greek Christians. The Roman Catholic Church operated the bureaucracy for the mostly illiterate Frankish aristocracy. Under the reign of Charlemagne (A.D. 771-815), the Franks persecuted Pagans in Bohemia and the Baltic regions. Pogroms occurred. Charlemagne attempted to destroy the Pagan faith of his ancestors and also allowed the Roman based theocracy to crown him "Holy Roman Emperor." Frankish society may have felt invincible and safe from Muslim, Byzantine or Pagan attacks. But following Charlemagne's death, the Franks fell apart 35 years later. This ended any myth of invincibility that might have developed. The greatest single European power through this period remained the Greek Orthodox Byzantine Empire. The struggling Byzantines did not mourn the Frankish demise. Over the next 250 years (A.D. 750-1100) the Byzantines held off new threats from Russians and Bulgarians to the north while slowly expanding against the Muslim states to the south. But continued, constant attacks by Mongols and then Turks from central Asia ended any hope of Byzantine invincibility.

Filling the power vacuum left by the Franks, Saxon and then Franconian emperors ruled the Holy Roman Empire. They gradually ceded temporal authority and territory to the Roman Catholic Bishops and Popes. After Pope Gregory VIII, much of Italy became a theocratic empire in its own right. Real temporal imperial power passed with Barbarosa (d. 1190). These "Papal States" held much of Italy and for 200 years fought off Arab attacks from the sea. From 1100-1300, the Papal States gained control of the greater Holy Roman Empire, while advocating the Crusades and witch hunts. But there was little feeling of a myth of invincibility, even from Christian neighbors. France, already separated from the Holy Roman Empire, was eventually joined by Spain, Portugal and other Italian states as independent kingdoms. Secular craft and merchant guilds governed growing cities. Their state religion remained Roman Catholic but they would not be dictated to by the Pope or confine themselves to the Latin language.

Meanwhile, Western European Christian Crusaders finally crushed the diminished Byzantine Empire. In 1204 the Fourth Crusade set up the short-lived "Latin Empire" in Byzantium's place. Byzantium was restored again in 1261, but never again gained prominence. Finally Byzantium disappeared as a state forever in 1453 through defeat to the Ottoman Turks. The Turks did more than take temporal power. They replaced Christianity with the Muslim religion. The Greek language was replaced by Turkish or Arabic. Turkish Muslim theocracy replaced Byzantine Greek Orthodox theocracy.

The Ottoman Turks were tolerant of Jewish and Christian religions during their control of most of southeast Europe and the Mid-East. From the late 1300s, the Ottomans were at war conquering neighboring lands culminating 150 years later in an assault of Vienna in 1529. Through the rule of Bayezid II and Suleiman (1481-1566), there was perhaps 100 to 150 years when the Turks felt safe from invasion and invincible. During this period, Portugal and Spain created their world empires. In 1571 a European fleet defeated the Turkish navy. First Venice, then the Holy Roman Empire, Poland and Russia, all in their turn, challenged the Ottomans militarily while Spain, Portugal, Sweden, France, England and finally Holland, challenged the Turks commercially.

By 1650 — the end of Europe's Reformation and religious warfare (Thirty Years War) — the Papacy had disappeared as a major temporal power. All of the other European states mentioned above were then only at most equals in military might and empire with the Turkish Empire which still included all of North Africa, the Mid-East, lands north of the Black Sea and Europe's Balkans. In 1683, Turkey felt strong enough for another, though unsuccessful, attempt at the conquest of Central Europe. But the Ottoman Turk's myth of invincibility had already been shattered by the rising European nations who continued to pick away at its empire.

International commercial conflict of the seventeenth and eighteenth centuries kept Western nations at war or preparing for war. In each of these states a generation may have indulged in the conceit of a myth of invincibility. More than one generation may have experienced the myth in France or Spain or Ottoman Turkey, but no empire's life span allowed the myth of invincibility to get near Rome's minimum 300 years. By 1800, France and England finally gained the premier status as Earth's two most powerful nations. England ultimately achieved the singular premier status after France's revolution and the fall of Napoleon.

After the Battle of Waterloo in 1815, England's society experienced a feeling of invincibility for 125 years ending with The Battle of Britain in World War II (1940). The phrase, "The Sun never sets on the Empire" was touted by several European empires. But "Britannia rules the waves" was England's alone. Its navy's control of the natural barriers of the English Channel and North Sea (German Sea) meant Britain's myth of invincibility grew directly, as with Crete, from having no fear of foreign invasion. By 1900 however, new economic and military challenges faced England from Russia and France. These old competing empires were joined by the newer empires of Japan, Germany and the USA. All these powers were racing to build large, modern navies. At the close of the twentieth century's two World Wars, Britain's power was eclipsed by the US. Only Russia's empire (renamed Union of Soviet Socialist Republics) presented any challenge to the USA.

The planet's imperial nations were greatly diminished by the loss of their empires during or shortly after the World Wars, except for the US and USSR. World War I and II destroyed any myth in Western society that their separate nation could guarantee security from invasion. The US occupied England (at her invitation) and the rest of Western Europe. The Russian-US bid for primacy led to the cold war. Direct conflict between the US and USSR did not occur due to mutual fear of destruction by nuclear weapons. Though war technology was not as advanced, this stand-off was not unlike the one that existed between Persia and Rome 2000 years before. Only after the recent collapse of the USSR,(1990) could Western society truly begin to entertain a myth of invincibility.

The US may have reached an economic peak in A.D. 1969 when it was wealthy enough to finance the Vietnam War, the War on Poverty, manned travel to the Moon, a favorable trade balance and a balanced federal budget. Though no longer as economically strong today, the US is still closest to a one-world super power this planet has seen in the West since Rome two millennia earlier or Crete and Babylon four millennia ago. The belief that the US is invincible, held by friend and foe alike, will persist beyond England's 125 year myth of invincibility. With the present level of technology and military, natural and human resources to support it, the myth of invincibility may last well beyond the Ottoman's, Byzantine's or ancient Egyptian's 200 years. The US not only rules the waves, but also the sky. This was clearly demonstrated to the people of the Earth via TV during the Desert Storm operation against Iraq in 1990 or in Bosnia in 1995. These operations made clear that none can challenge the US militarily.

Superior military tactics, organization, technology and supply network worked for Rome and works for the US today. The US myth of invincibility is even now forming in the minds and hearts (*Zeitgeist*) of the next generation of Earth's people. A future unforeseen power, climatic change or plague may threaten and sap strength. Overwhelming immigration from Latin America may tax the resources of the US. Terrorist attacks may cripple civil liberties and the urban system. But the US has the resources to hold these problems in check, maintaining US supremacy for three hundred years.

In the Roman model, the two or three generations that made up the last critical 100 years of the myth of invincibility created a new religion and theocracy to go with it. It was these generations who produced St. Augustine within the empire and St. Patrick outside the empire. There was enough safety from foreign invasion and time to allow spiritual revolution and investigation until society finally created and then accepted the new faith. This is the essence of a Spiritual Phase. Today in the US, the new Spiritual Phase has begun. If Euro-US society continues for 300 years feeling invincible as the Greco-Roman world did, another example of a single Western super power's myth of invincibility and Spiritual Phase will evolve a new cosmology. The inevitable cyclical process will, in turn, bring Western Civilization full circle to yet another Theocratic Phase.

When Rome's myth of invincibility gradually faded and then disappeared with the barbarian sack of A.D. 410, it was the new faith of Christianity already established as the state religion, to which Western urban society turned for hope and spiritual strength. The faith the US and Western society will turn to 350 years from now if New York City is sacked, can only be conjecture. But a comparative study of contemporary US and the Roman Spiritual Phase experiences may provide an educated guess.

III: The Spiritual Crises in the USA

The society of every empire has at one time felt their invincibility would last forever. Few were lucky to maintain the myth beyond a century. However there are reasons in addition to the momentum of a 2000 year cycle, that the U. S. will have a myth of invincibility spanning 300 years. Like Rome, the US began as a republic and will remain a republic in name until the plutocracy and Western society finds it more expedient to keep domestic order through dictatorship. Plutocracy can operate as a republic or a dictatorship. At present, the majority of the Senators and members of the House of Representatives are millionaires. This was also true of most members of Rome's Senate and assemblies. In order to realistically expect election, vast sums of money for campaigning and membership in the major political parties are prerequisite. Thus the US Republic is a de facto, two-party plutocracy like ancient Rome. Only self-interest expressed through republicanism stands as a bulwark against dictatorship or anarchy.

This system may continue in the US a generation or two longer than it did in Rome. In order to prevent dictatorship or theocracy, the Founding Fathers of the US separated church and state as much as possible. They allowed for social change by petition through a written secular constitution. They advocated free capitalist enterprise yet supported socialized education, postal service, roads and libraries. They clearly defined, separated and set limits on the legislative, judicial and executive branches of the government. Though Presidents Jefferson, Jackson, Lincoln, F.D.R. and Nixon, to name a few, challenged or disregarded the Supreme Court or Congress, the US Constitution created in the Secular Phase Age of Reason has still maintained ultimate power. To interpret the Constitution so as to allow complete rule by an elite faction or single party will require the legislature and the courts to hand over their powers to the executive branch of government.

The pressure of economic strain and popular demand for quick action by the state proved too great for Rome's Republic. Rome's 500 year long tradition of a plutocratic, republican system evaporated under Caesar Augustus. However, Romans continued to delude themselves that they were a republic right through Augustus' 41 year reign. The myth of invincibility was established at the same time. If the 400 year US republican-plutocratic tradition fades into a rubber stamp Congress, there are other traditions and institutions that will insure the US myth of invincibility for centuries. Military superiority shall continue. A large consumer market will continue to entice would-be rival nations into staying at peace and selling to the US. Popular music and fashion generated by the US shall continue to be aped and consumed globally. New York shall remain the financial capital of the world as well as the site of the United Nations headquarters.

Power in government and finance, like gravity in mass, seeks to increase itself. The greater the mass, the greater the gravitation. The pace of human hunger for concentrated power will manifest slowly if safeguards are kept in place. The clear separation and competition of the branches of government, anti-trust laws, labor laws, environmental laws plus the

Securities and Exchange Commission and public utilities commissions have all helped to check the growth of economic monopoly and concentrated political power in the US. But, momentum continues to build toward centralized power as the wealthy jockey for advantage. State and local government power has declined as urban and industrial interests increase sway in the federal government.

No longer feeling able to be effective, the individual in society rejects or becomes apathetic toward a distant government. Society has turned from healthy skepticism to frustrated disenchantment. The President was granted line item veto power in 1997. In 1913, Congress and state legislatures added a sixteenth amendment to the Constitution allowing the levy of federal income tax to redistribute wealth. But the Federal Reserve Board was also created at that time. The Fed's power to set official interest rates and control money supply limited Congress's power of the purse. Though the chairman of the board is appointed by the President, the possibility of inside knowledge, leaked by the Fed, allows enormous potential power. The nineteenth century British historian, Lord Acton stated, *"All power corrupts, and absolute power corrupts absolutely."*

Even with legal safeguards, the potential exists that a temporary military dictatorship will be legislated to deal with immediate real or perceived domestic crisis. Drugs and terrorism loom large in media and public concern. These threats have replaced the "Red Scare" of the past perceived socialist threat. The US plutocracy saved the west for democracy in the twentieth century. But what power on earth will be capable of destroying the US government if it becomes a dictatorship in the twenty-first century? Once a plutocracy and the society it governs surrender to the seduction of a secular dictatorship, the system may continue indefinitely until it is supported by or supplanted by a theocracy. This is the lesson of Rome after Augustus.

As Roman society became urban, it also became dependent on the state for income (earned or given), while extolling the self-reliant virtues of their past agrarian society. The state issued government contracts, subsidies and tax exemptions to stimulate industry and finance while providing welfare payments to pacify the poor. The illusion existed in Rome, and it exists today in the US, that one could be a rugged individualist like the self-reliant ancestors of the past frontier while working for a government contract or bureaucracy. This participation in big government and big business is seen as patriotic. In reality, dependence on the state, corporation or franchise is self-serving. The society has a vested interest in keeping and expanding the established system. Ultimately this thwarts sociopolitical reform that may actually improve the quality of life and expand economic and political democracy.

In Rome and the US, military supremacy is acknowledged and maintained, revenues continue to be absorbed by the military industrial complex. The plutocracy's representatives vote for spending that will provide income and security for the voting constituents and military defense. The voting third of the citizenry is informed or misinformed by mass media owned by the plutocracy. Lack of details concerning the actions of distant big government and business leads to emotional, under-informed decisions open to manipulation by an organized group with a slick ad campaign.

Minus real fear of foreign invasion or compelling economic disaster to create a common cause, the US Congress feels less compulsion to cooperate within itself. Society is less patient with partisan congressional interests. The influence of special interests frustrates individual political involvement or lends support for independent millionaires like Ross Perot and Steve Forbes in their bids for the Presidency in 1992 and 1996. Their appeal relies on the hope that millionaires are above bribery. Other parties or individuals are marginalized by the mass media because the media is not interested in issues as much as it is with selling advertisements, and gaining ratings from a public which appears to want to know more about possible winners. This relegates a political campaign to a sporting event. The media virtually blacks out other party platforms or ideas. The campaign trails of the American Independent, Reform Party, Communist, Nazi, Libertarian, Socialist, Peace and Freedom, Natural Law or any other parties are never brought into the living room through the "idiot box." Thus a candidate like lawyer and consumer advocate Ralph Nader received minimum exposure. Because he accepted no campaign funds as the 1996 Green Party candidate, he could not advertise extensively. His message exposing big business exploitation was not heard. The Reform Party candidate, Ross Perot, sued unsuccessfully to be included in 1996 presidential debates. A committee of five Democrats and five Republicans had chosen the participants.

Information and communication are technically available and simple to access. But there is actually too much information or disinformation which makes it difficult and frustrating for an individual to digest. Dry analytic reporting succumbs to negative opinionated reporting. This, in turn, encourages society's shift from healthy skepticism to cynicism. The networks often direct the focus for society by deciding what is or is not newsworthy.

The murder trial of O.J. Simpson in 1994 and 1995 took far more TV air time than the concurrent investigation of the murderous bombing of the federal building in Kansas City. Reports came in on a daily basis on the hostages held in the Mid-East during President Carter's administration, while hostages taken and never released under President Reagan's administration were rarely mentioned. President Reagan's administration was successful in cooling investigative reporting by rewarding reporters with scoops if they followed party line while ostracizing detractor reporters. Without timely information, these reporters got little support from their employers.

The few citizens who take the time to follow televised congressional proceedings or use resources such as the computer inter-net for personal investigation have minimum effect on society at large. The majority of society tries to digest what is fed to them in a headline or sound bite. In a glaring example of selective reporting, the US public heard a lot of news in the 1970s about genocide in Cambodia caused by the Khmer Rouge. Yet little was told about events on the island of East Timor occurring at the same time. Indonesia's military invasion, conquest and genocide of the Timorese began one day after a state visit by President Ford to Indonesia. The oil rich, strategic state was apparently given free reign with no official protest from the US. Cambodia and Timor are both insignificant foreign lands in the minds of most in US society. Given the cold-war mentality at the time, the media somehow determined genocide at the hands of communists in Cambodia was more newsworthy than genocide at the hands of a dictatorship allied to the US. This filtering or simplification of news, in turn, lends itself to the power of special interests.

Big business funds media organizations through advertisements or outright ownership. At the time of this writing, American Broadcasting Company (ABC) is owned by Walt Disney, Columbia Broadcasting

Company (CBS) is owned by Westinghouse, Fox Broadcasting is owned by News Corp. and National Broadcasting Company (NBC) is owned by General Electric. This plutocratic, media dictatorship influences issues and network accepted politicians in their pursuit of favorable press and votes. Perot was refused TV air time in his '96 campaign. Society more often assumes a sense of hopeless apathy. Thus the minority who actually turn out to vote lean toward short-term, self serving demands for the declining revenues. Legislative battles test society's patience as factions become less conciliatory over their demands.

This dynamic within a republican system thwarts bold action and social progress. In Rome of A.D. 200, the once sought after job of tax collector became a personal burden as the central government demanded more revenue from a shrinking middle class. The tax collectors had to dig into their own pockets if they didn't come up with their assigned quota. Tax collection was made into a hereditary position to force people to do the job and collectors went into debt or hiding when no better system was devised. Maintaining fiscal prosperity led to a static dictatorship, barely meeting society's social and spiritual needs. Past success tended to get in the way of positive change. Society clung to what had worked as opposed to what was needed to deal with present and future realities. Eventually Roman society abandoned the system of things altogether. This led Spengler to propose that upon creating a civilization, the culture dies. But a visit to Rome today shows the culture (society) of that Eternal City is not dead.

In the US, confidence in the plutocratic government is currently low among an increasingly cynical society. Wealthy special interests wield major influences on lawmaking. Thinly veiled bribes in the form of campaign contributions from tobacco companies saved the destruction, by a 1995 Congressional vote, of a $23 million federal subsidy for tobacco research. This costly subsidy had little support from most citizens. Funding from medical insurance companies and medical doctors groups went to mass media TV advertisements and lobbying congressional representatives in order to kill any medical service reform. This greatly contributed to the congressional defeat of the Democratic Party's plan for a more socialized medical program in 1994. While squabbles in Congress continued, medical costs soared unchecked or unregulated. Medical practice and drugs are big businesses and continue placing funds into congressional lobbies and advertisements.

At the time of the Founding Fathers, the medical field was barely a science. George Washington was literally bled to death when his doctors attempted to get rid of the "bad blood" they felt caused his illness. For eighteenth and nineteenth century society, folk medicine was as valid and common as medicine available to the wealthy through doctors. Drugs and medical instruments were homemade. Had medical science and technology advanced as far by the American Revolution as it had by the turn of the twentieth century, the Founding Fathers would have instituted some sort of medical system set up like public education, fire departments, mail service and free public libraries. The revolutionary socialism of the Founding Fathers would have demanded that national health equated to national strength, just as public education was the means to a free and informed citizenry.

Today US society is far from its secular, revolutionary, agrarian beginnings, yet clings to the romantic appearances of the past. In the agrarian time there was no public plan for medicine, so today's society has no tradition to lean on and feels insecure about change. The one-room schoolhouse was a traditional pillar of the revolutionary, agrarian past. So some sort of public education is acceptable to society. Having a tradition to lean on or not, change is getting more difficult to adapt to or institute for US society and its government. Post-cold-war military base closing has reduced and consolidated garrisons, but not lowered spending. Spending on welfare programs may be declining, but the poor's dependency on the state is not. The US government and society is either unwilling or incapable of bold or rapid change. As in Rome, less and less domestic revenue is going toward education, agricultural and industrial infrastructure. Meanwhile, government's military spending and society's consumer borrowing continues. The military guarantees a myth of invincibility. Consumer borrowing guarantees continuance of lifestyle and distractions from spiritual or political realities.

The Founding Fathers also wisely separated the physical centers of political power (Washington, D.C.), and economic power (New York). But the separation was not great enough. The megalopolis extending and joining these two cities we see along the east coast of the US today, is a manifestation of centralized political and economic power. This megalopolis world capitol has replaced the metropolis of Ancient Rome 2000 years ago. The major difference is in size between Rome and New York/Washington, D.C. All roads lead to Rome, or at present, New York and Washington, D.C. and back again, carrying trade and ideas. The ancient world became Rome and Rome became the world. This dynamic applies to Washington. D.C./New York today.

The idea of one world is again being realized through Western eyes. The rest of the world's population is often astounded at the excesses of US society and culture. A fellow Western traveler to the developing world, Tim Cleary, when asked about this excess, says, *"The US today is the planet Earth swallowed and digested then regurgitated back over the planet."* All the positives and negatives ascribed to the US by the rest of the world are an Americanized mirror reflecting beauty as well as warts.

The increasing disillusionment of the US society is not due to concern that the government can't defend or conquer other societies at will, but that the government of the US can't adapt or change enough to govern itself or society openly, justly, compassionately, or at all. Demagogues become popular in the news media as a restless society becomes cynical and supports simple solutions for complex problems that are selectively or partially presented in the news. Many alienated people, out of frustration with shades of gray, gravitate to simpler black and white solutions to complex moral, legal, political, economic or spiritual questions. The solutions are often provided by a single person or institution. Pat Buchanan's bid for the Republican Party presidential nomination in 1996 is a case in point. Buchanan's simplistic solution to illegal immigration into the US via Mexico was to virtually militarize the border. Seemingly impractical and racist today, this status may very well be a reality a half century from now.

Currently, the two party system continues with an occasional third party populist protest with no hope of winning. The choice for leadership in Congress or the Presidency returns to a Democratic or Republican Party member every two years. Once elected to office, any differences in practice seem minimal. Society thus feels more and more alienated, powerless and impatient. A sense that voting does little to change the system of impersonal distant government reduces potential voters by two thirds. For a secular nation founded on a systematic, republican principle, this presents a crisis. Humans appear to be incapable of governing themselves. This cynicism runs counter to the rational humanism of the Age of Reason and Secular Phase which gave rise to the US Constitution. Not willing to return to a Theocratic Phase, a call for divine interaction develops nonetheless. Whether or not humans are able to govern humans will vex society in the Spiritual Phase.

To counter domestic discord, nationalism with a divine blessing will become more popular, though it is not a secular or rational response. As in the US, a long tradition of relative religious tolerance and secular or spiritual speculation was well established in Rome. Two thousand years ago, Publius Virgil (70-19 B.C.E.) blended traditional mythology (religion) with Rome's rural beginnings to establish the sanctity or even divinity of the state. Virgil's poem, *Georgics* extolled the world of a farmer as the model for a world view. Virgil's *Aeneid* served with Homer's stories as a sort of moral text for the Roman Empire as Western society entered the Spiritual Phase. Virgil painted Rome as a vigorous independent polity as opposed to decadent Greece or other old empires. This is similar to the way US society has come to see its new world self relative to old world Europe and the rest of the planet. Past US presidents are deified in stone image at Mount Rushmore located in the Black Hills of South Dakota. Stories of patriotic virtue are planted in every school child's education. Young George Washington admitting to chopping down a cherry tree to his upset father or Honest Abe Lincoln walking miles to school through the snow everyday, are encouraged myths. The role of Native Americans is consumed by myth in the Thanksgiving story or Pocahontas. The unofficial national anthem of *America, America* grants "God's grace." A House Bill proposal of 1995 called for officially proclaiming the US a Christian nation. Today this moralistic nationalism honoring the past continues as disillusionment in the present secular republican process of government grows into uncertainty about the future.

Industries and banks set goals to be bigger, more profitable and international. Big business mergers combine capital and cut costs by eliminating duplicate operations and the employees of those operations. For example, drug companies have a short window of time before they lose patents and monopoly on their products. The merger of drug companies Pharmacia and Upjohn helped compensate for weak product lines they both retained after patents expired. The 1997 merger of aircraft builders

Boeing and McDonnell Douglas will have only Europe's Airbus as any competition.

US exports are led by aeronautical technology, pharmaceutical sales, computer technologies and movie and music entertainment distribution. These export industries depend on the buying ability of non-Western societies. World trade and communication bring home to US society how dependent their economy is on states and institutions, in partnership with multinational big business outside the immediate control of the US government. Economic organizations that transcend national sovereignty or control by the average US citizen make decisions that may directly or indirectly affect that individual. It appears to growing numbers in the US that through political influence and economics, merging banks and international capitalism subverts US society's aspirations through world organizations. In the nineteenth century, anti-Mason, anti-Catholic and anti-immigrant movements existed to fight what seem today as less complicated foreign conspiracies. The twentieth century list includes The Council on Foreign Relations, Tri-Lateral Commission, United Nations, Organization of American States, North American Free Trade Organization, European Economic Community and the World Bank.

Isolated by physical separation from other lands, the common US citizen or ancient Roman only observes other lands through the media and military or business service. Tourism offers a superficial survey of a foreign land. Today visits to 16 cities in three weeks is not uncommon. Immigrants whose numbers have increased since 1970 to 10 percent of the total US population paint a picture of lands they originate from. But immigrants carry with them discontent with their homeland's economic or political situation. All these perspectives give a less than balanced view of the outside world. A superiority complex on a mass level easily blends into nationalism and xenophobia. Meanwhile, the non-Westerner's view of the US comes through the rich tourist, Hollywood movies or military action.

The US has attained its myth of invincibility. But, like empires before, domestic discord is the price to be paid. The US will have a long time to deal with the benefits and consequences of its position. Civil rights, including the right to bear arms and to privacy, are being limited in an effort to curb rising crime and domestic terrorism. Law and order, or lack of it, has replaced national defense as government's prime and immediate focus in maintaining security. Only compassion from within US society and government openness can dampen suspicion and bring about needed cooperation domestically and internationally if the US is to live within its economic means and adapt to society's changing need for spiritual well-being.

But compassion is in declining supply in a society that clings to the myth of the rugged individualist. The myth persists that anyone can become wealthy if they work hard and are selfish. Compassion is something the Founding Fathers left to patriotic emotionalism, local volunteer community action and a line in the Constitution which states that the government will provide for the general welfare of the people. The Constitution was created through a systematic, scientific secular approach. It has worked well in the Secular Phase. But compassion involves the heart. Perhaps that is why the Founding Fathers preferred not to deal with it in the very rational, scientific and secular Constitution. In pre-urban US, volunteerism at the village level filled emotional as well as socio-economic needs. Local rural groups and individuals showed acts of compassion and cooperation with fellow humans and governments in the face of frontier challenges, environment, natural disaster or fear of invasion. The meliorism of the Secular Phase supported a general optimism towards the urbanizing future. Today it remains difficult to find purpose and place beyond immediate personal associations.

Currently the single most visible and symbolic world government institution is the United Nations. Many in US society do not support it. People who dislike the UN either feel it is too powerful or too weak. Those who disagree may cause the demise or alteration of the UN. Alternative groups or sects will offer their plan for an organized means to address planetary/Gaian problems. If Pax Americana continues long enough, loss of faith in the paradigms of the established national systems and attitudes will occur. A reformed world government shall prevail. The name given over to a future world government may no longer be the UN because even the concept of nations will seem antique. United Tribes or United People might better serve as a new label. But this is only a political-economic remedy. New paradigms will need to evolve to fill the emotional-spiritual gap created by the alienation of the individual in an

Euro-US, urban *Zeitgeist.* Only a universal spiritual movement shall rectify the loss of the village and Nature.

IV: Rome's Spiritual Phase

Rome experienced its Spiritual Phase in the first three centuries A.D. This period has also been labeled the Early Christian Era. A survey of that time illuminates the modern West's fast approaching future. When Rome's Spiritual Phase dissolved into theocracy, a new universal cosmology arose in Western civilization. The spiritual and philosophical movements participating in that evolution filled a vacuum caused by society's loss of faith in science. The cults and schools of philosophy provided hope in the face of cynicism toward the dissolving plutocracy-republic and the plutocratic dictatorships that followed. The West's spiritual future in the Aquarian Age is contained in the story of Rome's entrance into the Age of Pisces.

Rome's extended 300 year myth of invincibility witnessed the gradual death of the Roman Republic. In A.D. 69, the senate held enough power to declare Emperor Nero a public enemy. Upon Nero's removal, the bid for monarchy of the Augustan family chain of emperors (Augustus, Tiberius, Caligula, Claudius, Nero) failed. But succeeding emperors, supported by the plutocracy, ruled by military dictatorship until Rome's fall, 400 years later. Society went along with this for the most part, as they lost personal memory of a republican alternative. There was more concern for local law and order which assured safe travel for commerce. Under decisive dictatorships, standards of living and security could be maintained as well as the illusion of traditional Roman values. During the first century, remaining republicans were ruthlessly persecuted. The senate existed only as a vestige of tradition, holding little real power.

Continuing urbanization, corruption, anonymity, personal alienation and lack of compassion led Roman society to the investigation and creation of anti-establishment spiritual cults. Within the empire, many traveled and educated citizens were familiar with Greek philosophy and all the world's religions of their day. Retaining Secular Phase Hellenism, they systematically approached their spirituality. Incorporating the Golden Mean, they developed an almost Buddhist view that the material world was illusion. This logic allowed them to transcend concern over the tyrannical politics of their day. This left the spiritual realm as their true reality. Some became interested in religions and available cults in search of explanations for spiritual phenomena. The new cults intrigued many because the Greco-Roman mythologies seemed antiquated and familiar. Exotic cults such as Christianity caught their attention. For these Gnostic Christians, even the human nature and activities of Jesus were disregarded as not divine and thus irrelevant for study. In time, all strata of society shared in spiritual quests and the investigation of exotic spiritual ideas. From Egypt came the popular traditional and ancient mother deity cult of Isis. The Indian merchant community in Alexandria, Egypt, brought Indian trade along with Indian beliefs including Hinduism and Buddhism. Christian and Pagan lived and worked side by side and intermarried (as was the case with St. Augustine's parents).

For Christians in the first two centuries, there was not one clergy but only a loose affiliation or at best a confederation of churches. Indeed, there was little distinction between lay and clerical members. Depending on their geographic location, culture, language, neighboring religions, and level of education, each Christian group possessed only the most basic similarities to one another. The mysteries involved with baptism, study of Jesus' sermons, the passion play and the incorporated Pagan practice of sacraments were all the first Christians held in common. Such a generalized cult accepted all of society's classes in a spirit of belonging, understanding and compassion. This is the case with any cult. But minus a priestly elite, Christians could not be controlled or effectively countered by the rigid Roman state laws and religious dogma. Other competing cults such as Isis worship had a long estabiished priest class and dogma. Christianity also accepted all perspectives as members joined, worshipped in tandem with or quit other cults and added their ideas or inspiration.

The common term "Christian" was coined by Roman society after it came to understand the mythology of the cult. During the first hundred years, Romans called the cult the Third Race. The Third Race members (Christians) were not generally accepted. The Jews (labeled the "Second Race") along with the Third Race, were considered irreverent in their sexual debauchery, lack of patriotism and interpretation of love. Romans felt the northern German and Celtic tribes at least followed a pantheon similar to Rome's. Celts in Spain, Britain, Gaul and Galatia (Turkey) were pacified and incorporated into the empire. Germans served under the Roman eagle as loyal mercenaries. Other than the potential foreign (barbarian) political power of the Druid priests or Asian shamans, Romans felt little religious or spiritual threat from north of the Rhine and Danube rivers. Within the empire in the first two centuries A.D., the majority of Roman society saw themselves and fellow Pagans as the "First Race."

The First Race viewed the Christian cult, unlike the other Pagan cults, to be almost monotheistic like the Jews. Christians and Jews were found in every major Roman city but had little following in rural areas. Christians and Jews recognized no other deities than one called Jehovah. Unlike the Jews, Christians worshipped an additional personality called Jesus. The divine nature of Jesus was not yet clear, even among Christians. Christians uniformly believed Jesus was a Messiah who would shortly return to set the world right. Jews believed a messiah was yet to be revealed. The Jews were a traditional ancient religion; Christians were new on the scene. Both were apocalyptic religions that predicted a new world to come. The present was considered irrelevant. Roman society generally did not like the notion that any other power than Rome should rule the present and in the future. Being Jewish was a birthright. The Christian cult was initially split over whether to accept non-Jews. But within the next generation, Christians welcomed anyone who accepted the teachings of Jesus. They actively searched out converts throughout the empire.

In the informal and loosely run Christian leadership of that time, there were many women, challenging the paternalistic concept of a woman's role held by Roman society. Christians advocated martyrdom, as exemplified by Jesus, rather than violence towards others. This was a means of demonstrating their faith in Jesus as savior of the soul. Christians had turned human sacrifice from sadistic to masochistic. Conforming with gnosticism, matter (including one's own body) was seen as transitory along with material possessions and martyrdom was the ultimate human act of selflessness.

The concept of self-sacrifice was well established before Christianity. In barbarian lands during Rome's Spiritual Phase, the practice of human sacrifice was dying out, but was still common in rural society. Pagan cosmology held that the firstborn was conceived by divine insemination.

Therefore, if human sacrifice was made, it was usually the firstborn child given back to the Divine as an act of thanksgiving and a request for the Creator's blessing. The conception of Jesus through the union of Jehovah and his mother, Mary, was a prevalent belief. More often, the sacrificial victim died willingly in a state of honor and faith. Within the empire's urban centers, human sacrifice had become an entertainment or sport through the gladiatorial arena. Animal sacrifice remained very common in traditional Pagan and Jewish practice within and outside the empire's borders. Bloodletting of a bull was part of Persia's Mithra worship.

Beyond Rome's eastern borders lay Persia's empire. Persian traditional state religion, Zoroastrianism, advocated a sort of dual nature in the Divine. Good and evil were a constant, represented by two main deities. Persian religion contained the concept of a messiah as well. The Persian counterpart to Jesus was a deity/man named Mithra. He acted as a bridge for human contact with the Divine. Mithra religious practice called for a baptismal shower of bull's blood poured over the worshiper's body. The bull was suspended above the initiate at the temple alter and then sliced by a priest.

Mithraism, like Christianity, was another new contemporary cult which actively competed for converts. Mithra was very popular among Rome's soldiers and was probably not adverse to patriotic violence in the form of war. Christians only symbolically drank blood and ate the flesh of their messiah-martyr. Drinking wine to symbolize blood and eating a crust of bread to symbolize flesh no doubt appeared to be insincere or effeminate to a Mithra. Christian communistic disregard for the material world may have been perceived as piety by non-Christian contemporaries. Other cults from the East competed for the hearts and minds of society. The third century Manichaeans felt hedonism or partaking of the material world, including lust, was unavoidable. But a person could, through proper consciousness, partake of the material plane without being controlled by it. Thus one could be in the world but not of it.

It was not a difficult concept for Greco-Roman society to entertain Jesus or Mithra as the Divine in human form. The human-as-deity concept was well established in Rome's Pagan church. Greco-Roman traditional religion was alive and still popular. This old time religion of Rome was revived by adding Julius and Augustus Caesar to the Pagan pantheon post-mortem. Following emperors were made living man-deities. A living deity in human form was also a common concept throughout other non Greco-Roman societies within the empire. The Samaritans of the Eastern Mediterranean worshipped a self promoting man named Simon as their deity. In A.D. 140, he and his disciples spread the faith. But by A.D. 240, the sect was absorbed by other cults or disappeared.

Conversely, on the northern frontiers of the empire and in the provinces of Gaul, Britain and Africa, many Pagans accepted Jesus only as a prophet and not a deity at all. In the German tribes' form of Christianity, Jesus was seen as divine only in the context of a wise priest or holy man like some arch Druid. This concept was expressed by the Christian writer Arius of North Africa. Arianism (later termed the "Arian heresy") remained an issue well into the sixth century wars between Ostrogoths and Franks. Meanwhile, bi-theistic Christians centered in Egypt maintained Jesus was a separate deity from Jehovah altogether and worshipped both.

Like Simon the Samaritan's cult, Mithraism and Manichaeanism were absorbed into other cults and affected them. New precepts were introduced or reacted against by Christianity, while others were discarded. St. Augustine was Manichaean before becoming Christian. Augustine's rejection of the Manichaean acceptance of base human nature affected his concept of Christianity when he did convert. He brought in a negative position toward Manichaeanism where none had been stated before. Through his writings, he narrowed the definition of Christianity in general. Those who retained Secular Phase faith in agnosticism, rationalist philosophy and science, or the old pantheism of the Theocratic Phase influenced Christianity and the general synthesizing Spiritual Phase of the *Zeitgeist.*

Not every subject state within the empire accepted world government ruled by a divinely proclaimed Roman monarch or dictator. The year after Nero's demise, Rome ended a four year Jewish revolt (A.D. 70). The Romans destroyed the Jew's temple in Jerusalem. Fifty-nine years later (A.D. 129), the Jews waged a second three-year revolt. Emperor Hadrian dealt with this revolt by banning any Jew from living or visiting Jerusalem (A.D. 132). The Romans also rededicated the temple in Jerusalem to Jupiter, the prime deity of the traditional, Roman pantheon. Temple smashing was an act of religious persecution committed by an otherwise fairly tolerant Roman society. That tolerance was also tested by Christianity.

Christians within the empire experienced persecutions in A.D. 64-98 and a generation later in A.D. 121-180. Again, the Roman society, angered that Christians refused recognition of the state or any deity other than Jehovah or Jesus, persecuted Christians in A.D. 249-251 in an attempt to strengthen traditional values and Roman "old time religion." The appeal of a new age to come and tenacity and martyrdom of Christians won converts to the cult. State sanctioned monotheism was attempted in order to be relevant to the Spiritual Phase. Like Egypt's Akhenaton 1500 years earlier, Emperor Aurelian made the Sun the primary deity for Rome in A.D. 274. He established a new temple and priestly college for worship of the Sun. John Ferguson describes the Sun cult in his book, *Utopias of the Classical World:*

> *The form of the cult was Roman, but it might forge together in Roman patriotism worshipers of Apollo, Mithras and Elagabalus, and we cannot escape the association with universalism, social justice, and the birth of a new age.* (P. 179)

Ferguson continues to explain that Greco-Roman religion had been a function of the family and sprang from social and political relationships which influenced the state. He felt that for the Christians, in theory, religion was independent of any political or social order. Likewise, social or political thinking should be a function of religion. Three more generations passed before Emperor Constantine finally made Christianity a legitimate religion (A.D. 313) along with the others then present. After three centuries, the concept of Judeo-Christian monotheism became accepted or at least officially tolerated by Western civilization.

Constantine's family were worshipers of Aurelian's Sun. Ferguson states that it was from his family deity, the Sun, that the vision of the Cross came to Constantine. Following Emperor Constantine's elevation of Christianity as a state religion, Emperor Constantinius II attempted to support Arius's view that Jesus was a prophet rather than a deity-man. But the popular notion established in previous generations of Rome's Pagan state religion advocated a divine manifestation in the flesh. This belief was too strong among many Christians in Roman urban society to accept Jesus as anything less than an only begotten son of the Divine.

Monotheism and the decline of human sacrifice were the two major contributions of the last Spiritual Phase. This represented a major shift from Greco-Roman cosmology within the Western *Zeitgeist.* Whatever the practice, traditional or new, cults then as today offered cosmologies to explain mysteries that logic or science could not. They provided human fellowship, identity and compassion. Within the cult, an attitude and rationale was provided that gave meaning and solace to life under imperial, urban government and big business.

Had Rome lost its myth of invincibility in A.D. 276 rather than A.D. 410, it is doubtful that Christianity would have survived. At best it would have been incorporated into an existing, established religion with Jesus becoming just another lesser deity, Jewish prophet or forgotten altogether. Society would have been too concerned about immediate physical survival to allow the speculation that early Christianity tolerated. When religious tolerance occasionally evaporated, it was due to society's disdain for a lack of patriotism. This resulted in periodic persecutions of Druids on the frontier or Jews and Christians in the empire's cities. The democracy or anarchy, that Christianity enjoyed at that time, included not joining the Roman military. Such behavior is not conducive to the physical survival of any state. Rome would have turned to the religion of their ancestors in the face of foreign threat and crisis.

But Rome's myth of invincibility did continue for another 100 years. During the first three centuries of the Piscean Age, a sense of physical security allowed for the tolerance necessary for free speculation on new ideas. There was enough time to actually experiment with practicing alternative beliefs that were presented to Roman society. The change over to a new belief system, mythology and theocracy was not immediate. It moved to such a station in the hearts and minds of Western society by degrees. The wealthy and educated elite had little reason to alter traditional beliefs which supported their status in society. But time and human curiosity allowed investigations to wander with the myth of invincibility permitting the needed security.

As interest in all beliefs increased, the wealthy leisure class and academically educated pondered meaning beyond just physical observation. Society's poor and less educated had fewer resources, but speculated just the same. The poor had the added need to rationalize or understand why they were in the lower station in society. They also had less to lose in the material realm. In the fading Secular Phase, science, reason, and rule by humans without divine guidance became less trusted by an impatient and cynical society. The secular republican system served plutocracy driven by greed. Just as in the US today, civil liberty in Rome was gradually exchanged for physical security from street violence. Over generations, Roman republican government became more static and corrupt. Cynicism and apathy increased. Republicanism required an informed society and the information was not forthcoming from the distant imperial capitol. Human reason and republicanism were ironically replaced by "Divine" rule of the Caesars in Roman society's search for traditional values and a higher moral and ethical ground. Western society longed for a cosmology that included an uncorrupted one world government, demise of urban alienation, love and peace, and a universal route to a simpler unity with the Divine.

V: The New Theocracy

Christianity did not rule the state as hoped. Instead, the state sponsored Christian Church became an organ of government. In the service of the state, other religion was condemned. Other Christian churches came under attack as well. The tolerance and spiritual freedom of the Spiritual Phase faded into the religious tyranny of the approaching Theocratic Phase. Roman dictators and bishops attempted to create orthodoxy and a common official religious dogma. Sun worship had failed and Greco-Roman Pagan myths were increasingly antique. At Nicea, Greece (A.D. 325), a meeting of Christian leaders decided that Jesus was divine. They established as doctrine that he was the "son of God." Many leaders protested by not attending. The decision was made after some debate and a majority vote, rather than consensus of all representatives of Christendom. Arianism was denounced as heresy. Partisan politics had entered the scene. The Christian Church pulled away from its cooperative, inclusive, confederate, accepting and compassionate nature. Traditional Roman paternalism infused the church with male leadership that edged out women leaders. The Holy Spirit within the Christian trinity became sexless although originally it carried a female connotation. To centralize control, the church continued to define itself more narrowly as the myth of invincibility disappeared. St. Augustine favored this theocratic approach and has since been rewarded for his written expression by Roman Christendom as a "Father of the Church."

Pagan women leaders were no longer to be tolerated either. A mob of Augustine's fellow North African Christians murdered the beautiful and brilliant Hypatia in Alexandria (A.D. 415). She was the head of a Neoplatonic school. By the fall of Western Rome (A.D. 476), Nestorian, Syrian, Armenian, Egyptian (Coptic) and Ethiopian Christian churches along with all Pagan churches were outlawed by the state as unofficial. However, the Roman Christian theocracy's enforcement was not successful in rural areas and cities outside the crumbling empire. Rome's lasting gift to Western civilization was a new theocracy and dogma based on a narrow, urban, paternal interpretation of Christianity.

Dealing with urbanism during the myth of invincibility was the challenge of the Spiritual Phase in Rome. The changes from an agrarian to an urban society that affected all classes, Roman and non-Roman, ran in tandem with Christianity's rise. There is little in the New Testament that relates to a relationship of humans to the earth other than references to the Old Testament of the Jews. The cross incorporated by Christians as a symbol predates Christianity. Spaniards invading America found the Pagan Mayas already using the cross symbol. A Celtic cross with a circle enclosing the nexus was well known among pre-Christian Europeans. Used in Egyptian hieroglyphics, a similar but completely enclosed cross represents the word "city." Perhaps the nexus of crossroads as the origin of cities was the inspiration for the symbol. Cities, not the countryside, of the empire were the centers for Christians. Monasteries established only islands of Christianity in the rural landscape. But not only roads meet in cities. Ideas and beliefs also meet, synthesize and transform.

The symbolic Jesus on the cross was used to focus on his compassion and sacrifice for humanity's redemption. But the cross also symbolized where faith and reason come together. In this epiphany, where timeless intersects with time, a trivial object becomes all and profound for an instant. This second of illumination, termed "moment" by Romantics or "satori" by Buddhists, leads to complete understanding and inspiration.

The word "Pagan" in Latin means villager or people outside the city. A large number of Pagans were present in cities through the fifth century as well. So, it appears "Pagan" was a symbolic word to describe anyone outside the Christian "City of God." Much of Europe's countryside remained Pagan well into A.D. 1000. Slavic and Norse Pagans held off Christian conquest into A.D. 1200. For rural people, recognition of Nature, growing and harvest seasons, fertility, thanksgiving and length of the day were as important as getting along with fellow humans. Over time, accommodations were made by Christians to Pagan celebrations for natural phenomena (Christmas, Easter, days of the week named after Pagan deities, etc.). But city folk didn't directly live off the land or sea. They were more concerned with the Divine's relationship to society and the individual than watching the weather.

Outside the disintegrating empire and its theocratic control, St. Patrick and St. Brigid developed a naturalistic, non-urban Christianity in Ireland. There were no cities in barbarian Ireland. Christianity took hold and survived while being isolated as Western Rome was overrun by Pagan German tribes. Christians from all parts of the empire escaped to the Irish safe haven. These urban Italians, Greeks, Spaniards, Syrians, Egyptians and Gauls joined with residents like St. Patrick, St. Brigid and Columcille to build flourishing monastic cities. These were the first urban centers of Ireland. Pagan Druidism and reverence for Nature was blended into Christianity there. Women maintained a high station relative to the Roman Christians. The monastery city of Kildare was co-ed.

It was not from urban Rome, but from rural Ireland's missionaries that the rural people of Europe were Christianized. Up to that time (A.D. 600-800), Christianity was confined to surviving Roman cities. Gradually the Irish naturalistic approach was co-opted and then eliminated by the Pope's administration. With the passing of the Irish missionary movement in rural areas, urban Christian theocracy, supported by local warlords and clerics, secured the countryside for Roman theocracy. By A.D. 1200, the Roman theocracy was sponsoring or sanctioning forced conversions to Christianity in Scandinavian and East Baltic regions as well as witch burnings all over Europe. St. Francis of Assisi's Franciscan order did emphasize recognition of the divinity in flora and fauna. The Franciscans no doubt attracted Pagans wishing not to be accused of witchcraft by the Roman theocracy. The Franciscans were finally accepted by the Pope (A.D. 1209) after great opposition within the Roman church theocracy. Perhaps some people still retained the Irish approach to Christianity.

> *He is the Sun of Righteousness, that is the Sun of Justice.*
> *No one knows when Jesus was born, but Christmas was*
> *transferred to the winter solstice, the Sun's birthday.*
> *Constantine's god was always the god of power, never Love.*
>
> John Ferguson, *Utopias of the Classical World,* p. 180

Chapter Six

THE SPIRITUAL PHASE TODAY

1: The End of Dogma

Breaking from past dogma to accommodate emotional needs, as well as intellectual cynicism, was the challenge for ancient Rome's urban society in the Spiritual Phase. In Greco-Roman society, Christians provided a new path after the break from their Secular Phase. We have yet to see what group and cosmology will point the way as the US and Europe travel into yet another Spiritual Phase.

At the end of the nineteenth century, vestiges of the Theocratic Phase remained, exemplified by the monarchies of powerful Western nations like England and Germany. But Secular Phase republicanism was also established to varying degrees. The spectrum ranged from secular republican France and the US to the autocratic Russian Orthodox theocracy of the Russian Empire. Young and wealthy urbane Russians reacted to the static theocracy still ruling Czarist Russia. These "Nihilists" were mostly found among university students and in academic circles. They were literate and able to study and visit secular nations like France or the US. Nihilists knew there was an alternative to theocracy. They also noted the failures of secular humanism or faith in science and technology. Unable to effectively change their society, they stepped outside society to experiment with different values, realities and lifestyles. Many denounced the existence of the Divine in the traditional Russian Orthodox Christian sense. Yet English, US or French constitutional secularism and faith in pure science or reason was also questioned. Nihilism went beyond the romanticism of the eighteenth and early nineteenth century which found spiritual solace in the ideal of a biblical "return to Eden" or the "Golden Age" of Greco-Roman mythology. Romantics felt human effort could bring humanity to a self-actualized reunion with the Divine.

Jacobins, also rejected by nihilists, attempted to establish science as a religion. The beliefs of Jacobins and Romantics were in keeping with the Secular Phase hope for a new millennium realized in the French Revolution. Nihilists were influenced by the existential idea that life is a series of personal decisions as to what is right or wrong. They felt these decisions create responsibility for one's actions. Nihilists attempted to transcend the dogma originating in both the Theocratic and Spiritual Phases. This is also the basic goal of the Spiritual Phase.

But the nihilists were not necessarily existentialists either. Their attempts to synthesize science and religion expressed itself in different ways. A popular figure among young Russian aristocrats was Madam Blavatsky. This spiritualist married a Russian aristocrat and eventually founded the Theosophical Society. As the title implies, this group attempted to blend the existing theologies, occult, science and philosophy into one field of study out of which they hoped a new formula for world order might develop. Rather than such spiritual investigation, other nihilists advocated violence to bring down established authority in order to allow a new system to emerge from the ashes.

Following an assassination attempt on Czar Alexander II by a student in 1867, Russian education was greatly censored to support church and state. This incident and following reactionary measures by the government against personal intellectual freedom created more discontent toward the Russian state. Terrorism through attempted and often successful assassinations of public officials and the Czar was the continued reaction of some nihilist groups such as the "Will of the People." Their goal was to bring down established Western systems, whether constitutional republics or remaining theocracy. They wished to create a vacuum to be filled by a future utopia responsive to the needs of peasants and workers. Alexander II was finally assassinated by a nihilist's bomb in 1881. Though greatly suppressed as a result, the nihilists continued to be active through the turn of the twentieth century. However, the majority were neither violent nor consumed with spiritualism. Most preferred publishing revolutionary statements and working secretly among peasant groups. The counter culture nihilists of Russia were ultimately absorbed, exiled or eliminated by the Russian Revolution (1920s) and the dictatorship of Joseph Stalin (1930s).

But nihilism and existentialism survived in the rest of Europe. After World War I, the counter culture baton was passed on to the "Bohemians" of the cafes of Paris and Berlin. Western modern art exemplified the expressions of the counter culture's *Zeitgeist.* Toward the end of the nineteenth and into the early twentieth century, visual art moved from impressionist through dada and cubism to surrealism and abstract. In popular music, classical moved to light classical, operetta, musicals and jazz. Looking at society and the world in a new way was the inspiration. Traditional models lost relevance. New approaches and paradigms for a new age were sought.

Europe's exiles including bohemians immigrated to the US. In return, the US counter culture exported jazz originating in its ex-slave class. The counter culture "Swing Kids" of Germany were listening to outlawed swing music and jazz well into the Nazi period of the 1930s. "Things American" gained popularity as Hollywood came into its gilded period. Three movies of 1939 exemplify the US sense of optimism carried through to the "happy ending." John Steinbeck's novel, *The Grapes of Wrath*, was made into a moving picture. The movie, *Wizard of Oz*, offered escapism from the economic hard times. *Gone With the Wind*, provided the historical perspective of post Civil War hardship overcome by perseverance. Every movie house around the world who showed these movies brought home the plight of rural people dealing with adversity. The 1930s was the decade when the majority of the US population became urban dwellers. Through the '20s and '30s, counter culture concern for the underclass and alienated urban dweller was expressed politically by labor unions, nationalism, women's suffrage and socialist movements. The plutocracy responded to the Great Depression with the New Deal programs in the US or socialist dictatorships in Europe. World War II followed.

"Beatniks" came on the scene in the US with the post W.W.II economic prosperity. Beatniks did not share in society's expanding materialism and optimism in the fifties. Like the nihilists and bohemians, this counter culture group was cynical. They identified those in society being excluded from the American dream due to economics, education, race or politics. Folk music joined abstract art, jazz and poetry as a means of expressing solidarity.

In the prosperous early 1960s, cynicism began to dissolve among the youth within the counter culture. A positive attempt to include society's alienated was made. President Kennedy supplied the credo for the early sixties when he implored citizens to *"Ask not what your country can do for you, but what you can do for your country."* The Peace Corps, established by Kennedy, sent idealistic young missionaries of the American way to the Third World at a grass roots level. Continuing civil rights legislation and enforcement gave hope to minority races and the poor. President Johnson's Great Society continued to feed the *Zeitgeist* of optimism in the mid-'60s. This attitude of positive change fostered a feeling that anything was possible. There was hope that the dispossessed could be included, and change in society's attitudes toward civil liberty, economic-political democracy and racial equality was possible. This spirit was embodied in the "Hippies" of the mid to late 1960s and early 1970s. The hippie movement also erupted in West Europe. Post war prosperity returned there only a decade after it did in the US. The number of those under thirty participating in counter culture activity expanded due to the post war "baby boom."

In the US at that time, poetry of the romantics or the beatniks was eclipsed. Rock and roll and blues replaced folk and big band music as an effective medium, bringing Western society's classes and races together. Pop music recordings also became the common art form to transfer ideas across the Atlantic. Europeans danced to lyrics informing them about surfing and Motown; New Orleans, Memphis, Chicago, New York or San Francisco. In the US, place names like Soho, sunny South Kensington, Knights Bridge, Strawberry Fields or Liverpool rang exotic. Electrically amplified music has continued to be a global communicator though incredibly eclectic in the '90s. Today musical forms include: acid, rap, folk rock, new wave, hip hop, grunge, new age, Christian rock, world beat, reggae, punk. But the youthful high expectations, impatience and idealism were dashed by the continued Secular Phase system. The plutocracy's vested interests thwarted economic democracy through big business and big government. Cold war political restraints, the Viet Nam War and President Nixon's Watergate scandal created profound distrust of secular government. With economic uncertainty and greater spread between the haves and have-nots in the late '70s and '80s, cynicism returned to the counter culture. The baton was passed to "Generation X" in the '90s.

All titles applied to the counter culture (romantic, Jacobin, nihilist, bohemian, beatnik, hippie, generation X), like Christian, Satanist, Mithra or Manichaean, were initially ascribed by others than group members. If the first Christians called themselves anything, it might have been Ecclesiasticals. Hippies used the term "freaks" to describe themselves. At that time, a popular Crosby, Stills, Nash and Young song, on their *Deja Vu* album, referred to long hair as a "freak flag." This exemplified an attempt to transcend nationalistic, secular or religious causes represented by a flag or other symbols.

All these groups (modern and ancient) were urban in origin. Even though Jesus had rural roots, both his trade as a carpenter and proximity to large Hellenistic urban centers kept him abreast of the world culture at that time. Gospel writers Paul, Mark and John preached in cities, not on hilltops. Like early Christian monks, many hippies fled from cities, rejecting urbanity altogether. They investigated less chaotic and less alienating rural lifestyles including organic vegetable gardens and self constructed rustic homes. Jug Band music became a popular expression of this simpler ethic. Some of the popular bands playing this music were Jim Kweskin's Jug Band, Nitty Gritty Dirt Band or early Grateful Dead. The ideal for many was the relatively less technical life of their agrarian era grandparents rather than their suburban parents. A reattachment to the rhythms of Nature was a magnet. In this sense hippies were romantics.

The mostly middle class members of the hippie movement were in actuality born and raised as urban creatures. The ideal of personal self sufficiency, rugged individualism or communizing and the poverty that resulted from such lifestyles wore thin on many. By the mid 1970s, most returned to the cities to join those of the counter culture who had never left. The counter culture found solidarity in their larger numbers in the urban setting or in isolated rural enclaves. Community developed through communes or cooperatives.

Counter culture groups operate within secular society as critics and detractors (anti-thesis) of the status quo (thesis). What has been very different from all the modern counter culture groups mentioned above and the anti-establishment groups of the last Spiritual Phase, is that Christians had Jesus in common, Mithras had Mithra and Manichaeans had Manias. There is yet to be any one Secular Phase personality, from Karl Marx, Freud and Nietzsche to Timothy Leary or Billy Graham, who could come near the position of a messiah. Christians had the Passion Play and sacraments in common. Other than smoking usually illegal hashish or marijuana, there are no common sacraments or rituals today in the counter culture. However, that there is not any single leader may be the central contribution of the coming Spiritual Phase, just as abolition of slavery is the contribution of the last Secular Phase. Musicals generated by the '60s and produced in the '70s, such as *Godspell*, *Jesus Christ Superstar*, *Tommy*, and *The Wall*, emphasized the limits of following any single leader.

Since the 1960s, many counter culture individuals have re-investigated traditional politics and Christianity. They have worked within the established economic-political system and scientific establishment that many had initially rejected. The spiritual end result of the hippie movement was the revitalized born-again Christian movement, the present deep ecology environmental movement, and what has been dubbed the "new age" religious movement. These three movements share a basic end time belief; their *Zeitgeists* incorporate the idea that Western society's present system of things will end. They reject the constructs of both the Theocratic and Secular Phases. But the three movements face the end time inevitability differently by acting and preparing accordingly.

II: Christians

From the first generation of Christians to the present one, there has been a belief that theirs was the end time. Christian end time is expressed in various forms. There is an academic distinction between millennialism and millenarianism. Millennialism ascribes generally to biblical end time predictions, in symbolic or literal terms. Millennialists are found within traditional orthodox Christianity and millennialism is a major component of Calvinist churches including Methodist, Baptist and Presbyterian. Millenarianism is a radical and literal interpretation of biblical end time prophecy. Millenarians are more prone to commit to exact date for end time, while millennialists do not. However, the distinction between the terms is often not very clear. Many millenarians may hold an affiliation with a less radical millennialist church body. A millennialist congregation of Baptists, Methodists or Quakers might include radical members or splinter congregations who are millenarians. As a result, not all Methodists and Quakers are millenarians. A literal rather than symbolic biblical interpretation is also difficult to determine at times. The term millennialism will be used in this book unless in a direct quote.

The early Christian prophet Montanus and prophetesses, Priscilla and Maximilla predicted the end time arriving in their lifetime. This Montanus movement faded when Maximilla died in A.D. 179 without experiencing the "Second Coming." Many of Europe's wealthy class of A.D. 1000 gave their material wealth to the church and sat in coffins on New Years Eve. They expected the return of Christ and the beginning of a war between the forces of Christ and Satan, led by an antichrist. They believed Christ would be victorious, raising the good people from the grave to join living good people who were to be saved. All non-Christian and bad people were to be cast into Hell. Those saved would be returned to Earth and begin a "Heaven on Earth" utopia lasting 1000 years.

Christopher Columbus believed he was spreading Christianity so the world could get the apocalyptic message before the end time he felt was due to happen in 1650. This date curiously coincides with the end of the bloody Reformation wars. In the seventeenth century, Oliver Cromwell's English Calvinist army felt they were doing Christ's work by killing Roman Catholics who were loyal to the Roman Pope in preparation for the Second Coming. Calvinists felt the Pope personified the antichrist. Though Cromwell's reign of terror failed, end time belief continued into the Secular Phase.

In England, Ann Lee, the founding prophetess of the Believers in Christ's Second Coming (Shakers), was seen as a female Christ or second Eve bringing a new millennium in 1792. Most Shaker converts were women who found feminist liberation from childbirth and male domination in Shaker doctrine. Shaker dictates included sexual separation, sexual equality and celibacy. Richard Brothers, a self proclaimed prophet and Prince of the Hebrews, placed end time at November 19, 1795. Following him, believers in the English prophetess Joanna Southcott thought she would give birth at age 64 to Shiloh, the new messiah in 1814. Southcottian feminism charged women with the responsibility of redressing Eve's original sin and initiating the millennium. Calvinists (Puritans), Shakers and members of the Society of Friends (Quakers) carried the neo-Montanus, millennialist tradition to America. Thus modern Christian end time predictions or millennialism began in Europe (England), spread to America and via missionaries, throughout the world.

In 1844 William Miller, one time Baptist preacher, had one million people in the US believing Jesus would return on October 22 of that year. Joseph Smith delivered his prophesy, including end time prediction, giving rise to the Mormon Church of the Latter Day Saints. For many millennialists, the US Civil War was the fulfillment of end time prophesy. Though the end did not come, end time myth continued as a central millennialist theme in fundamentalist Christianity. As recently as 1994 in the US, a radio and TV call-in host, Harold Camping, asked his followers to get ready for "The Coming" in late September or early October of that year.

Millennialism is a major component of fundamentalist and born-again Christianity. Each generation of millennialists has seen their time conforming to end time prophesy found in the Bible's books *Daniel*, *Revelations* or even *Psalms*. Modern fundamentalist Christian history in the US came out of, and in reaction to, the Secular Phase. The Age of Reason and American and French Revolutions brought social change. For many people this was *"uncomfortable, bewildering, traumatic,"* according to historian J.F.C. Harrison. In his book, *The Second Coming: Popular Millenarianism 1780-1850,* he states:

> *Familiar landmarks disappeared, assumptions about stability and normalcy were no longer unquestioned, the sources of authority to which men looked for guidance were not convincing as they had once been. A new ideology* [millenarianism] *to take account of the disruption or weakening of the old social order and to sanction new aspirations was needed.* (P. 219)

He also states that millenarians of the early nineteenth century were either unaware of the rational and scientific intellectual trends of the day, or *"...were, like [William] Blake, repelled by them"* (p. 217).

But William Blake (1757-1827), like the English writer Gerrard Winstanley (c. 1609 to c. 1660), broke from fellow Puritans by individualizing apocalyptic prophesy. Winstanley's Inner Light Protestants even developed a Christian communist community in 1649-50 called the Diggers. The Inner Light faction took all biblical prophesy metaphorically and applied to a single person's spiritual development as romantics did 150 years later. Innocence of the infant was likened to Adam. Heaven and hell existed within each person, not in the sky or under the ground. The fall, confession, redemption and salvation were stations contained within each individual's life, not all humanity in unison. Still, attempts to universally reconcile literal biblical prophetic interpretation and science continued through the Secular Phase.

In the 1840s, a contemporary of Miller and Smith, John Darby of Great Britain, led a faction called the Plymouth Brethren (Darbyites). Darby felt the "Rapture" when Christ returns just before the end of time, marked the beginning of the end time. Darby devoted much energy to making literal and logical sense out of the books of *Daniel* and *Revelations.* He tried to validate the established religion of his day for the contemporary, Secular Phase audience. The Secular Phase demanded a rational explanation even of mysteries and prophecy. To counter scientific skepticism presenting religious stories as past mythology or at best parables, Darby presented various biblical quotes as facts in support of an end time thesis. Society was changing to an urban one. Philosophical and sophisticated spiritual alternatives abounded. Darby employed the scientific method used by the scientific historians and social scientists of his day. He used reason to counter rational statements discrediting the Bible. Darby's followers had found a means within the secular approach to lend credibility to fundamentalist Christianity.

Later in the US, Charles Hodge of Princeton University and others also applied the scientific method. They picked apart the Bible's verses and concluded that the Bible was without any error in any way. Historian and psychologist, Charles B. Strozier explained in his book, *Apocalypse: On The Psychology of Fundamentalism in America*, how the notion of inerrancy took shape in the 1870s:

> *Enough carefully selected facts on a given problem yielded an answer that amounted to truth. In the spiritual realm, the search for Truth was subject to the same method. Close biblical analysis*

> *of a text thought to be without error proved the scientific validity of God's revelation to humans. Blind faith was unnecessary. One only needed to accept the validity of the scientific method.... These Calvinist scholars pored over the Bible and its meanings in an attempt to formulate a theology relevant for the new world of post war* [US Civil War] *uncertainty.* (P. 185)

In Hodge's three volume work, *Systematic Theology*, published 1872-73, he argued that the Divine dictated every word to the writers of the Scriptures. The major self-justifying statement of proof (or fact) lay in *Jeremiah* 1:9, *"Then the Lord put forth his hand, and touched my mouth. And the Lord said unto me, Behold, I have put my words in thy mouth."* Eric W. Gritsch, Lutheran author and professor of church history described the Princeton theology in his book, *Born Againism.* He said, *"They* [fundamentalists] *are provided with a 'theologic' which establishes the desired harmony between faith and reason"* (p. 35).

The US Civil War ended the ruralism and socioeconomics of landed aristocracy. The result was sanctified urbanity, science and industry. Two thousand years earlier, Secular Phase urban Romans and their Pagan cults, incorporated Greek rationalism, foreign deities and the traditional man-as-deity concept. This was a response to their society's disinterest in or disenchantment with traditional pantheistic beliefs of rural origin. That milieu produced early Christianity. Christianity increased democratically as dictatorship continued, middle class declined and society wished for an end to the system they lived under. Harrison, in *The Second Coming*, states:

> *Where a class or group suffers a lowering of its standard of living in terms of wealth and status, where the poor get poorer, or where oppression of various kinds increases, social discontent may be channeled into millenarianism.* (P. 221)

For many, in the changing nineteenth century society (A.D.), there was a need to understand the Bible in concrete, black and white terms that accommodated a rapidly industrializing, confusing, urban, secular society. The notion of the verifiable inerrancy of the Bible became more important than sixteenth century Lutheran blind faith developed in the Theocratic Phase. By the turn of the twentieth century, fundamentalism in the US came into its own as a great reactionary answer to Marxism (which had its own secular, romantic utopian millennialism). Paradoxically, the fundamentalists bought into the rationalists' systems and theories they were reacting against. These included Darwinism, Marxism, psychology, scientific criticisms and any other new ideas or non-Christian religions emerging out of the Secular Phase. Like scientific historians who validate by using facts to state a case, fundamentalists came to use biblical quotes as facts rather than parables or metaphors.

Fundamentalist Christianity thus operates within the belief system and mentality of the Secular Phase just as Satanists operate within Christian parameters. Satanists reject Christianity, yet they still operate within a belief system and mythology dictated by Christianity. Definition of what is good or bad, divine consequences, the nature of Jehovah, Jesus and Satan are shared by both Christian and Satanist. Similarly, fundamentalists attempt to adapt traditional Protestant Christianity to new realities and the changing *Zeitgeist*. Only seeing the Divine as a transcending prime mover or some master mechanic (deism) gives little personal connection or spiritual emotion. At the same time, viewing the Divine as a grandfatherly, gray bearded Jehovah sitting in the clouds seems childish and hardly an answer to the agnosticism of the Secular Phase. Many Romans no doubt came to view statues of Zeus skeptically 2000 years earlier.

Today in the US, one third of the population are not members of any organized church while 90 percent of the total population state a belief in the Divine. The spiritual needs of this non-attending third of society, who nonetheless believe in the Divine, are not met by today's churches. Much of this is due to anti-clericalism. Fundamentalism is currently popular because it attempts to minimize clericalism. But neo-Paganism is also gaining popularity because the shamanistic lay members and clergy democratically mix and share authority. Paganism contains cosmology which transcends both Christianity-Satanism (Theocratic Phase) and science (Secular Phase).

The vocal and well organized fundamentalist churches in the US today continue to demand that society follow fundamentalist morals and fundamentalist biblical interpretation. Even other Christian churches such as Unitarian, Self-Realization Fellowship, Latter Day Saints, Rastafarian, Lutheran, Coptic, Greek and Russian Orthodox, Santagrian, Episcopalian or Roman Catholic are rejected by fundamentalists. For fundamentalists the first four are examples of modernism, deism, Asian mysticism or false prophet following. The latter seven represent antiquated churches founded during the Theocratic Phase. They are seen as too steeped in doctrine, tradition and clericalism to allow true communion with the Divine or Holy Spirit. The liberation theology practiced by Roman Catholic priests in Latin America is deemed too secular or liberal. It also competes with fundamentalist missionary activities. Presbyterian and Methodist churches are acceptable as they play into the origins of recent fundamentalist history. But they too are viewed as mainstream, clerical and without the radical edge.

One tenet of that radical edge is that a singular, dramatic, cathartic change must occur in each Christian's life to be truly saved when the end time also suddenly and violently arrives. The statement by Jesus to Nicodemus: *"...unless one is born anew, he cannot see the kingdom of God" John* 3:3 is central. Of course fundamentalists define the process of being "born again." Some acceptable fundamentalist churches include Assembly of God, Church of the Nazarene, Calvary, Pentecostal, Baptist and evangelical organizations such as the Billy Graham Evangelistic Association or one centered in Dr. Schuler's skyscraper, the Crystal Cathedral.

Fundamentalists look to the mystical and prophetic *Book of Revelations,* where it was stated that there will be a battle at the end time. This battle will involve the forces seen by the Western *Zeitgeist* as good against bad, on the Plains of Armageddon, in today's Israel. The Jordan River will fill with blood, but the forces of good will prevail. Jesus will return and all good Christians, whether in the grave or not, shall be saved and placed into a heaven on earth. Belief in the above thesis, and predicting its occurrence is basic to fundamentalism. In *Gods of Eden,* William Bramley studies the causes of war:

> *Revelation can be used to predict an imminent "End of the World" at almost any historical epoch. The prophecy is constructed so that the symbols can be interpreted to represent whatever historical events happen to be occurring at the time one is living. This is precisely what has been done with Revelation ever since it appeared, and it is still being done today.* (P. 136)

In World War I, there was a Battle of Armageddon at the location placed by the *Book of Revelations* (Battle of Megiddo, September 19-23,1918). The German Empire supplied and advised their allies, the

Turks' "Kingdoms of the North" *(Ezekiel* 38, *Daniel* 11:40), in Turkey's bid to hold its empire. The other "Kingdom of the North," Britain, pulled in *"Armies of the East" (Revelation 16:12)* from colonial India and Australia (plus Jewish volunteers) to defeat the Turks. This battle is noted in military history for employing the first effective use of air power for strategic strikes rather than only reconnaissance, dog fights or random bombing. Twenty years later, Hitler's *Blitzkrieg* perfected this strategy in W.W.II. German V-2 rockets and Allied carpet bombing matched biblical proportion, *"...and fire came down from God out of heaven." (Revelation* 20:10.)

The modern weapons employed in the Battle of Megiddo would seem beyond science fiction and be difficult to describe to the contemporaries and author of *Revelations* in A.D. 95 when that book was written. While fundamentalist Christians interpret the Bible literally, few even know of this relatively recent battle. Certainly the Nazi generated tribulation that fell upon the Jews fifteen years later could find its way into Biblical interpretation. The person of Adolph Hitler as antichrist, who proclaims peace, prosperity and new world order to his followers but brings destruction in the end, could easily fit a fundamentalist biblical interpretation. The general conflagration of WW I is considered the beginning of end time by one church.

Jehovah's Witnesses (JWs),founded by Charles T. Russell in 1884, believe the prophesied end-time battle began with W.W.I and is still raging. It is true that the Earth has not seen a time of peace since World War I, yet there have been conflicts, wars and rumors of wars somewhere on the planet at any given time before. Nonetheless, JWs feel the fighting will stop and 144,000 chosen people will be taken up by Christ. Few fundamentalist groups other than JWs believe Christ has returned quite yet. Thus most fundamentalist churches see the JWs as an illegitimate cult. JWs are also ostracized for their fundamentalist doctrine which places little emphasis on Jesus. They do not believe in the Trinity and Holy Ghost. This runs counter to other fundamentalist churches such as the charismatic Pentecostal Church. Pentecostal members experience the Holy Spirit's instructions to speak in tongues as occurred in the original Pentecost. JWs reject Christmas and other religious holidays due to their Pagan origins. Being anti-nationalists like the first Christians, JWs refuse to enroll in the military or pledge allegiance to any nation's flag. This also sets JWs apart from other fundamentalists who are often very nationalistic.

However, fundamentalists did acknowledge W.W.I to some extent. Celebrating the end of World War I, a conference was held in Philadelphia, May 1918. The Darbyite focus was on the British conquest of Jerusalem and the imminent return of Christ following the tribulations of the war. The following year in Philadelphia, a World's Conference on Christian Fundamentalism was sponsored by the periodical, *The Fundamentalist.* Five committees were created to defend fundamentalism from modernist errors and mainline denominations. These committees were to accredit Bible schools, foster fundamentalist periodicals and thought in educational institutions, organize Bible conferences and expand overseas missionary activities.

In the 1920s and '30s, schisms between fundamentalists within the Presbyterian, Methodist and Baptist traditions developed. A magazine called the *Crusader's Champion* advocated fundamentalist involvement and influence in government and public education. The magazine was the mouthpiece of the Bible Crusaders of America founded in 1925. The Crusaders attempted to influence anti-evolution laws in education through public demonstrations. They supported William J. Bryan's representation of the State of Tennessee's right to enforce an anti-evolution law upon biology teacher John L. Scopes. Mr. Scopes had been fined one hundred dollars for teaching Darwin's theory of evolution at Dayton Central High School. In July 1925, the American Civil Liberties Union employed Clarence Darrow to represent Scopes and contest the constitutionality of the law. As the trial unfolded, the cool logic of Darrow exposed the limits of biblical inerrancy reasoning and the fundamentalist emotionalism expressed by Bryan. The resultant embarrassment discredited those in society who supported fundamentalism. The *Crusade's Champion* ended publication in 1926. Fundamentalism left the secular arena but continued. In 1927, Aimee Semple McPherson started The International Church of the Foursquare Gospel at Los Angeles, California. She was the first to broadcast millennialism on radio through the 1930s. In 1941 the American Council of Christian Churches was founded to provide a united front for the fundamentalist cause.

The following year the slightly less radical National Association of Evangelicals was formed with the help of young Billy Graham. This later group allowed for focus on conscience and laws of Nature as well as Bible inerrancy. Returning to populist, traditional tent-meeting revivals, Billy Graham launched a mass media campaign in 1949 that was more ecumenical. In that same year, the World Pentecostal Fellowship was organized in Paris to counter the more ecumenical and non-fundamentalist World Council of Churches which had organized the previous year. In his book *Born Againism*, Gritsch concludes:

> *The born-again movement is part of a widespread dissent from the mainstream of American Protestantism which had become linked to popular ideals and patterns of American life: patriotism, manifest destiny, Anglo-Saxon self-confidence, the common folk's social and economic aspirations, and whatever the American dream and the Constitution promised.* (P. 103)

By the 1950s, Pentecostals softened and backed off from ostracizing other fundamentalist churches completely. Some Pentecostal groups no longer required speaking in tongues as a tenet. In 1956, the Billy Graham Evangelistic Association was the result of the shift toward inclusion. A more tolerant fundamentalism again attempted dialogue with the secular world and mainline churches. The famous Pentecostal minister, Oral Roberts, became a Methodist in 1965.

The appeal of the Christian fundamentalist movement today relies on its encouragement of the fear that the end time is close but not quite here. Currently most fundamentalist Christians believe Jesus will call his flock in the next generation, if not sooner. This notion creates an urgency or angst, that pressures individuals or encourages individuals to be saved and become church members as soon as possible. Few fundamentalists will acknowledge, like JWs, that the world is already experiencing tribulation or that it may last for endless centuries. In the US there are automobile bumper stickers that proclaim "Jesus is coming." This aptly describes the Christian fundamentalist mentality.

Fundamentalist Christian tradition holds biblical credence to a two thousand year period for renewal and change. Interpretation based on "days" mentioned in the Bible is stretched to equal years in human experience. The book *Daniel* states "*...Unto two thousand and three hundred days; then shall the sanctuary be cleansed.*" 8:14 As long as these Christians keep waiting and looking for signs of Christ's return, all that is good is yet to come. The present is spent preparing for the end time, saving souls and exposing "bad" people, unbelievers and the antichrist. But the writer or writers of *Revelation* may have been writing symbolically about current events 2000 years ago, knowing that history repeats itself. The fact that the US would replace Rome is not important because the characters and dynamics remain constant. Thus the author had a "revelation" that Rome would inevitably fall and Western civilization would again create an ultimate super power like Rome. Fantastic physical descriptions aside, the author saw the world ruled by an evil "Beast" identified by the number "666." *Revelation* states, *"Let the one that has intelligence calculate the number of the wild beast, for it is a man's number; and its number is six hundred and sixty-six."* (13:18.) The number six in Jewish Talmudic numerology represents humans. Seen in that context, *Revelation's* 666 and the Beast clearly represent humans and human inability to run human affairs. Likewise, 66.6 is the product of dividing the number 30 into 2000. Some may thus see 30 as representing the age at which Jesus went into the wilderness, overcame temptation by Satan and began preaching. Perhaps the inspiration is simply the division of 666 generations (thirty year periods) into a 2000 year long age that must pass before a new age begins (Age of Aquarius) and Jesus returns to do battle with the Beast. Also, .666 is another way of stating the fraction two thirds. This fraction may represent the feared majority of society that will persecute the compassionate one third minority who don't attend state dictated church, don't follow traditional dogma and will be able to recognize the true messiah. *"... the third part of men killed" Revelation* 9:18 *"And the rest* [two thirds] *of the men which were not killed by these plagues yet repented not..." Revelation* 9:20 Interpretations go on and on. Yet even with biblical symbolism, complexity and vagueness, fundamentalists have created a literal interpretation of the end time, developed a doomsday mythology and insist that it is the truth. Thus, fundamentalists, caught in their Secular Phase systemology, believe the Beast will actually appear as physically described in the Bible, horns and all.

Fear of future events, consequences and outsiders is very effective in maintaining group cooperation or a theocracy. But this *Zeitgeist* is often closed to dealing with present, complex socioeconomic realities or evolving rationally into the future. This *Zeitgeist* of fundamentalist paranoia precludes recognizing the coming of a messiah or heaven on earth. A second coming would bring an end to the fundamentalist power base that is dependent on maintaining fear of the consequences of Jesus' impending return.

If all society believed that the Messiah *has* returned (at least in spirit), individuals could live out that reality, like Winstanley or Blake, rather than exist in a state of anticipation like Miller or Camping. No longer waiting for the future, perhaps fear would be dispelled and heaven on earth would be realized. Perhaps this will be in the new gospel given by the end-time angel described in the *Revelation*, *"... having the everlasting gospel to preach unto them that dwell on the earth."* 14:6 The utopia of libertarian compassion would finally prevail here and now. However, utopian social experiments usually do not last much beyond the generation of their founders, (monasteries, kibbutzim and Mennonites aside). Societal criticism is greater toward the compassionate in their midst than toward the fearful.

Due to its remaining radical millennialism and Secular Phase approach toward rational and emotional needs, fundamentalist Christianity will be the shock troops in defense of "old time religion." According to Gritsch:

> *The born-again movement therefore represents the classic restitutional ideal: to bring to life again the ancient, golden age of Christianity when sinful people were renewed by walking and talking with Jesus, who came to make the world ready for the kingdom of God....* (P. 104)

By A.D. 3000, Christianity's position will be consigned to past mythology as the Greco-Roman myths are seen today. Given the persecution of Christians at the time when *Revelation* was written, and the examples of then recent and contemporary Roman emperors Tiberius, Caligula and Nero, the author of *Revelation* could have determined that when the end time did come again, it would play out similarly to their then recent tribulations. Others who have read *Revelation* or *Daniel* prefer a more general analogical view. Some discount these books altogether as so much hallucinatory gibberish. Nonetheless, it is possible to read biblical descriptions as myth, as parables for ethics, or for historical and spiritual perspective. Much of what is today called "New Age" religion reads the Bible in this way, blending biblical passages with other holy works and histories.

III: New Age

The Piscean Age was significant to early Christians. Astrologers at the time of Jesus recognized that the Piscean Age was dawning. The symbol for Pisces is a fish. The fish symbolism used by Christians fit well, for Jesus and Christians were seen as *"fishers of men" Matthew* 4:19 symbolically saving souls through the coming age. During the periods of persecution, a Christian drawing an arc in the sand was an invitation for a fellow Christian to communicate in secret. The other Christian would add an intersecting arc, creating a fish-shaped symbol. The two Christians then felt safe in their mutual cultic trust. At present we are leaving the Age of Pisces begun at the time of Christ and Augustus, 2000 years ago (see fig. 3).

The genesis of the label "New Age" stems from new agers placing significance on Earth now entering the Age of Aquarius. The New Age movement incorporates Christian and non Judeo-Christian end time beliefs found in many other established religions including Native American faiths, Taoism, Buddhism and Hinduism. New Age (or "New Thought") perspectives range from deism to predestination. Impatient Christian fundamentalists and new agers alike feel that time is again at hand. Both groups feel the end of the present Piscean system of things will soon be upon us all. But new agers feel the Age of Aquarius will be a time of democratic evolution leading to harmony, understanding and heaven on earth. This is not unlike eighteenth century romantics who hoped a like change would come with the American and French Revolutions. Christian fundamentalists, by contrast, see a great climactic battle followed by a 1000 year theocracy ruled by Jesus. Whether Jesus' arrival will come at the beginning or end of that millennium remains a point of interpretation and controversy.

As with the modern Christian fundamentalists, new agers in the West can be traced back to reaction to a changing secular world. Astrology had been a component of folk belief through seventeenth and eighteenth century Europe. It was referred to in popular pamphlets and almanacs of the time, including Ben Franklin's *Farmer's Almanac.* Herbalists and white or black witches retained a place in the reality of the poorer classes. The Age of Reason's educated wealthy class relegated such belief to superstition. Yet the occult, mysticism and secret societies such as Masons or

Rosicrucian, remained popular among that class. Spiritualists and seances gained popularity among the poor, wealthy and rising middle class. There was a reinvestigation of ancient Celtic religion and belief systems of America's Native Americans and a fascination with the "noble savage." By the end of the nineteenth century, organizations like Madam Blavatsky's Theosophical Society or the Fraternal Druids were part of a list of responses to the Secular Phase. New sciences included psychology, phrenology, light therapy, sociology, archeology, anthropology, Egyptology, social Darwinism and Marxism. England's colonies of India and Southeast Asia exposed Eastern religion to the English speaking world.

Modern India's Hinduism was introduced on Western soil by Vivekananda at the first World Parliament of Religions in Chicago in 1893. His form of Hinduism accepted the teachings of Buddha, Jesus and Mohammed. It was established in the US in 1894, (and later England), as the Vedanta Society. Interest in Hinduism and Buddhism steadily increased in the West. Greater contact with Asian cultures came after World War II along with more translations of Hindu and Buddhist holy literature into English. It is out of the Vedanta tradition that transcendental meditation was presented to the West by Maharishi Mahesh Yogi in the 1960s. Maharishi gained fame for tutoring the English rock band, the Beatles. Vedanta influenced Deepak Chopra, whose holistic, metaphysical, integrative approach to medicine has created great interest and popularity in the 1990s. Peter Occhiogrosso wrote in his article, "Swami Bruce and the Future of Vedanta in the West," in the Nov./Dec. 1995 *Yoga Journal*:

> *Vedanta's appeal lies partly in its powerful philosophical nature but partly also in its tolerance of other religions, a characteristic suited to the increasingly secular and pluralistic culture of the West.... and appears to have had a similar impact on Western intellectuals earlier in the century, from Christopher Isherwood to Aldous Huxley to Joseph Campbell.* (P. 80)

The practice of yoga and Asian martial arts have expanded perceptions of the Divine in the West. The blending of Kriya yoga with Hindu-Christian cosmology came to the West through the Indian, Paramahansa Yogananda. He addressed the International Congress of Religious Liberals in Boston in 1920 stressing the universality of all religions in what he termed "science of religion." Unitarianism and the Baha'i Faith also gained popularity in the 20s, emphasizing universal approaches to the Divine. Great interest in Egyptian religion came with the opening of King Tut's tomb in 1922. Common ground was also found among new agers in the reverence for Nature contained in Chinese Taoism, Native American shamanism, Celtic Druidism and nineteenth century romanticism.

After World War II, reports of unidentified flying object (UFO) sightings and encounters increased. This supplied a more scientific rationale to divine occurrences. The notion that ancient astronauts have meddled in human affairs over time has gained popularity, expressed in books such as Charles Fort's, *The Book of the Damned* (1919) and *New Lands* (1923) or the 1970s best seller, *Chariots of the Gods* by Erich von Daniken. William Bramley's book, *Gods of Eden*, puts forth the theory that human warfare is encouraged by "custodians" from other planets to keep humans from realizing spiritual potential and to make sure they remain subservient to the aliens. The beliefs expressed by the Scientology Church place Earth as a pawn in an intergalactic war that rages even now. Other new age beliefs in "higher beings" and angels incorporate alien visitors from outside Earth or undersea Atlanteans as advanced beings who periodically visit us. The Unarius Education Foundation expects 33 space ships from the Pleiades constellation to land in 2001. A visitor to the town of Mt. Shasta, California, will find many citizens who believe in the existence of a "Lemurian" city inside the great sleeping volcano that is the town's namesake. The late Carl Sagan headed a project attempting to pick up extraterrestrial radio signals called Search for Extraterrestrial Intelligence (SETI). Steven Greer, head of North Carolina's Center for the Study of Extraterrestrial Intelligence (CSETI), initiated contact and communicated with UFOs at Sea Breeze, Florida, in 1992 and again at Mexico City in 1993. Group consciousness, high power lights and electronic beacons were employed. It was reported that UFOs arrived and then signaled back the simple patterns projected by Geer and the SETI group. Holy and historical writings from traditional religions often provide a basis for new age conjecture or interpretation. The Virgin Mary may have been artificially inseminated by a spaceman described as an angel in the Bible. Ezekiel may have been lifted up by a spaceship described in biblical texts as swirling wheels and whirlwind of fire (*Ezekiel* 1:4 & 3:12-14). Upon the fall of the Aztec city of Teotihuaca'n (Mexico City) to Cortez' Spaniards, a UFO danced on the walls of the city after a heavy mist descended. Reincarnation and guardian angels are part of new age cosmology. Channeling into the spirit world, other dimensions or past lives is also a new age practice.

Fanciful as the ideas, revelations and emotions may be, new age beliefs may be seeds of a new world religion. Currently it is popular mostly with white middle class people in the West. But like early Christianity, it is democratic and tolerant of all ideas. Yet both new agers and fundamentalist Christians demand personal transformation and seek societal transformation. New age shares various beliefs with Christianity including a time of tribulation for humankind which will bring on a new age of divine rapture. Revelation and prophecy play a large role in their mysticism. Both look to a future utopian heaven on earth reserved for the righteous. But there are also some very real differences. Charles B. Strozier stated in his book *Apocalypse*:

> *Perhaps both New Age and fundamentalism are plowing the same apocalyptic ground. We are in it, and it is in us. It cannot be escaped, though there is much uncertainty about our responsibilities toward it, and the role of violence in the move from the old (age) to the new (age). But what opens up at the other end for the New Agers is quite a different picture of the millennium from that of the fundamentalists. In the inclusive utopian images of the New Age, global justice and equitable distribution of resources prevail. The sacredness of "Mother Nature" is respected. There are neither executioner nor victims in a world of peace. And instead of a present God or resurrected Jesus leading the faithful, each individual is an empowered and fully realized human being.* (P. 247)

September-October, 4 B.C.E. or 2 B.C.E. have been placed as the time of Jesus' birth. To fit his return neatly within a two thousand year cycle, the years A.D. 1996 and 1998 might be placed, as they fall precisely two millennia after 4 and 2 B.C.E. As 2000 years ago, the search for compassion beyond what is available through traditional religion and science is already taking new agers into the inspection of other traditions, philosophies and systems. But they are not early Christians. They are not Essenes, whose tradition Jesus learned through his mother.

The inclusive, universalist approach of new age differs from today's fundamentalist Christian exclusive, paranoid approach. The return of Jesus or any personality is unimportant. However, new age respect for Nature is reminiscent of the early Irish Christians and St. Francis. Equality of the sexes and high positions held by women within the new age movement are similar to early Christianity as well. New agers have no set doctrine or single leader, past or present. Basic Christian compassion for fellow humans, study of religions other than Christianity, study of shamanism and of ecology are all part of an evolving, Gaian cosmology. Ancient shamanism, traditional world religions, and new practices and rituals are being synthesized. In present Western society, belief in the myth of invincibility has only begun. Under the relative tolerance allowed by an extended myth of invincibility, even fear of the future will not be enough to frighten people into one belief or another. Centuries must pass before a synthesis is formed and adopted by more than the Western middle class. The good luck of the Chinese and druid dragon or Aztec winged serpent must be reconciled with St. George the dragon killer.

IV: ENVIRONMENTALISTS

Acknowledgment of the importance of a healthy ecology and human connection to Nature brings a third spiritual movement into focus. It may appear that the environmental movement is purely secular due to its scientific, rational and systematic approach and direction. But a spiritual aspect is evident as well. Like the fundamentalist Christians and new agers, the origins of modern environmentalism lies in reaction to the Secular Phase. The ecology minded environmental movement shares the shadow of end time fear. The environmental movement also has a violent element that disdains technology.

In turn of the nineteenth century England, the Luddites set about destroying factories and mills, though the Luddites cared more about their loss of employment due to steam technology than ecology. The fear of unrestrained technology was echoed in Mary Shelley's 1818 novel, *Frankenstein,* in which the human attempt to create immortality through technology runs amok. In the 1927 movie *Metropolis* by Fritz Lang and Thea von Harbou, the elite depend on a machine named Moloch which demands consumption of mindless labor and sacrifice by enslaved workers. A twentieth century Luddite counterpart may be found in the Monkey Wrench Gang of the late 1960s and early '70s. This group set about wrecking equipment used to build dams and exploit natural resources in the southwestern US. And the spirit lives on in the present group dubbed the Sage Brush Rebellion which has taken responsibility for blowing up US Forest Service buildings. The Sage Brush Rebellion portrayed the US Forest Service as caring more about logging, ranching and mining interests than trees and coyotes. The Earth First organization does not trust big government or big business to conservatively manage the planet's resources. Terrorists have spiked trees to destroy saws and machinery in the sawmills. Violence has been used in the name of animal rights through blowing up facilities conducting scientific experiments on animals.

Some have taken up arms for what they see as a war between human greed and Nature. Squeaky Fromme attempted to assassinate President Ford in 1975 to somehow save the redwood forests of California. The FBI has implied that the Unabomber's murderous attacks are somehow connected to saving the Earth's ecological balance. The 3500 word manifesto of the alleged Unabomber, printed in the *Washington Post* and *Oakland Tribune*, describes his disdain for the technological "system." He felt the system robs the individual of liberty, dignity and power and destroys the environment. It stated that the social battle today is not between left and right political factions; the manifesto criticized both for supporting technology. It advocated individuals and small groups doing battle against those in control of advanced machines and the elite who create and operate them.

> *The system has already caused, and is continuing to cause, immense suffering all over the world. Ancient cultures, that for hundreds of years gave people a satisfactory relationship with their environment, have been shattered by contact with industrial society, and the result has been a whole catalogue of economic, environmental, social and psychological problems.*
> (Paragraph 168 of the manifesto, *The Oakland Tribune,* Sept. 21, 1995.)

But most environmentalists have used peaceful means. "Back to nature" eighteenth and nineteenth century romantics and naturalists included inspiring personalities such as Jean Rousseau, Alexander von Humboldt, Charles Darwin, John Muir and Theodore Roosevelt. Organizations and activist groups have worked for change in un-ecological government and business practices. The Sierra Club, founded by the nineteenth century naturalist John Muir, lobbies to set land aside for preservation and animal protection. The Jacques Cousteau Society, named after its French founder and developer of the aqua lung, seeks to protect the oceans from industrial pollution and over-fishing. The international and political Green Party began in reaction to acid rain destruction of Germany's Black Forest. The Society for the Prevention of Cruelty to Animals (SPCA) has been joined by a more militant group called People for the Ethical Treatment of Animals (PETA). PETA advocates vegetarianism, alternatives to use of animals for scientific research, industry and clothing. PETA made an unsuccessful legal attempt, through the US Supreme Court, to end animal sacrifice by the Christian cult, Lukumi Babalu Aye, Inc. PETA also lobbies for the protection of endangered animals from extinction. They advocate ending fur coat production. Pets Are Wonderful Support (PAWS) is yet another animal advocate group. Animal rights activists have illegally released lab animals. Green Peace mobilizes their ship, the Rainbow Warrior, on the high seas to upset whale hunters and monitor dolphins killed through commercial fishing practices.

There is fear and desperation in Western society concerning the powerlessness of the individual worried about ecology, relative to the apathetic urban society that gains its livelihood from industry that often pollutes. This sends the worried individual into environmental groups which translate into political action. The US government has responded with the National Environmental Policy Act under President Nixon, followed by the Clean Air Act, Clean Water Act, Marine Mammal Protection Act, Endangered Species Act, Safe Drinking Water Act, and Toxic Control Act. However, enforcement of these laws brings some convictions and violators are fined, but no person goes to jail. Even a million dollar fine does not effectively dent the economics of a multi-billion dollar, multi-national company. But such a penalty would ruin a small business. Fluorocarbons, asbestos, DDT, and lead used in paint and fuel along with other products of industry have been banned in the US. But capital and industry are not bound by borders.

In Australia in the mid 1970s, US toothpaste companies still peddled their products in lead tubes after lead tubes had been banned in the US.

In 1989, Chinese state TV ran an advertising campaign to sell freon-using, Chinese made refrigerators to its giant domestic market. In 1990, trucks regularly sprayed DDT through Turkish neighborhoods for mosquito abatement. Industry's destruction of tropical forests in Southeast Asia, Africa and South America continue to destroy those ecologies and Earth's oxygen supply. More than oxygen is taken from the indigenous people in those areas.

In one case, Shell Oil's industrial practices ecologically devastated areas of Nigeria resulting in the displacement and impoverishment of the local people. In 1995, environmental activists protesting the situation were condemned to death by the Nigerian dictatorship, hungry for oil income. Such examples have caused environmentalists (and the Unabomber) to remain skeptical of all governments. Western governments could pressure developing nations and multi-national corporations to act more ecologically responsibly. Conditions could be placed on military assistance, foreign aid and private economic aid. This, of course, would greatly upset trade and is unrealistic in the eyes of industry and the plutocracy still very invested in the Secular Phase of the *Zeitgeist.* Recognizing the need for technology, environmentalists have called for non-polluting, conservationally "appropriate" technology. Industries involved in the manufacture of solar-based power generating photovoltaics, organic farming, waste recycling and management have developed into big business as a result of "thinking green."

There are scientific end time theories that the earth will be swallowed as the sun turns to a red giant, or that an earth destroying giant meteor will strike the planet. But environmentalists feel that humans are going to kill themselves into extinction, along with all life forms, much sooner. Here the environmentalists are on common ground with new age and traditional Hopi prophecy. Some see the apocalypse as a state of war between human greed and Nature. Rising rates of skin cancer or cancer in general have direct environmental causes. The development of genetic engineering has frightening potential. New industrial diseases like sick building syndrome or carpal tunnel syndrome add more uncertainty.

Causes and effects of global warming or global cooling also present theoretical, scientific end time scenarios. At present these theories fall into the realm of scientific myth, along with Darwin's Theory. But, there is also hard science supporting environmentalist emotionalism. The ozone layer in the earth's atmosphere is being destroyed. Global temperature is rising as carbon levels increase. Oxygen-bearing forests are being destroyed. Methane levels are increasing. Human created toxins are negatively affecting ground and surface water as well as the biosphere. The earth's deserts continue to expand. Growing human population is taxing natural resources. Based on these facts, environmentalists make educated guesses about future end time scenarios. Many in the environmental movement feel an urgency that this generation or the next shall determine earth's survival as we know it. In this sense, angst is shared with fundamentalist Christians and new agers. This angst transfers to compassion for all life. It generates empathy and anthropomorphizing over the plight of stray dogs, test animals used by the cosmetic industry, or how livestock is treated and slaughtered.

For environmentalists and new agers compassion transfers to the emotional need for spiritual identity or union with something greater than just preserving earth for future human generations to exploit. The overwhelming realization of the interdependence of all forms of life can ultimately lead to the emotional-spiritual acts of hugging a tree or swimming with whales. When water, weather, geologic and food chain cycles are studied, the interconnectedness of the physical world spills into the interplay of energy vibrations which are measurable in terms of frequencies. Vibrational quantity and quality (vibes) and physical manifestations are aspects of the Divine. "Deep Ecology" is the label given to this spiritual response coupled to science. A virtual return to Eden is the biblical context for the environmental movement's goals.

As with fundamentalist Christianity and new age, the environmental movement feels that the Secular Phase system of operating must and will change. Unlike the new agers, both environmentalists and fundamentalist Christians are more militant and evangelistic. All three groups feel changes will have to be of a spiritual nature in order to alter the *Zeitgeist* of humanity (Spiritual Phase). "Facts" are systematically used for support. But environmentalists and new agers employ a holistic, physiomatic Spiritual Phase appreciation of Gaian cycles and patterns in order to transcend Theocratic and Secular Phases of the *Zeitgeist.* All see change involving the whole earth. Fundamentalist Christians see the change divinely dictated to humans while new agers and environmentalists see self-actualized humans paving the way for the Divine's grace.

V: The End of Past Religion

Religion is not the only exploiter of human ignorance and paranoia about the Divine. Governments find fear of divine judgment helpful as well. In W.W.II, Germans went to war with "*Gott mit uns*" (God is with us) written on their belt buckles. Atheist Stalin and Communist Party doctrine aside, Russian troops turned to Jesus or Mother Russia when facing death. American's sang the World War II ditty of *"Praise the Lord and pass the ammunition... we're on a mighty mission."* The US has used the Divine as an ally of the state, as has every empire including Rome. Sacrifice for the Greek city-state or the "senate and people" of Rome has been described earlier (Chapter 3) The ultimate sacrifice of giving one's life requires caring more for others (family, friends, or homeland) than one's own safety. This involves society's cooperation driven by fear of the enemy, or evil incarnated in the enemy. A world without fear is a common human dream rhetorically shared by all religions and governments. Yet fear and compassion are the catalysts for human cooperation. The participating individual within society must be sustained by one or both of these emotions.

The educator, William Glasser, developed a simple list of human requirements for a successful individual within a group. Glasser feels, after basic material survival needs such as food and shelter, everyone in society needs basic feelings of empowerment, freedom, fun and belonging. Fear of losing these needed feelings will cause the individual to join a subgroup or counter-culture that does fulfill these needs. Often individuals will join a gang, religion or support a government even if that gang, religion or government denies the same basic needs to individuals of another religion or society. Thus religions or governments, like street gangs, can become exclusive rather than inclusive.

In 1955, a humanist psychologist, Abraham Maslow, developed a five step hierarchy of an individual's social development. Maslow felt the number of individuals able to reach the higher levels of his scheme drop as individuals work their way to the highest level. At the first level, physiological needs such as hunger or thirst are the primary human concern. Achieving this first level, individual humans strive for a sense of physical safety. While Maslow did not expand his hierarchy beyond the individual, it does not take a great leap of logic to apply his pattern to a whole society striving for physical safety during a nation and empire building period. Having achieved this safe state (myth of invincibility), individuals (or society) may go on to a third level. The individual yearns for a sense of belonging. This can mean joining a group within society that has a shared belief system. Since physical safety is no longer a concern, angst is transferred to joining an organization supplying rationales or understanding of life in the hereafter and what truth is. At the fourth level, there is the individual's ego need for esteem or "making a mark" in life. Few achieve this goal according to Maslow, and fewer still reach the ultimate fifth level of self-actualization. At the fifth level, Maslow believed, the full human potential is realized. Societally, governments support the third and fourth level, defining truth and censoring speculation. A set dogma forms to enforce the paradigms. If a myth of invincibility continues, Maslow's fifth level is possible. At the fifth level, the individual(or society) transcends dogma. Here government, religion or gangs are no longer needed. The potential for society to self-actualize is utopian anarchy and anathema to a theocratic or secular system.

A government or church can't control an individual or group who holds and takes for granted Maslow's first four basic needs unless the individual or group is willing to give credit to the established church or state for their status. But compassion for even enemies of the state, without fear, transcends control by both theocratic or secular government. Mahatma Gandhi, Martin Luther King and the first Christian practiced this truth through passive resistance campaigns. Those caught in levels one to four overwhelm those at level five with their needs. So rather than end government altogether, society periodically replaces it, if the old government doesn't provide the needs identified by Glasser or Maslow. In this process, the self-actualized are employed to help form a new religious or governmental organization or they are eliminated and exploited post mortem. Every 2000 years Western civilization's self-actualized transcendentalism (and its martyrs) helps to create a new cosmology and religion in the milieu of the Spiritual Phase and extended myth of invincibility.

In the last Spiritual Phase there was enough time for the old myths to be destroyed or incorporated into new mythology returned to the fourth level. Western society's return to the ego based fourth level brought theocracy. Attempting to supply the physiological needs and safety of the third and second levels, theocratic government reigned over a Dark Age.

After plague, war and starvation reduced society to the first level, society again began the climb up Maslow's hierarchy.

Presently within the US, there are seven well-established religious traditions. These are Christian, Jewish, Muslim, Hindu, Confucian-Taoist, Buddhist and shamanic-animist Pagan. They represent the major faiths of the planet. There are tiny congregations leftover from the Arian Age such as Zoroastrian or Druze. Within these are major schisms such as Shiite and Sunni Muslims, or Mahayana, Tibetan and Hinayana in Buddhism or Greek Orthodox, Roman Catholic, Protestantism and Satan worship in the Christian tradition. Within all these there are a myriad of sects, cults, orders, monastic and mystical deviations. There are crossovers such as the Sikhs who combine Muslim and Hindu traditions or Self-Realization Fellowship combining Indian yoga with Christianity.

Within each congregation, each individual, while being a member of a church, sect or cult, still acts out their life slightly differently than the person worshipping next to them. Yet both may listen to the same sermon or read the same holy book. The individual acts individually even if they attempt to conform to the group. Religion is actions based on a faith. Two people may state they have an identical belief, but how they express and act upon their common faith is always, even if slightly, different. Seen in this context, there are as many religions as there are people on the planet. Yet, for security or the need to belong, most will identify with one of the faiths mentioned above or perhaps two because of intermarriage. Even those who put faith in science, whose tenets are the scientific method, have a belief system based on pure reason and skepticism. Psychiatrists are the priests and capitalists are the aristocracy. While being skeptical of fundamentalist Christian theory (religious myth) many in secular Western society accept scientific theory as reality. Thus the theories of John Locke, Adam Smith, Darwin and Marx are mythologies of the Secular Phase. Others profess atheism. This doctrine is a belief in disbelief as a means to the truth. A statement of faith in a negation is still a faith. Opposite teams can be involved in the same game. Persecution between groups is the extreme result of such competition. In the Spiritual Phase, Roman Pagans attacked Christians. In the following Theocratic Phase, Roman Christians persecuted Pagans.

Today the Pagan Europeans' horned deity of the hunt is personified as the Devil at Halloween (Druid New Year's Eve). The horned deity was dubbed the Devil by zealot Christian theocracy. Pagans persecuted by the Christians had three choices if they didn't want to give up their connection to Pagan traditional belief systems. They could join the Christian church, exchanging past deities for Christian saints, as done by the German Mystics and European peasants alike. They could practice their shamanic-animist Nature religion in secret at the risk of being condemned as witches if discovered. They could reject Christian tenets and Jesus, yet buy into the Christian cosmology and demonization of Paganism. In this sense they acknowledged the Bible through non-acceptance. These Pagans rejected Jesus, while worshipping what the Christians called the Devil and accepted the Christian-given label of Satanist for themselves. In Erica Jong's book *Witches*, (beautifully illustrated by Jos. A. Smith), she states:

> *Let us make it clear: a Satanist is a renegade Christian.... Satanists...accept the Christian duality between good and evil; Pagans do not. Satanists...have utterly bought into the Christian world view. Pagans see good and evil as intimately allied, in fact, indivisible.* (P. 52)

Jong continues:

> *The Satanist, for his part, is locked into Christian definitions, names, cosmologies, and paranoias.... Christ is all powerful in his* [the Satanist's] *mind or he wouldn't constantly war against Him. To the Pagan, interested in transcendence, not revenge, Christ may be seen as a prophet, a bodhisatva...pointing to spiritual liberation. The Church is seen as a secular organization — a real-estate conglomerate, a powerful lobby for the oppression of women....* (P. 53)

The horned deity of the hunt did not become evil until Christians made it so. Well before the persecution of traditional Pagan beliefs by Christian theocracy, the Pagans persecuted the new ideas found in Christianity during the last Spiritual Phase supported by the Roman government. Though many Christians feel they will one day be persecuted again, it is more likely Christians will persecute others in a vain attempt to hold onto traditional Christian religion. Currently, the competition between new spiritual ideas and religious tradition in the West has not reached such violence or intolerance. It takes generations of skepticism, discussion and acknowledgment before enough individuals within society admit past fears of the Divine were unfounded and that a new transcending belief system is needed. At that point, traditional religion (Christianity) will feel very defensive and turn hostile.

Until the twentieth century, freedom of religion for much of society in the US meant freedom of religion within Judeo-Christian boundaries. Since the 1960s, the definition has turned to universal religious libertarianism including Eastern religions and animism. Science is yet another religion or mythology for some. But, 150 years from now, this benign tolerance may no longer be the case. Reviewing the past in a Hegelian context, Paganism (thesis) and Hellenism (anti-thesis) were transcended by Christianity (synthesis) to form a Christian theocracy (thesis). The theocratic Christians were in turn challenged by secularism (anti-thesis). The new synthesis will be a yet to be labeled transcending faith, developed as the Spiritual Phase dissolves (see fig. 1).

If Pax Romana gives us any lesson, it is that after 300 years of an established world order and myth of invincibility, no traditional, established government or religion will survive in its original form. Will Durant wrote in his concise book, *The Lessons of History*, *"One lesson of history is that religion has many lives, and a habit of resurrection"* (p. 49). Two millennia from today, like Greco-Roman mythology, Christianity will be an historical footnote for scholars and romantics, incorporated into a new universal catholic faith.

A future messiah may not issue a message until older than 30 and may live seven decades like Louis the XIV or Buddha. Jesus may not come back, rather, her name might be Jane. Few, if any, Christians or Jews will recognize the Messiah should one appear, for their interests and cosmology are locked in dogma and theocratic or secular politics typical of any established religion of a past age (or phase). Christians may be part of the two thirds (.666) of society that persecutes those being saved by a Messiah. The threatened Christian establishment, encouraged by the state, may act under direction of the antichrist or "Beast" in sheep's clothing. This may not turn out to be a human or beast at all, but a human created and programmed super computer that gets beyond human control! Novelist Mary Shelly's Frankenstein's monster concept is a fear expressed again by George Orwell's novel *1984*, Aldous Huxley's *Brave New World*, the science fiction movie *2001 A Space Odyssey*, and the Unabomber. If the Beast does take human form, it may not be a solitary person, but rather persons in an institution or group that a future Messiah will rebel against. This could be an established institution (United Nations, US Presidency, Trilateral Commission, union of churches etc.) that has become corrupted, oppressive, tyrannical and deified. The Beast and/or Messiah may turn out to be extraterrestrial. The future holds as many scenarios as the imagination can create.

Using biblical terms like "Messiah" or "Beast," a past example may be examined both objectively and spiritually with a physiomatic approach. A little less than 2000 years ago, the first Christians saw the Roman Caesar as a personification of the Beast. For most of Western society, Caesar Augustus, while alive, acted as a benevolent dictator extolling the republic. He allowed controversy and relative freedom of speech within his rubber stamp senate and judiciary. He also allowed himself to be re-elected term after term. He garnered so much executive power that upon his death, the republic also died as less and less power rested in the senate. Augustus' 41 years of leadership defined and established the borders of the empire. He initiated peace and prosperity within the empire that lasted for two centuries and established a world order. Internal strife and the empire's split in two (A.D. 350) eventually came to pass. But the myth of invincibility against foreign conquest, initiated under Augustus, was not extinguished until the sack of Rome by German Visigoth tribes in A.D. 410.

To most of Western society, Augustus appeared more than human. The senate proclaimed him a deity post-mortem. Turning Augustus and following living emperors into deities also helped the established plutocracy to rule by executive whim with divine blessing and military support. Traditional religion was attempting to meet contemporary society's ideal of a human/deity implanted since Alexander the Great (300 years before Augustus). Traditional faith was competing with new and exotic ideas. As personal memory of life under the republic died, questioning the actions and laws of a ruling deity became not just unpatriotic treason, but also blasphemy toward the Divine. Still, as long as the myth of invincibility prevailed, spiritual speculation continued among members of society in the Spiritual Phase. With the end of the myth of invincibility, Hellenism, traditional Paganism and the counter culture (Christians, Mithra, Mani) synthesized and were finally co-opted by the state for mutual security. The human/deity cosmology was transferred to Jesus. Priest craft and new dogma rather than human discourse moved the synthesis to Theocratic Phase thesis. (See fig. 2.)

Logic, justice or civil rights in Rome and thus Western society came to be dictated by the Divine (Theocratic Phase) rather than rational human intellect and law ascribed to human effort (Secular Phase) or tolerance and compassion (Spiritual Phase). Describing these days, Thomas Cahill wrote in his book, *How the Irish Saved Civilization*:

> *The intellectual disciplines of distinction, definition, and dialectic that had once been the glory of men like Augustine were unobtainable by readers of the Dark Ages, whose apprehension of the world was simple and immediate, framed by myth and magic.* (P. 204)

Cahill goes on to describe the case made for the primacy of the Roman theocracy and view of Christianity over the democratic Celtic view of Christianity. He documented the synod held in A.D. 664 at Whitby Abbey, Northumbria, England, presided over by the Celtic abbess Hilda.

> *Even the "Romans" at Whitby presented their point of view in the new way. They did not argue, for genuine intellectual disputation was beyond them. They held up pictures for the mind — one set of bones versus another. Indeed, the Northumbrian King, who ruled in favor of the Roman party, did so because he imagined that Peter, Rome's supposed first bishop, to whom Jesus had, in a metaphorical phrase, given "the keys to the kingdom of heaven," would use those keys to lock the king out of heaven if he ruled against Rome.* (P. 204).

In a Theocratic Phase of the *Zeitgeist*, previous religions along with any new ideas die, are incorporated or are driven underground. Western civilization must then wait for yet another Secular Phase to bring old and new ideas to the surface again. This brings theocracy into question and reason and science are proposed as an alternative. With the Spiritual Phase, static theocracy and narrow science are transcended and synthesized until a new religion (and Theocratic Phase) is born.

VI: The End of Past Government

At present, the ruling elite of the US represented by a little less than

535 wealthy legislators, who make federal laws for nearly 300 million citizens, is conscious of Roman history and resists complete executive power. The separation of powers set by the wisely constructed US Constitution may very well slow the arrival of an almighty executive person, group or institution. But the world is getting smaller due to technology. Legislative battles and nationalism will only slow inevitable ratification of trade agreements with other nations, global communication and dealing with global health, ecological, military and immigration problems. As moral and economic quality of life deteriorates in the societal view, it will be the seemingly inept law makers (Senate and House of Representatives) not the law enforcer (Presidency) who will appear to stand in the way of society's aspirations. Society has already moved to a more cynical mentality. A popular pro government bumper sticker directed against protest of US government policy in the 1960s stated, "America, love it or leave it." This was replaced by a new sticker in the 1990s stating "I love my country, but I fear my government." The cynicism of the beatniks and skepticism of the hippies (or freaks) has taken hold within contemporary Western society.

The West is looking for more compassionate, responsive government with safeguards against those un-elected individuals running the bureaucracies who seem to take advantage of their positions. Providing for the general welfare is subject to graft and corruption generated by tempting offers in exchange for inside information or preferential action. Preferential treatment and information benefits special interests in search of government contracts or favorable laws. Because of its distrust of government, the middle class, encouraged by the wealthy, fear too much compassion by government in the form of direct revenues for the poor. The poor fear discrimination and exploitation by the middle class and wealthy who seemingly run the state and society. Due to lack of education and misinformation, the poor more than middle class are politically apathetic. But when squeezed too hard, the poor react violently through theft or riots. For public safety then, some of the poor's needs are addressed, only to be challenged again by the middle and wealthy classes at a later, more passive time. The common denominator is greed.

Meanwhile, the middle class incomes available for consumer spending decline as the costs of living increases faster than wages. This results in rising consumer debt as people use credit cards to maintain their lifestyles. Less middle class income also restricts the tax base. The wealthy (as was the case in ancient Rome) pay relatively little tax, and the poor pay even less. Low skilled jobs garner less and less relative pay due to competition with cheap labor overseas and illegal immigrant workers domestically.

Terrorism fuels society's fear of anarchy by urban bombing or gassing. A strong efficient executive seems more appealing to much of society as partisan congressional squabbles continue. Insuring a myth of invincibility remains a priority. The 1995 military spending bill passed by Congress provided seven billion dollars more than the Pentagon asked for! Though national and domestic security is entrusted to the centralized federal government, society's distrust of big government grows. Attempts to decentralize non-military spending and federal power have been made. The federal Congress has given more freedom of action to the local governments. But this freedom carries the burden of economic costs and responsibilities. Local governments strain to fund services at the levels demanded by society for medicine, education, public works, police and fire protection. Paradoxically, the cost of local government increases the need to levy local taxes. Local governments go into debt. The call for federal help becomes necessary as local government can't deliver. Already this status exists in times of natural disasters, major corporate failures or aid for the poor.

In 1995 the House of Representatives gave democracy away to efficiency. Power was consolidated when the number of committees was reduced. Chosen committee heads were given term limits. The effect of these actions was to place greater power into the hands of the Speaker of the House. Discussion and debate were limited at the committee level. These actions were in stated response to the public's demand for more legislative action. But deadlock slowed political action and paradoxically increased society's frustration.

Complete power in the hands of a single plutocratic party has yet to occur in the US. Generals have become Presidents, but the military has not yet taken the US government overtly. To date, a single party has only briefly held power in two of the three branches of government. No party or faction has gained an overwhelming majority for long or controlled the Supreme Court. The people of the US are not yet desperate enough to let the plutocracy create a single party state. However, the near future holds potential for desperation sufficient to tip the scale in favor of demagoguery, oligarchy or dictatorship. The common denominators here are order, and compassion for those exploited due to greed. Losing a positive, personal memory of a republican system, benevolent dictatorship will become an enticing alternative.

As with Rome B.C.E., immigration is a growing problem for the US and Europe A.D. and will continue, bringing new demographics, changing culture and values in Western Society. In the Roman example, Huns drove German and central Asian groups en mass into the empire. This eventually brought an end to Rome's myth of invincibility. An event such as major disease or war may drive relatively massive numbers across the US border causing the US society to lose its myth of invincibility. Economic downturn as in the Great Depression of the 1930s would be a much greater crisis in an urban, technologically dependent future. The US is no longer rural and society is quickly losing personal memory of living without the luxuries of the city. Demagogues like Louisiana's Huey Long (1893-1935) will be in demand.

The US will long maintain the will, ability and resources needed to contain such events before their impact is so complete. In the ongoing myth of invincibility, society will continue to get weary of uncertainty concerning domestic physical and spiritual well-being, while foreign military invasion will seem an ever dimmer possibility. Yet generation after generation will continue with business as usual. The continuing, gradual decline in the standard of living, shrinking globe and growing population will grind along. The church and state will hold their static forms, based on tradition. Appearances of an imminent end time will be more obscure. Those individuals, cults or organizations claiming a dramatic, even violent end time within the near future will lose credibility among an increasingly apathetic and cynical society.

Still, a consensus will continue to exist throughout society, for centuries to come, that whatever the future, the present political, economical and spiritual system can't last and must change someday. To counter this lack of confidence and to keep order and power, the government will rigidly continue to resort to expedient measures to check increasing social and ecological challenges. Western society will also have three major well-established spiritual movements to look to for guidance. The genesis of the available ideas will be those expressed today by new age religious groups, fundamentalist Christian churches and the environmental movement. During the Spiritual Phase, government will become irrelevant as society's loyalty shifts to the demands of these movements. A resultant new religion will come to pass as the end time for Western secular governments arrives. The plutocracy's oligarchy or dictatorship in existence three centuries from now will incorporate the new synthesized religion to maintain power and create a theocracy in response. This new theocracy will bring the end to the Spiritual Phase and launch Western society into a new Theocratic Phase as surely as the acts of Constantine and Justinian did in A.D. 300.

> *That is his "world-history," the history of a steadily increasing, fateful rift between man's world and the universe — the history of a rebel that grows up to raise his hand against his mother.*
>
> Oswald Spengler, *Man and Technics,* p. 44

Chapter Seven

NEW RELIGION

1: A Survey

The components of a future world religion can be forecast if the three contemporary spiritual movements — new age, fundamentalist Christian and environmental movement — are compared. What they have in common will prevail. Contrasts will be reshaped or eliminated. The early Christian period is our last example of this process. Its evolution in the last Spiritual Phase must also be considered as an historical perspective for the approaching one.

New age is attempting to synthesize, but does not subscribe to Judeo-Christian original sin and accompanying guilt. New agers feel humans can consciously affect how the end time plays out and also prepare for it. In this sense new age celebrates the capacities of the human spirit to effect change. This places new age in the Secular Phase humanist camp with the aspirations of eighteenth century romantics. New age vision of the future millennium is democratic and evolutionary. All people are self-actualized as saints or Buddhas. New agers seek to place equality of the sexes in a co-dependent Taoist dualism. Reverence for "The Goddess" is great among new agers, connecting it with shamanic Paganism.

Fundamentalist Christians uphold the paternalistic, Western Judeo-Christian tradition. They subscribe to cosmology developed in the Theocratic Phase of the *Zeitgeist* stated in Secular Phase terms. They use a Secular Phase systematic approach to validate their literal interpretation of the Bible. Faith is placed in being the Divine's chosen and thus saved in the end time. Fundamentalist Christians shed personal human responsibility for the end time or state of the planet. They credit the events of end time completely over to divine and satanic influences on humans. They see the apocalyptic change to heaven on earth as dramatic, sudden and violent. There is still time to save souls. But they pessimistically feel it is too late to save the planet. Whatever resources remain are divinely given for the consumption of humankind. Many feel humans have a divine mandate to use up what is left of earth's resources. Fundamentalists are theocratic monarchists as they visualize a future ruled by Lord Jesus.

The environmentalists use the Secular Phase, systematic approach placed in scientific terms. Scientific fact validates their cause more than the other two movements. Yet environmentalists also possess a mythology and cosmology. They see stewardship toward the earth as a personal responsibility of each individual and an evolutionary step toward the new millennium. They look to an ecologically educated, rational humanist society saving the planet. Reverence for the earth and Nature (Gaia), brings the environmental movement into common ground with the new agers, placing both in the Spiritual Phase spirituality of Deep Ecology. New agers and environmentalists support use rather than abuse (management versus total exploitation) of the earth.

All three causes present elements of theocratic-style dogma and a Secular Phase systematic approach to validate tenets of their faith. Yet they also call for a new system and *Zeitgeist* that transcends both theocratic and secular elements. They are evangelistic. Their debates are the essence of the synthesizing practiced in a Spiritual Phase. Given time and freedom to practice, society will come up with a cult addressing the need for spiritual libertarianism and political security with universalist compassion for Nature and all classes and races. Emphasis on Mary, mother of Jesus and a female Holy Ghost (Sofia) has existed in past Christian theology, and may again become a fundamentalist response to changing sexual roles and women's rights. A less paternalistic future theology has a precedent of female empowerment expressed by the Christian cult in their first three centuries. Personal transformation is common to all three groups and will be part of a new faith. But it will need a common label other than "self-realized" or "born-again" to distance from Secular Phase psychology or Christianity.

During an extended myth of invincibility, the state may periodically feel threatened enough to persecute a new cult, providing martyrs. In ancient Rome during its myth of invincibility, Christians were seen by society as not only unpatriotic, but blasphemous due to their resistance to military service and non-recognition of the emperor/deity. Christians were condemned as atheistic for not worshipping any deity but Jehovah. The first Christians held "love feasts" providing food, fellowship and equality for all classes and the sexes. The love feasts, underwritten by wealthy Christians, ended because not all who attended could leave behind their hedonistic practices. The gatherings became too popular, lost spiritual focus and went out of control. Christians were often described as sexually promiscuous due to loose interpretations of love which may have slipped into lust. Early Christian sexual equality ran counter to establishment paternalism. Christians were even seen as the cause for natural and political disasters. They were accused by traditional religion of being in league with deities ruling the underworld (a Pagan style Satanism). These prejudiced charges are not that different from those made by many of today's traditional society or fundamentalist Christians against new age cults.

Pagans and new agers are seen by many current fundamentalist Christians as being in league with Satan, sexually promiscuous, atheistic and unpatriotic. Lack of patriotism is often leveled at environmentalists as well when they object to government policy or business practices that may be destructive to the earth's ecology. The eariy Christian love feasts were little different from the love-ins of the 1960s. The first '60s love-ins were spontaneous with minimum organization and supplied with donated food. All classes and races were invited. Love-ins quickly gained electrically amplified music, drowning out participants' tambourines, flutes, acoustic guitars and chants. Religious experience was lost as food booths began charging money and hard drugs and methamphetamines took over. Today's open air, hedonist rock concert is the legacy.

In ancient Rome, most early Christian converts initially came from the lower and middle classes. They found identity in Jesus, their carpenter messiah. Ritual was basic and simple. The water, bread and wine (ritual cannibalism of the body of Christ), the name of Jesus and the cross were the sole sacraments. Blind faith in biblical miracles and mysteries of baptism and Last Supper supplied spiritual solidarity. There was no set dogma or calendar of religious events. All the religions and philosophies of the Arian and beginning Piscean Ages were added to a simplified, unorthodox Jewish tradition. There was only one commandment handed down by Jesus when he stated, *"This is my commandment, That ye love one another, as I have loved You."* (*John*, 16:12.) This command superseded or contained all other Roman or Jewish commandments. It was wide open for interpretation and incorporation. Over time, elements of the previous Theocratic and Secular Phases were incorporated for a wider audience. As the wealthy or more academically educated joined in with the illiterate, poorer classes and slaves, reason and philosophy brought theology to the cult. Gnostics attempted to provide a rational concept that could even include the science of the day and make faith in Christ acceptable to more of society. In time, other Pagan sacraments were added such as anointing, the laying on of hands, use of sacred oil, salt or incense.

The birthday of Mithra, a rival intermediary to the Divine, was incorporated as the date for Christ mass, honoring the birth of Jesus! Wine used as the symbolic blood of Jesus and water used for baptism was perhaps more acceptable to urban types than Mithra baptism in bull's blood. The Jewish Hanukkah holy days also corresponded to the present fictitious birthdate of Jesus. Christmas was also conveniently near Winter solstice, celebrated (then and to this day) by many Pagan-animist groups. This being a holy time for humans since the beginning of human history, it is perhaps one recurring celebration that will be with us 2000 years from now. But the label given to that holy time of human connection with the Divine and Nature will not be Christmas when it is again incorporated into a new religion.

There was a need in the opening Piscean Age, as today at the onset of the Aquarian Age, for one unifying, universal belief system for one world. As a contrasting example, the popular Isis cult provided a mother image and the tradition and chic of Egyptian religion. But it was based on an established goddess rather than a contemporary. It operated under the terms and *Zeitgeist* of traditional cosmology. By the third century the Christian cult was a catholic church with all the solemn and precise ritual, priests, sacrifices (human sacrifice in religion was disappearing in all faiths by the second century) and holy ceremonies. In this sense Christianity could rival any traditional or new Pagan cult or church. Isis, Diana or Venus were incorporated into the currently sexless Holy Spirit and the Virgin Mary. Christian theology, developed in its first two centuries and was practiced another 100 years before it became the dogmatic state religion and theocracy under Emperor Constantine. Early Christianity began organizationally with elements of episcopalian (rule by bishops), presbyterian (rule by elders), or congregational (rule by church members) systems of authority depending on the local inclination and culture. By A.D. 350, Roman Christianity developed into an episcopalian paternal structure, outlawing the democracy, alternative systems or what the state saw as the anarchy of the church. Dogma was developed in their recent past for modern, urban conditions and needs of the Piscean Age. But Christianity still needed evolution to relate to the more rural Dark Ages.

The fifth century Irish Christians were isolated from the episcopalian church in Rome by the invasions of the Pagan Franks who took Gaul and the German tribes (Angles, Saxons and the Jutes) who took England. The Irish carried on in a congregational mode. The bishops or elders were often elected to their positions by local congregations. This model was consistent with tribal democracy. The Irish church leaders would suggest rather than dictate their wishes. St. Patrick was a contemporary of St. Augustine, but they were as different as city and country. Patrick was less concerned with sexual matters and tolerant of the Celtic reverence for Nature. Irish monks and priests wore the white robes of the shamanic-animist Druid priests they were replacing. The Irish turned from a mythology containing a frightening pantheon and human sacrifice, to a tolerant loving and caring Jesus who represented the ultimate human sacrifice. Patrick, once a slave himself, fought to end slavery. Slavery, human sacrifice and intertribal warfare ended in Ireland by the end of Patrick's life (A.D. 461).

The Irish Christian worshipped Nature as a manifestation of the Divine. Roman Christians worshipped only the Divine creator but not the creation (Nature). This alone set Patrick apart from urban, Mediterranean Christian leaders. Urbanity had severed connection with Nature which was only appreciated as something to be consumed or used by humans. Ireland had no cities. Cahill stated in his work, *How the Irish Saved Civilization*:

> *Patrick's gift to the Irish was his Christianity — the first de-Romanized Christianity in human history, a Christianity without the sociological baggage of Greco-Roman world, a Christianity that completely inculturated itself into the Irish scene.* (P. 148)

There was no coercion or bloodshed in Ireland's conversion, only encouragement.

Without cities, there was no Roman style diocese or need for bishops in Ireland. So abbots and abbesses became the church leaders. Literacy and scholarship was encouraged among the masses, not just the church elite, in the inclusive Irish Christianity. Patrick accepted women into the church as the early, pre-theocratic Christians had. St. Brigid, converted by Patrick, was a druid as well as an abbess. This affiliation with shamanistic, druidic tradition was not seen as a contradiction in Irish eyes. Cahill described Brigid's acceptance of Christ and establishment of the monastery of Kildare:

> *She is reputed to have taken the veil on the Hill of Uisnech, Ireland's primeval navel and the mythical center of its cosmic mandala. Her monastery began as a sort of Green Martyrdom under a huge oak, the sacred tree of the druids — thus, Kildare, which means "Church of the Oak."* (P. 173.)

The "Green Martyrs" were Irish monks who, armed with copies of the beautifully illustrated Book of Kells, effectively converted the rural Celtic, Germanic and North Italian rural folk of Europe 250 years later. Urban Roman Christian leadership had little concern for rural folk. At the same time (A.D. 700-800), Spain and North Africa came under Muslim control. The Greek Orthodox Byzantines and recently christianized Franks were pressing in on the Slavic Pagans with their own brand of Christianity. Once Christianized by the Irish, Europe's rural Christians were incorporated over the passage of time by the aggressive, urban Roman church. As part of the ongoing synthesis, Rome's Christians had to concede to the inclusion of a few Pagan vestiges such as May Day, Christmas, Easter eggs and, for the Germans, naming the days of the week after Norse deities. Tues, Woden, Thor and Fria were assigned Tuesday, Wednesday, Thursday and Friday. The sun and moon were given homage on Sunday and Monday while the Roman deity Saturn was given Saturday. The Druid's New Year (Halloween) became the Christian's All Saint's Day. Rural areas joined the Theocratic Phase.

At this point Western civilization had come full circle, moving through the Spiritual Phase and completing the establishment of the Theocratic Phase begun four centuries earlier. Narrowing and confinement of spiritual speculation within one tradition continued for at least the next 800 years. Forced conversions and witch hunts were the modes for persecuting Pagans, women's status and Manichaeans (who re-emerged as Bogmolis or Cathari through the tenth to fourteenth centuries). The Irish Christians remained outside the controls of the Roman Christian theocracy until the Norman-French and English invasions, c. A.D. 1100.

The contrast between the values and approach of the Roman and Irish Christian movements is significant. These differences should be kept in mind when projecting into Western society's future spiritual and religious development. Though the new religion of Christianity had become the state religion of Rome by the end of that Spiritual Phase, rural Europe did not join in the new theocracy until much later. The urban Romans were not trusted by the rural folk while the provincial Irish were. Yet in the end, Roman Christian theocracy carried the day because its organization included narrower interpretations, and its bureaucratic hierarchy was more efficient in controlling society. Since control is what warlords are interested in, it was natural that rural chiefs should ally with an approach to religion that actively pursued power and wealth. As long as the emerging aristocracy got a share of the wealth and power, they gladly enforced the will of the Divine as dictated by the Roman Christian priest class. Piscean Age Deep Ecology died with the Druids, Irish Christians, witches and St. Francis. Hellenism's romantics were consigned to monasteries.

In the last and recent Secular Phase, groups were again freed to pursue a new cosmology. Placing hope in the American and French Revolutions, romantics developed secular terms for a new millennium they felt was soon to come. The end result was Socialism. At the turn of the twentieth century A.D., Baha'i faith in the last days of the Ottoman Empire came out of a Turkish myth of invincibility. Baha'ism offered a universalist attempt to transcend nationalism, sexism, secularism and theocracy. Had the Ottomans kept their "Pax" for another 200 years, Baha'i may have become the Turkish state religion. But reaction to military defeat in World War I and a reformist leader, Mustafa Kemal Ataturk, created a more secular Islam drawn from Turkish "old time religion." Without any state sanction, Baha'i will remain as a scion of Shi'ah Islam. Marxist and Baha'i precepts may contribute to a world catholic religion of the future or be absorbed and lost to history. But they offer modern, tentative examples for the future.

As Western society moves into the Spiritual Phase now descending upon us, control of technology and power will continue to be sought. The vision of a world government made from a confederation of nation-states will compete with a vision of a world unified by a cooperative of small local groups. Initially, under the luxury and tolerance of a long myth of invincibility, the global, cooperative networks will transcend secularism's nationalism and ancient theocracy. They will assume a physiomatic, holistic Spiritual Phase approach. There will be no need for priest craft or bishops. Shamans and elected wise persons will suffice as was the case with the early Irish Christians. Politically, the forces of decentralization, tribalism and local interests will challenge a world order based on a confederation of nation-states. The world confederation which is already realized in the United Nations, will strive to maintain national integrity for the member nations as an efficient means of communication, trade and societal control. This is a systematic, logical approach in keeping with the Secular Phase of the *Zeitgeist* which spawned nationalism and the UN.

But the world confederacy of nations, whose name may no longer be the UN, will retain the global police force and prevail. As foreign threats challenge the myth of invincibility, authority will defer to the service of a central world order that defines the Divine's will. This theocracy will serve the West's continued concentration of wealth and power. The decentralized cooperative, Spiritual Phase approach will attempt to apply appropriate technology in the hands of small groups and individuals to communicate and trade democratically, transcending nationalism. The Hegelian appeal of coming full circle to human self-actualized unity with Nature and Christian unysis with the Divine, will remove existential science. Thus, the spiritual, physiomatic approach will wash the secular systematic approach from society's personal memory and *Zeitgeist.* But decentralized, high tech pastoralism is also utopian. Actuating such romantic anarchy would inevitably lead to the age-old cycle of theft, revenge, conquest, militias, consolidation of wealth and a return to power politics. A new religion and dogma would replace spiritual freedom as an institution like the UN incorporates and establishes that new religion as its own. Ecologic deprivation and separation would return as the Spiritual Phase fades into a Theocratic Phase.

Placing so much power of the temporal as well as spiritual realms in one institution may become necessary for planetary survival, but the cost will be a return to a long Theocratic Phase. Alternative approaches to a new official religion will be tolerated as an efficient recruiter. Over time, as occurred with the Irish Christian movement, the theocratic state church will incorporate or eliminate any divergence from orthodox dogma in order to consolidate even more control. Localism, alternative beliefs and spiritual anarchy will again be outlawed in favor of security and central authority using a narrow definition of the Divine as a rationale. This is a bleak future, but it is as inevitable as the rain. Consolation may be found in that the return of such theocratic tyranny is centuries away.

Leaving the Age of Aquarius two thousand years in the future, a retrospection on the present might see the U. S. still very much a republic. This is consistent with where Rome was 2000 years ago, if only in name, under the leadership of Augustus from 27 B.C.E. to A.D. 14. But it will take some time before "Hail to the Chief" has the same connotation as "Hail Caesar" did. The persecution of sub-cultures or cults is not yet as severe in the US as in Imperial Rome. Yet acts against racial minorities and anti-animist, anti-Catholic, anti-Mormon, anti-Jewish or anti-women discrimination have occurred from time to time. In the Utah War, an army was sent to subjugate Mormon power (1857-58), forcing mediation. The slaughter by the US military at Wounded Knee was a direct result of racist fear of the Native American's Ghost Dance religion (1890). Ninety-five years later, in 1985, a back to Nature group, called Move, was bombed in Philadelphia when they resisted eviction from their residence. Police and firefighters stood inactive as fire cremated the group's members and their children plus 61 adjoining residences in the Black neighborhood. The freedom of Religion Act of 1993 was passed by Congress in an attempt to curb discrimination toward "recognized" religion. Yet an investigation of charges concerning a two hundred dollar sales tax due on a gun led to the Branch Davidian massacre by federal troops in 1994. After Congressional hearings in 1995, it is still not clear why the fundamentalist Branch Davidians were attacked at their Texas compound by the police and military. As an offshoot of the Seventh Day Adventist Church and in existence since 1935, they were a recognized religious group. Perhaps it was only a case of over-zealous law enforcement agencies. Still, religious persecution is a valid concern for the future.

In the US, all but three Presidents and the great majority in Congress have been Protestant Christian; the US government is de-facto Protestant Christian. This is the case even though the Constitution specifically states that religion may not be used as a requirement for holding public office. The US government has been generally unsympathetic towards other belief systems. It has maligned, through false propaganda or ridicule, various racial minorities, laborites, communists, religious cults, Native American religion and most recently hippies. The clash between the vision and values of the traditional Protestant Christian or secular humanist US society and the spirituality of the hippies, is symbolic of the conflict between the Secular and Spiritual Phases. Though the Spiritual Phase is currently resisted by the majority of society and its governments, the momentum of the *Zeitgeist's* cycle continues, forcing society to contemplate and understand the spiritual milieu of the 1960s.

II: BEATS AND FREAKS

The scenario for the next millennium has been laid out. But the course of the next century is more relevant to those living today. Understanding the hippie phenomena as it relates to future trends is essential. Hippies greatly affected the last wave of the born-again fundamentalist Christians, new agers and environmentalists who will, in turn, begin to synthesize a cosmology that will be a new religion two centuries from now. This in turn will synthesize into the world religion of 1000 years in the future. Much of what current society understands about hippies is either demonizing or romantic and often far from the truth. The author will relate personal memory, acknowledging the difficulty of recounting such a recent social phenomena objectively. Observations and conclusions are based on youthful first hand experiences as they unfolded during the 1960s in California from San Francisco to Laguna Beach, greater

Orange County and Los Angeles County to Humboldt County, as well as in visits to Hamburg, Germany, London, England, and Chile.

First, the term "hippie" was never in the lexicon of the '60s counter-culture. The need to describe the counterculture of the '60s was symbolic of prejudicial categorizing from a gray, secular world in need of a label. A tenet of the '60s counter-culture was abolition of labels. Yet they referred to big business and big government as the "Establishment." They called each other by their names, nick-names or new names, such as River, Prairie Rose or Wild Flower, or referred to each other in general terms like "man," "head," "long hair," "dude," "old man," "old woman," "chick," "cat" or "freak." Freaks joined or inspired many civil rights, anti-war and other counter-culture groups. Their input added to the Rolling Stone magazine, Vegans, organic farm movement, radical feminists, Queer Nation, Hari Krishna, Christian congregations, charities, the Monkey Wrench Gang and New Left organizations such as Students for a Democratic Society (SDS) or Maoists. Other than musical groups, only a few purely freak groups achieved any labels. These were the diggers of San Francisco or the provos of Amsterdam and London and finally the yippies in New York. A group of "Merry Pranksters" rolled across the US exposing the more hedonistic side of freak life. These anarchist groups were leaderless in any formal sense.

Freaks were influenced by the earlier beatnik movement as outlined in the last chapter. Beats provided literature, counter-culture lifestyle examples and information including use of cannabis and hallucinatory drugs. Mostly under the age of 30, the Freaks read and listened to the over 30 critics of traditional Western values, among them, Alan Watts, Ken Kesey, Dr. Timothy Leary, Richard Alpert, otherwise known as Ram Dass, Allen Ginsberg, Gary Snyder, Aldous Huxley, Hermann Hesse and Jack Kerouac. Religious leaders and saints, living or dead, from Eastern and Western traditions, were studied as well. But while the freaks studied these elders, few would ever be dictated to by them. None would admit that they followed them. In *California Dreams*, edited by Dennis Hale and Jonathan Eisen an article that appeared in *Ramparts Magazine*, March, 1967, by Warren Hinckle titled, "A Social History of the Hippies" stated:

> *Kesey sensed that the hippie community had soured on him. He had committed the one mortal sin in the hippie ethic: telling peo-*

ple what to do.... At thirty-one, Ken Kesey is a hippie has-been. (P. 335)

Freaks were people who in the mid to late 1960s and early '70s, dressed unconventionally and dabbled in alternative philosophies and life-styles. They were willing to work but did not feel Calvinist guilt for taking a vacation; they advocated "dropping out" of society to introspect and create a vision for their individual destiny. Recreation came to mean re-create consciousness. Unlike much of US society at that time, the excuse of sports or hunting or a business trip was not needed to rationalize why they were not working at a job for monetary gain. These people were happy to climb or hike and enjoy the wonder of Nature, art and science. They were "turned-on" to learning, as one of them may have put it — reminiscent of a Secular Phase Romantic, Spiritual Phase Irish Green Martyr or Theocratic Phase Franciscan. While freaks cast out the suit and tie or girdle and bra for themselves, they were tolerant of those who didn't. This libertarian attitude was expressed in the phrase, "do your own thing." The credo of "peace and love" included celebrating all the differences among humans, as long as those differences were non violent. Length of hair or facial hair became a statement by these people only after the media took notice and ridiculed them. The neo-Franciscan message was that length of hair, or type of clothing is not a measure of the person.

This statement had been exemplified by young St. Francis of Assisi to his wealthy, textile merchant father. St. Francis stripped naked in front of his father, symbolically and physically rejecting material wealth by casting off his fine garments. From that time on, he wore only sack cloth. In a 1967 discussion, taped at the Center for the Study of Democratic Institutions, Arnold Toynbee called St. Francis *"....the earliest drop out in* [modern] *Western History."* St. Francis was a counter-culture icon along with other past and present holy ones, aesthetics, shamans and philosophers. Many freaks also identified with the persecution and trials of early Christians and witches alike.

The European custom of women not shaving legs or underarms was adopted by many US freaks as a statement against vanity and for economic, non-consumptive practicality. Facial makeup and hair permanents were rejected as vain in the same sense as Puritan ancestors or fundamentalist Christians of their grandparent's generation did. But mid-20th century US society generally saw these behaviors as rejection of basic positive values and somehow unclean. It is curious to note, as the freaks did, that to be a "painted lady" was a negative image with sinful connotations among the fundamentalist Christians well into the 1950s, however, perhaps in order to distance themselves from the counter-culture freaks, many fundamentalists paradoxically embraced makeup in the 1960s. Tammy Baker, the recently discredited television evangelist who uses vast amounts of face makeup, is an example.

The freaks attempted to achieve the US ideal of the rugged individualist in the face of what appeared to them as ever increasing conformity to big business, control of big government, anonymity, urbanization, and separation from Nature and the Divine. Speaking as an outside observer, Hinckle describes freak philosophy in *A Social History of the Hippies:*

> *They talked about reducing governmental controls, the sanctity of the individual, the need for equality among men....*
>
> *Despite a disturbing tendency toward quietism, all hippies* ipso facto *have a political posture — one of unremitting opposition to the Establishment which insists on branding them criminals because they take LSD and marijuana, and hating them, anyway, because they enjoy sleeping nine in a room and three to a bed, seem to have free sex and guiltless minds, and can raise healthy children in dirty clothes.* (P. 331)

"Sleeping nine to a room and three to a bed" is not uncommon in the third world nor even in nineteenth century America, but it was a disturbing image for most of twentieth century middle class Western society. Initially freaks' sexual roles were very conventional, but altered as the women's consciousness movement evolved. Looking to the past, freaks saw their frontier, rural forefathers and foremothers, early Christians, shamans of Native American and European Pagans and Asian religions as examples of alternative spiritual directions.

Along with the beats, surfers presented a lifestyle example and mysticism for freaks. Surfers professed an intimate connection with Nature through the power of an ocean wave. This translated into a sort of religious-mystical experience which applied generally to Nature. Youthful surfers and freaks were unconventional and cultic. They vacillated between minimalist practicality and hedonist excess. Freaks also identified with racial minorities excluded from middle-class society and the Establishment. Like the beats, bohemians, nihilists or romantics before them, freaks rejected the conventional methods of traditional religious and governmental politics as well as confrontive collective bargaining used by labor and management in business. Like the nineteenth century nihilists, freaks attempted to transcend traditional political operations, but more like early Christians or Mahatma Gandhi (d. 1948), they also employed co-operative methods and emphasized love. Hinckle continues, *"The hippie choice of weapons is to love the Establishment to death rather than protest it or blow it up (hippies possess a confounding disconcern about traditional political methods or issues)"* (p. 331).

The Freaks' economics was closer to the Native American custom of potlatch in which the wealthiest person of the village holds a feast and party for the whole village resulting in that person's poverty. Poverty brought status. Survival was guaranteed by the next potlatch redistribution. Many Freaks survived by similar means. Many did not work during those prosperous times because there was discrimination in government and industry toward hiring any "long hair." Others refused to work in industries or for the government, including the military, if they felt such employment would help the industry or government agency in harming or exploiting other humans or the planet. They did create their own co-operatives, businesses, schools, medical clinics, arts and crafts.

The West's fashion industry was no longer the dictator of style with these "alternative culture" folk, nor the cosmetic industry, automobile industry, housing industry or any company producing that which was believed of poor quality and/or for status only. Sand candles and homemade cards made wonderful Christmas gifts. This attitude was misrepresented by the media and society as anti-materialism. In fact this trend expressed anti-consumerism. While hitchhiking, a major mode of travel, many got dirty but few would turn down a shower if one was offered. Unlike European cities, there were few if any public showers in the US cities. Yet these romantic-nihilist voyagers were stereotyped as "dirty" with all the negative connotations that word brings. Akin to Calvinist mentality is the dictum that "cleanliness is Godliness" and dirty people were sinners.

Many freaks returned to the Christian fundamentalism they had earlier criticized or rejected. In the introduction to this book the author supplied personal memory of how this played out in Humboldt County. Some freaks became weary of the responsibility that came with the freedom they advocated. They felt guilt or loss for having left the "old time religion" they grew up with. Others had experienced divine states under the influence of LSD. They searched for a means to digest the experience through biblical literalism. Others didn't have the patience or education to understand the eastern philosophy embraced by the beats. As freaks entered the fundamentalist churches, they demanded a purity in faith which revitalized the born-again movement. They challenged those who attended services only for social reasons. So, giving themselves to the Lord, they placed decisions of conscience outside human will and into the hands of the Divine, as defined and dictated by the elders of the church. This included letting themselves be drafted into the military. Society labeled them "Jesus Freaks."

Although freaks approached politics unconventionally, they were aware of policies and events surrounding the civil rights movement and the Viet Nam War. New York freaks attending political protests playfully bantered about the term "Yippie," standing for Youth International Party. But the title was taken up seriously by the label hungry media and reflected society's need to assign leaders, such as Abby Hoffman, to a spontaneous, leaderless movement. The only unifying creed of the yippies was peace and love. Another author presented in *California Dreams* was Hunter S. Thompson, whose article, "The Nonstudent Left," first appeared in *The Nation*, Sept. 27, 1965. Thompson addressed media and government misconceptions of student unrest at the University of California at Berkeley at that time. Thompson wrote:

> *Terms like "Cal's shadow college" and "Berkeley's hidden community" became part of the journalistic lexicon. These people, it was said, were whipping the campus into a frenzy, goading the students to revolt, harassing the administration, and all the while working for their own fiendish ends.* (P. 319)

Thompson goes on to state:

> *Assemblyman Don Mulford, a Republican from Oakland...thinks he knows that the outburst last fall was caused by New York Communists, beatnik perverts, and other godless elements beyond his ken. The students themselves, he tells us, would never have caused such a ruckus.* (P. 320)

As with the early Christians, hippies opposed war, preferring passive resistance. Unlike the Christians, no leader was wanted or trusted, from past or present. The people society called Hippies were also similar to early Christians in that much was ascribed to them that was greatly exaggerated. Christ's command to love was combined with the freak's demand for peace.

Because most freaks preferred smoking illegal cannabis to drinking more toxic alcohol, and experimented with hallucinogens which were legal until 1966, the press made LSD-advocate Timothy Leary appear to be a spokesman or leader of a movement that ironically advocated spontaneous, anti-dogmatic anarchy. Unable to compete with the media hype and misrepresentation, a hippie effigy was buried by freaks, in San Francisco in 1967, proclaiming the "death of the hippies." But the hippie label could not be erased. The numbers in society who identified with or supported counter-culture philosophy actually increased. Psychedelic drugs used for psychological or shamanistic practice and investigation became a means for recreational escapism. By the early 1970s the drug scene was out of control, with the help of organized crime, submerging responsible drug use in a sea of society-wide hedonism.

Free love in all its myriad expressions was distilled by the press into the most sordid examples. Mass media reported on sexually transmitted diseases, destruction of traditional sexual roles and the exploits and murders perpetrated by Charles Manson's followers. This further stigmatized all freaks in society's eyes. A press headline exposing nudity or unwed partners sold more papers than an explanation of a circle of people holding hands saying Om. Sex sells. As mainstream society heard the stories and accounts, most accepted the maligning and rejected freaks. Others embraced the media's exaggerations and emulated disinformation and presentations of the hippie subgroup. Consumers of mainstream media thus perpetrated the stereotypes fostered by that media, government and industry. The fascination with the media-generated mythical hippie lifestyle quickly translated to consuming the fashion of anti-fashion.

By the mid '70s, the fashion and advertising industry capitalized on the new trend. Industry was aided by entrepreneurial freaks, as it incorporated counterculture styles and art. Outfitters for camping, hiking and back to Nature activities became yet another profitable business. Illicit and legal drug use soared. The multi-billion dollar legal drug industry supplied the demands of a society caught in a fit of uncertainty about the present and the future. Cocaine, heroin and methamphetamines gained popularity along with a return to alcohol as drug of choice.

In the late '70s, romanticism in the form of a '50s nostalgia craze assumed that the years before the '60s were somehow simpler and easier to comprehend. This was expressed through the TV serial *Happy Days* or the movie *Grease.* The music industry gained immense profits through rock and roll's popularity. Rising costs of production and recording technology forced musicians to conform to packaged formula and music developed for mass consumption. The "underground" independent radio stations and record companies, often started by freaks, were bought up by giant media networks such as Warner Brothers and CBS. A form of stylized ballroom dancing called "disco" became popular along with funk music and competed for popularity with counter-culture world beat music and Jamaican reggae. Politics, spiritual and social comment declined in the poetic lyrics of pop music. In the '80s, the epitome of the '60s troubadours, Bob Dylan, became a fundamentalist Christian. The *Star Wars* movies presented new realism in science fiction and metaphysics contained by "The Force." Social critic and ex-Beatle, John Lennon, was assassinated in 1980.

Initially cynical, then skeptical but optimistically challenging spiritual, socioeconomic and even technological paradigms, beats and freaks dissolved into mainstream Western society. They opened the way for the skeptical pragmatism of "Generation X." The legacy of the beat-freak's sub-culture of the '50s, '60s and early '70s was a heightened awareness of rapid technological progress that demanded social and spiritual change. Consumerism continued as an appropriate behavior for society, but with demand for better quality. The Ford Motor Company even came up with a slogan used by their advertisers, "quality is job one." The auto industry delivered more fuel-efficient vehicles with seatbelts and pollution controls as standard equipment. Consumer protection was legislated. Labeling on products listed ingredients and health hazards. According to the NBC evening news (11/30/95), tobacco smoking declined from 40 percent of the US population in 1965 to 20 percent in 1995. Freaks entered the job market as civil rights suits ended bans on long hair for entrance to public institutions (including Disneyland). Demonstrating a work ethic and ability in middle management as well as creative entrepreneurealism, a new label developed. "Yuppie" stood for young, upwardly mobile people and it caught on because the old hippie stereotype of anti-Calvinist, un-American laziness could no longer be supported.

Whether yuppie, hippie or freak-induced, a shift in the Western *Zeitgeist* did occur in response to prosperity, the dawning of a myth of invincibility and new world order. Use of verbiage from the '60s reflects attempts to express that shift. Many words and ideas from the freak's vocabulary have been co-opted by mainstream society. An example is the greeting, "Have a nice day." Originally this was an attempt to find a greeting that conveyed some real, non-superficial meaning beyond just hello or a nod. A "trip" came to mean a person's issue or state of being rather than a physical journey. Just as a person could be on a bad or good trip, a person could send or receive good or bad "vibes" (vibrations). "Rush," used by today's military jet pilots, described physical, emotional and mental exhilaration. To destroy became to "trash," used later in computer lingo. This term is being replaced by "recycle" in programs like Windows 95.

A person's "bag" or "gig" described their vocation or avocation. A home became a "pad." Reflecting technology, a person could "turn on or off" to an interest, or "tune in or out" a topic. Depression became "bring down" or "bummer." Intoxication became "wasted." The list continues: "where it's at," "do your thing," "sock it to me," "rip-off," "uptight," "hang/hung-up," "blow your mind," "drop-out/in," "mellow," "go with the flow," "flashback," "burn out," "spaced," "freak-out," "shack-up."

The impact of the beats and freaks continues: from computer development and computer language to health food, ecological awareness in architecture, agriculture and industry. Organic farming, natural childbirth and holistic, integrative medicine of the nineteenth century and third world advocated by freaks, continue today in reaction to the archaic, static and expensive practices of the American Medical Association, agribusiness and drug companies. The light shows of the '60s are now global and popular as ever, exemplified in the Acid House dance raves the author attended at Brighton Beach, England, in 1989 or on the beach 10 kilometers north of the Gaza Strip, Israel, in 1991. The music has become more technical. Even though the acoustic instruments and innocence of love-ins have disappeared, the appeal of tribal, oceanic ecstasy continues. The ancient circular Taoist symbol once commonly seen as hippie graffiti became a logo for a clothing line. The medieval "peace sign" symbol resurrected by freaks, went on textile patterns in third world countries and is still demonized by fundamentalist Christians. The "hippie trail" blazed through the third world by freaks traveling in a less than five star mode "with the people," is still alive and well in the '90s. Local economies cater to backpackers by providing treks, meals, beds, curios and intoxicants.

The post World War II beat-freak sub-culture was part of the first generation in modern Western society to perceive what the extended myth of invincibility might bring in terms of change and spiritual exploration. Freaks were idealistic enough to attempt the realization of a new age, unlike the more pessimistic beats before or more pragmatic Generation X after. Only eighteenth century romantics may have been so confident that they could bring real universal change of consciousness. Failing at society wide self-actualization, freaks were nonetheless the vanguard of what Spengler termed "proto-mysticism." He felt this occurs when the culture attempts to spiritually deal with its past, technologically altered present and rapidly changing future. Spengler felt twentieth century Western culture had gone beyond the confines of modern history and was in its death throws in the 1920s when he wrote. In *The Decline of the West* Spengler states that the soul of culture hearkens back to a seemingly better past and

> *... in Romanticism looks back piteously to its childhood; then finally, weary, reluctant, cold, it loses its desire to be, and, as in Imperial Rome, wishes itself out of the overlong daylight and back in the darkness of proto-mysticism, in the womb of the mother, in the grave.* (P. 75)

This gloomy prognosis reveals Spengler's misinterpretation of Nature. Apparently he thought physical death equates to the death of the soul as well. What he did not see is that the "womb of the mother," after gestation, will give birth to an altered society and a reincarnated immortal cultural soul and spirit.

The Secular Phase that gave birth to the Age of Reason and the US, is being discredited or revised as fundamentalist Christians, new agers and environmentalists attempt to define the future direction of Western civilization's *Zeitgeist*. They all hold visions of imminent change. But when New Years Day of the year 2001 comes and goes uneventfully, dashing all predictions of a sudden and dramatic end of time and new millennium, it will discredit Christian and new age prophecy alike. If no major dramatic ecological disaster befalls humanity, the environmental movement may even lose appeal. But the Spiritual Phase will not end. The proto-mysticism leading to a new cosmology, new thought and someday, new religion originated in large part with the beats and the freaks will develop. Controversy and doubts shall continue to synthesize another 200 years at least, but a new hybrid theology will evolve.

> *Science and technology may create a religious vacuum by bringing previously accepted religions into discredit, but they cannot fill this vacuum themselves; it will be filled by religions of some kind.*
>
> Arnold Toynbee, *Surviving the Future,* p. 47

CHAPTER EIGHT

CONCLUSION

The present and emerging phases of the West's *Zeitgeist* found a singular expression through the picture of planet earth taken from the surface of the moon in 1969. The rationale for the Secular Phase of the *Zeitgeist* was vindicated by space travel. This represented the culmination of technology's lineal progress. The view of "one world," alone in space, was graphically driven home. This placement and fragile existence of earth within the cosmos excited profound, mystical awe reminiscent of the Theocratic Phase. But the spectacle created more than past cosmology could deal with. An intense wonder about earth's and human's place in Nature ensued which demanded new thought. Thus the Spiritual Phase's time had come. The Theocratic Phase of the past had played its role, attempting to adjust to or resist alternative cosmology. Apocalyptic fear of end time is its best defense. But Western society turned its faith from theocracy (thesis) to science and reason (anti-thesis). This secular anti-thesis provided alternative explanations for the cosmos and the Divine. But the sublime view of tiny earth was greater than what theocracy and antiquated religion or even Secular Phase science could explain.

Today the demands increase for the survival of this fragile planet and humankind. Resources are devoured as technology attempts to provide material needs and desires. Society has also become disenchanted with reason and science. The basic needs of belonging, compassion and love are not delivered by the tools, systematic approach and scientific theories in this post industrial, currently dawning Silicone Age. The Silicone Age denotes technology's advance from the Iron Age. But stone, bronze, iron or silicone, fashioned by humans are only artifacts affecting human perception and lifestyle. Yet humans perceive and live through their *Zeitgeist.* Technology plays its part, but it only pushes or pulls the *Zeitgeist's* predetermined cycle. Technology is pulled or pushed by the *Zeitgeist* as well. The *Zeitgeist's* cycle does not vary as it reflects human nature and Nature's cycles. Though never static, Nature and human nature do not change.

The ancient world, ending with the Roman Empire, was different and perhaps more brutal than the present. But society's basic, social and spiritual needs have not changed. The appeal of observing a fellow human being on the edge, challenged by mortality and perhaps escaping death, is greater than watching the actual act of death. The state sanctioned deaths of gladiators are today replaced by accidental deaths in boxing, football or auto racing. It doesn't matter if such drama is caused purposefully, accidentally or by Hollywood's special effects. People still gamble on and encourage the risks of the sport event. Military hand-to-hand combat has been refined to weapons of the air with the detachment of a video game or terrorist's bomb. But conflicts continue and blood still flows in the streets and countryside. Slavery has been replaced by the wage slave, state welfare and the credit card. Rational observation and recording of Nature has been given the title "Science." Theocracy that was before based on the fear of the Divine expressed through the deities of polytheism, has been reincarnated through monotheism into the expressions of saints. Philosophy and religion are still with us. The personality cult within society continues. The separation from Nature due to moving from a rural society to an urban society are ongoing. Timeless emotions that range from love to hate are still in evidence.

Skepticism of theocracy and its discredited myths and dogma also keeps the Theocratic Phase dated. Attempting to transcend both the Theocratic and Secular Phases to attain a more basic spiritual synthesis, has again returned Western civilization to a Spiritual Phase of its *Zeitgeist.* The three recurring phases make up the parts of Western society's *Zeitgeist* cycle. With each turn of the *Zeitgeist's* 2000 year long cycle, technology's lineal progress shrinks the world furthering political and economic unity. But the individual concurrently becomes more alienated from Nature and fellow humans in the process. Society requires a new cosmology to bring individuals together and accommodate technology. When political and economic unity inevitably disintegrate, Western society is left with a new religion and a theocracy starting the *Zeitgeist's* cycle over again. In accordance with their needs and station, individuals either advocate their current phase, extol the past phase or look forward to the realization of the approaching phase. Thus, Western society is eternally involved with the three phases of the *Zeitgeist's* cycle.

The Theocratic Phase endures 1,400 years, leading to the Secular Phase lasting 250 years. The Spiritual Phase follows, running 350 years. The three phases total 2000 years. This is followed by yet another Theocratic Phase. Parallel events spawned by the *Zeitgeist* recur two millennia apart with a differential variable averaging 50 years or less, plus or minus. The Spiritual Phase includes an extensive environment of peace and security caused by the advent of a minimum 300 year myth of invincibility. The luxury of tolerance and open speculation synthesizes into a new faith. When the myth of invincibility ends, speculation declines or is outlawed by theocracy. This signals the end of the Spiritual Phase. Thus a new Theocratic Phase returns, co-opting the new religion. These phases reflect the cyclical nature of the Western society's mind, heart and *Zeitgeist*. The *Zeitgeist's* cycle has created traditions that go back to the religion of Melchizedek (*Genesis* 14:18, 22) in 2000 B.C.E., and the origins of today's Christianity, begun 2000 years ago.

The 300 year myth of invincibility arrives only once within the 2000 year cycle. Only a single, undisputed super power can maintain a military peace long enough to establish a world order lasting more than a generation or two. Such a super power existed in Akkad-Babylon of the Fertile Crescent and Minoans of Crete, 4000 years ago. Ancient Rome was the super power of the Mediterranean world 2000 years later. Currently the US possesses all the requirements for continuing its status as a super power another three centuries. The Spiritual Phase requires such a super power in order to provide the critical elements of: (1.) a 300 year period of national security, which allows, (2.) an extended myth of invincibility, given to experimenting with and synthesizing alternative, new and old practices and belief systems until, (3.) spiritual speculation, evolution and revolution continues long enough to erase personal memory of any previous phase. As in the times of the early Christians, an initial minority, followed in time by a significant sector of society, attempts to actualize transcendence of the existing myths, traditions and logic. These attempts are eventually synthesized and embraced by much of society and its plutocracy as the *Zeitgeist* moves into a Theocratic Phase. In the face of foreign threats, tenets developed in the Spiritual Phase are reduced to dogma. Society finds little time or energy to devote to spiritual speculation as the Spiritual Phase leaves society's personal memory after a few generations. This leads to a new universal "world religion." In the gloom of another Dark Age, the *Zeitgeist* is ultimately infused by dogma, a narrowing definition of the Divine and church bureaucracy. This occurred with Christianity as it emerged from a Spiritual Phase only to become the agent of the ensuing Theocratic Phase.

Even though humankind's *Zeitgeist* operates cyclically, human technology *does* move linearly into the future. Thus technology needs to be kept in perspective as it pushes or is pushed, and pulls or is pulled, by the orbiting, spiraling, *Zeitgeist* of Western society. In the Secular Phase, many nineteenth and twentieth century historians were caught up in scientific bias created by the secular, systematic environment and technological progress of the Industrial Revolution. Urbanity separated them from Nature and they were duped into seeing technology's movement as the major component to measure a society by. Thus they surmised that all realms in the study of history play out in a lineal fashion.

But, what they did not recognize was that in accordance with Nature, the biology, mind, heart and soul of individuals or a society operate cyclically. This cyclical aspect of existence is consistent though it may be stretched or compressed like a coil spring and cause the 50 year plus or minus variable. The lineal and systematic historical approach is merely documentation of one aspect of a holistic, cyclical, physiomatic reality where the past, present and future may blend. This is why history as seen by ancient Greeks, tribal societies or other non-Western cultures cannot be comprehended by "scientific historians."

As Western society continues living without fear of foreign attack for the next three centuries, old theocratic and secular myths will no longer be adequate as even fear of divine consequences ebbs. The *Zeitgeist* shall attempt to transcend, aided by the breath of a new vocabulary expressing expanded paradigms of a Spiritual Phase. In time, personal memory of the centuries long theocratic-secular conflict will pass. But society's attempt to transcend will fail. Nonetheless, a synthesis will congeal into a thesis producing a new, global religion. This synthesis will be the fulfillment of the Spiritual Phase. The Spiritual Phase of Akkad-Babylon and last experienced in Greco-Rome, is dawning on the Euro-US now — right on schedule. Understanding the presently emerging Spiritual Phase is most relevant.

Today in the US, the rural, rugged individualist of the past who became personally involved in how the community and nation was run, is disappearing. Those holding a personal memory of a rural past are dying. In an urban setting it is too easy to tune out Nature and fellow humans. While headphones keep many listening to their own personal music, society occupies a self-indulgent, narcissistic reality. Trees of understanding are lost in a forest of overwhelming information that comes through personal computer, TV or radio. The computer network allows communication with others without ever seeing the other party or hearing their voice; intercourse ends with the flick of a switch. Answer phones filter unwanted calls. The urban, alienated individual gives over security and civic responsibilities to the state in exchange for loss of civil liberties. Taxes are paid on salaries earned directly or indirectly from government spending or subsidy.

Christianity assumes the role of the state sanctioned religion that Paganism did in ancient Rome. Initially, Christianity (and later Islam) were spiritual revolutions attempting to transcend Pagan theocracy and prevailing secularism. Christianity rose in the spiritual milieu of demands for better human to human relationships and urban survival. Eventually Christian spiritual movements became rigid theocracies. Today there is a triad of contemporary spiritual movements attempting to again deal with the present theocratic-secular conflict and human-to-human-to-Nature relationships. These three movements also profess an end time that calls for an imminent change in the system of things. They form organizations of common cause, yet disdain institutionalization or static bureaucracy and clericalism.

The fundamentalist Christian movement expects the Divine to intervene on behalf of humans and violently actuate the end time. The environmental movement believes human effort will bring either complete destruction through humanity's self-destructive nature or a self-actualized construction of a "Deep Ecology" utopia. The new age movement, incorporating shamanism and science, strives for a society that becomes divine through human effort aided by divine grace. Sadly, such dramas will not unfold suddenly or so completely. But change will occur.

The Christian's heaven on earth, communist's self-actualized utopia or the romantic's return to a golden age Eden recognized the circular historical pattern. These ultimate goals provided more drama and meaning to existence than human participation in an endless, repeating cycle. But the failure of the French Revolution to realize an "Absolute Idea" dampened the optimism. Seeing the Reign of Terror and Napoleon's rule, romantics turned from expecting a new age in political and physical terms. Hope was retained in changing humanity's world view rather than changing the world. The nineteenth century turmoil culminating in the calamity of World War I and the Russian Revolution still did not deliver Christian or Marxist utopia.

Economic depression of the 1920s and 30s, the rise of Stalin, failure of democracy, Nietsche's emphasis on power rather than education as human purpose, Spengler's pessimism, dada art and jazz, all reflected doubts. Doubt turned into cynicism toward all systems or a longing for systems promised by millennialism. For the cynics, history appeared to be locked in a Hegelian dialectic with no conclusion or return. History came to be seen as a chain of events moving on a linear tract, measured by technology's progress. Far from getting better, many felt the human condition could only get worse with over population and continued fragmentation from each other and Nature.

However, with the subtle approach of the Spiritual Phase, society will call for science and art to attempt reconciliation of differences and acknowledge their co-dependence. This holistic approach is physiomatic and transcends the systematic approach used in the presently waning Secular Phase. A synthesis of science and religion through Deep Ecology or integrative medicine may provide avenues. Technology, urbanization and their impact and movement will be considered along with the requirements of Mother Earth and the demands of the Divine.

Noam Chomsky has used the terms "Libertarian Socialism" to describe what he feels will be needed to allow civil liberties, yet provide the cooperation needed to maintain global order and planetary survival. The silicone dependent media technology, oil based transportation technology and population growth, continue to expand human interaction but not necessarily communication. Meanwhile, the urban *Zeitgeist* loses its appeal as society recognizes it is no closer to utopia than it ever was. Western civilization is in search of meaning.

In the romantic tradition, McKenna feels a return to human connectedness with Nature will come through what he terms an "Archaic Revival." In *Food of the Gods* he postulates:

> *We need to think back to the last sane moment that we, as a species, ever knew and then act from the premises that were in place at that moment. This shift in viewpoint would enable us to see plants as more than food, shelter, clothing, or even sources of education and religion; they would become models of process. They are, after all, examples of symbiotic connectedness and efficient resource recycling and management.* (P. 97)

Fundamentalist Christians may go back 2000 years and extract from the Greco-Roman world the story of the birth of a messiah. In a modern parallel millennialist scenario, a nativity could be expected in 1996 or 1998, bringing the birth of a present day messiah! But this is unlikely. The specific replay of the event is less significant than the prevailing *Zeitgeist* surrounding the event. Thus we *can* look forward to a Spiritual Phase of the *Zeitgeist* if not the return of Jesus. In any case, society will have to triumph over technology and control it, or like the biblical "Beast," technology will appear the savior servant but emerge as society's master. All these considerations must be in place when the myth of invincibility dissolves and society clambers for a new dogma three to four centuries from now.

But Nature's cycles do not conform to the goal oriented needs, technological progress and vanities of humans. It is true that the future holds no ultimate state. There will be no final revolution, Armageddon, self-actualized *Zeitgeist* or final synthesis. Nonetheless, human nature dictates that we attempt a return to Eden. This must be accepted as the fate of the West.

> *For inquire, I pray thee, of the former age, and prepare thyself to the search of the fathers:*
>
> *(For we are but nothing, because our days upon the earth are a shadow:)* Job 8:8-9

Only two or three centuries of time will present to Western society and the planet what the face of the new world religion will be. The message will be carried through to the Aquarian, Silicone Age. There will have to be a clearer understanding of the dynamics of Nature's cyclical axiom. This axiom must be studied, applied and incorporated into all fields of study for Gaian survival. McKenna speaks for many neo-romantics and beat-freaks when he states in *Food of the Gods,* that we need a new *"paradigmatic image"* that can take us

> *through the historical choke point that we can feel impending and resisting a more expansive, more humane, more caring dimension that is insisting on being born. In the current global crisis we cannot fail to take its techniques seriously, even those which may challenge the divinely ordained covenants of the constabulary.*

McKenna proposes that shamanism provides an *"exemplary model"* (p. 253).

Now learning about and respecting the Divine and its creation will have to replace ignorance, and fear of the Divine. Basic human respect and civil liberty must be coupled with civil responsibilities. A true world faith must be one that all classes, cultures and their languages can ascribe to. Society should retain the valid tenets common to all of the seven traditional faiths on the planet today discarding any that foment separation from Nature. A libertarian "live and let live" attitude must be an added tenet. While containing a rational philosophy, society must also feel good about blindly following valid, old and new tenets. The commonly accepted tenets must be coupled with a sense of mystery and planetary fellowship. Interpretation of cause and effect, life or lives after physical death, marriage, birth control, the stewardship of plants and animals and the roles of children, men and women will all require definition. Accommodations for child and elder care must be made less institutional. Women will have to be accepted and assigned other roles in the new mythology that reach beyond virtuous mothers or sexual temptresses. Fundamentalist Christians have already returned to women the role of prophetess. New agers have rediscovered the wise woman, wicca and the goddess. Environmentalists speak in terms of Gaian "Mother Earth."

Already it is apparent that to love the earth, as well as fellow humans, must be included as a specific tenet for planetary survival. There must be an honest investigation into the definitions and role of socialism and individualism, casting out past perceptions, prejudices and myths surrounding those terms. For their own survival, plutocracy's governments must change spending priorities to further relevant education, economical holistic medicine and global food distribution. Angst, stress and any number of psychological disorders will need treatments that work without drug dependence (legal or illegal). Military spending must greatly decline along with nationalism.

But these noble and ancient goals will be buried in the confusion of a Dark Age when investigation, revelation and tolerance ends. It is folly to expect better or worse than the past has delivered in terms of the *Zeitgeist.* The military-industrial complex and drug merchants will present a resistance to such aspirations. Male dominion will resist female advancement beyond the present five percent of corporate heads who are women. Nationalism will remain an effective tool to rationalize division for a world government to "divide and rule." Yet, compassion and reason must be synthesized in order to adjust to technology, transcend and resolve conflicts inside us all, between each other and between individual liberties and responsibilities toward society and Nature. Western civilization will again create the cosmology and mythology to accommodate for another 2000 years. We can look optimistically toward the near future as a period of creativity, spiritual investigation and evolution, if not revolution. Though utopia is the vision, we must recognize that it was steam technology, not the Absolute Idea or Christianity that allowed slavery to be replaced by the wage slave. Human sacrifice has only changed its label from religious act to sport. Computers and economics may limit the horror of massive war. But murder will continue as a consequence of life in keeping with Nature's cycle.

The concerns and issues described above will be decided through a physiomatic blending and updating of the present belief systems expressed in the marketplace of ideas and emotions. The differences in perspective are as diverse as the colorful textiles worn at the ghats on the Ganges River in Benares, India, and the black and white clothes of worshipers at the Wailing Wall in Jerusalem. Synthesizing the differences and effecting change will be a long and difficult task. The first step must contain a revival of cyclical understanding to develop realistic expectations, adjustment to Silicone Age technology and accommodation to Nature's demands. Accepting human differences in a one world society is the mission of Western civilization's unfolding Spiritual Phase *Zeitgeist.* This mission will create a new cosmology. Human nature will require a theology in order to digest the new cosmology. In time this will synthesize into a new world religion. The new religion will set dogma that technology and spiritual need shall again, in time, challenge. As Nature cycles, so do humans' Zeitgeist. Forever.

BIBLIOGRAPHY

Abrams, M.H., *Natural Supernaturalism: Tradition & Revolution in Romantic Literature.* WW Norton & Company Inc., New York-London, 1971.

Allen, Gary, *None Dare Call It Conspiracy.* Concord Press, 1971.

Armstrong, Karen, *A History of God.* Ballantine Books, New York, 1994.

Barraclough, Geoffrey (editor), *The Times Atlas of World History.* Hammond Inc., 1984.

Bramley, William, *Gods of Eden.* Avon Books, New York, 1993.

Burke, James, *Connections.* Little, Brown and Co., 1978.

Cahill, Thomas, *How the Irish Saved Civilization.* Bantam Doubleday Dell Publishing Group, 1995.

Chardin, Pierre De Tielhard, The Phenomenon of Man, Harper and Row, New York, 1965

Cicero, Marcus Tullius, *Treatises on Friendship and Old Age.* The Harvard Classics, New York, 1909.

Comprehensive Concordance. Watchtower Bible and Tract Society of New York, Brooklyn, NY, 1973.

Cooper, Milton W., *Behold a Pale Horse.* Light Technology Publishing, 1991.

Cowles, Virginia, *The Romanovs.* Penguin Books, London, 1971.

Crane, B., Christopher, J.B., Wolff R.L., *A History of Civilization, Vol. I.* Prentice-Hall, Inc., 1967.

Durant, Will and Ariel, *The Lessons of History.* Simon and Schuster, New York, 1968.

Durant, Will, *The Story of Philosophy.* Garden City Publishing Co. Inc., New York, 1943.

Eisen, Jonathan and Hale, Dennis (editors), *The California Dream.* Collier Books, New York, 1968.

Ferguson, John, *Utopias of the Classical World.* Cornell University Press, Ithica, New York, 1975.

Gritsch, Eric W., *Born Againism: Perspectives on a Movement.* Fortress Press, Philadelphia, 1982.

Hamilton, Edith, *The Greek Way.* WW Norton Co., Inc., 1943.

Harnack, Adolf, *The Mission and Expansion of Christianity.* Harper and Brothers, New York, 1962.

Harrison, John F.C., *The Second Coming: Popular Millenarianism 1780-1850.* Rutgers University Press, 1979.

Hawkes, Jacuetta and Christopher, *Prehistoric Britain.* Pelican Books, London, 1943.

The Holy Bible (Old & New Testaments), King James Version. Grosset and Dunlap, New York, 1931.

Holy Bible (Old & New Testaments), Peoples Parallel Edition. Tyndale House Publishers, Wheaton, IL, 1981.

James, Simon, *The World of the Celts.* Thames and Hudson Inc., New York, 1993.

Jones, A.H.M., *Constantine and the Conversion of Europe.* Penguin Books Ltd., London, 1962.

The Kingdom Interlinear Translation of the Greek Scripture. Watchtower Bible and Tract Society of New York, Brooklyn, NY, 1985.

Kaiser, Rudolf, *The Voice of the Great Spirit.* Shambhala Publications, Inc., Boston, 1991.

Kitto, H.D.F., *The Greeks.* Penguin Books Ltd., London, 1951.

Jong, Erica, *Witches.* Harry N. Abrams, Inc., New York, 1981.

Langer, William L. (comp. and ed.), *An Encyclopedia of World History.* Houghton Mifflin Co., 1948.

Leon-Portilla, Miguel, (editor), *The Broken Spears.* Beacon Press, 1966.

Lindsey, Hal, *A Prophetic Walk Through The Holy Land.* Harvest House Publishers, 1983.

Marx, Karl, *Das Kapital* (abridged). Henry Regnery Company, 1967.

McKenna, Terence, *Food of the Gods.* Bantam Books, 1992.

McNeil, William, *Arnold Toynbee: A Life.* Oxford University Press, New York, 1989.

Menzel, Wolfgang, *Germany: From The Earliest Period, Vol. I & II* (trans. by Mrs. George Horrocks). Peter Fenelon Collier, New York, 1899.

Occhiogrosso, Peter, *Swami Bruce and the Future of Vedanta in the West.* Yoga Journal, Escondido, CA, Nov/Dec 1995.

Paine, Thomas, *Common Sense.* Penguin Books Ltd., London, 1986.

Piggott, Stuart, *The Druids.* Penguin Books, London, 1974.

Richards J.A. (editor), *The Outline of Knowledge, Vol. II (Religion & Philosophic Thought).* J.A. Richards, New York, 1924.

Sklar, Holly, *Trilateralism.* South End Press, Boston, 1980.

Spengler, Oswald, *The Decline of the West* (abridged). Alfred A. Knopf, Inc., New York, 1962.

Spengler, Oswald, *Man and Technics: A Contribution to a Philosophy of Life.* Alfred A. Knopf, Inc., 1932.

Strozier, Charles B., *Apocalypse: On the Psychology of Fundamentalism in America.* Beacon Press, 1994.

Toynbee, Arnold J. and Edward D. Myers, *Historical Atlas and Gazetteer (A Study of History, Vol. XI).* Oxford University Press, London, New York, Toronto, 1959.

Toynbee, Arnold, *Arnold Toynbee, History and the Hippies* (audio tape). Center for the Study of Democratic Institutions, Santa Barbara, CA, 1967.

Toynbee, Arnold, *Change and Habit, The Challenge of Our Time.* Oxford University Press, London, 1966.

Toynbee, Arnold, *Surviving the Future,* Oxford Press University Press, New York and London, 1971.

Wells, H.G., *The Outline of History, Volumes I & II.* Garden City Books, Garden City, NY, 1961.

World Book Encyclopedia. World Book-Childcraft International